An Enduring Tension

An Enduring Tension
Balancing National Security and Our Access to Information

Emily Berman, editor

International Debate Education Association

New York, London & Amsterdam

Published by
International Debate Education Association
105 East 22nd Street
New York, NY 10010

This book is published with the generous support of the Open Society Foundations.

Library of Congress Cataloging-in-Publication Data

An enduring tension : balancing national security and our access to information / Emily Berman, editor.
    pages cm
 Includes bibliographical references.
 ISBN 978-1-61770-094-1
 1. Freedom of information—United States. 2. Government information—United States. 3. National security—United States. 4. Transparency in government—United States. I. Berman, Emily.
 JC598.E64 2014
 323.44'50973—dc23
                              2013033051

 **IDEBATE Press**

Typeset by Richard Johnson
Printed in the USA

Contents

Acknowledgments

I would like to thank the authors who either authorized their existing work to be reprinted or contributed original material to this volume. Thanks also go to Martin Greenwald and Eleanora von Dehsen at the Open Society Foundations, whose assistance and support have been invaluable.

Introduction

Executive secrecy is one of the monarchical customs, plausibly defended, and certainly fatal to republican government. . . . How can a national self-government exist without a knowledge of national affairs? or how can legislatures be wise or independent, who legislate in the dark upon the recommendations of one man?

—John Taylor of Caroline, U.S. senator from Virginia
An Inquiry into the Principles and Policy of the Government of the United States (1814)

On taking office on January 21, 2009, President Barack Obama pledged that his administration would operate with "an unprecedented level of openness" to "establish a system of transparency, public participation, and collaboration" as a means of "strengthen[ing] our democracy and promot[ing] efficiency and effectiveness in Government." Just like innumerable public leaders that came before him, however, President Obama has found that these aspirational sentiments are easier uttered than realized.

President Obama's decision to release publicly several memos discussing the legal justifications for the CIA's interrogation practices in the years immediately following the attacks of September 11 illustrates the difficulty. The memos were drafted during the George W. Bush administration by the Justice Department's Office of Legal Counsel, or OLC—a highly respected office whose role is to provide legal advice to the president and the executive branch agencies, usually regarding legal issues of particular complexity and importance. These particular memos were written in response to CIA requests regarding legal limits on the treatment and interrogation of suspected al Qaeda leaders. They describe in detail multiple controversial interrogation methods, including the use of "waterboarding," in which a detainee is immobilized on his back, his face is covered with a cloth, and interrogators pour water over his breathing passages, creating the sensation for the detainee that he is drowning. After describing these tactics, the memos go on to make a legal argument—an argument disavowed by subsequent Justice Department lawyers as highly flawed—that such tactics are not barred either by U.S. laws or international treaties against torture. Journalists had reported on the memos' existence as early as 2004, and nongovernmental organizations had for years in the courts sought their public release, lawsuits that the executive branch had resisted with vigor.

The debate over whether the president should release these memos was heated. On the one hand, the memos clearly included information highly relevant to any public debate regarding the value of the CIA's interrogation program, what interrogation tactics ought to be approved, and how detained suspected terrorists ought to be treated. At the same time, Leon Panetta, President Obama's CIA director at the time, argued that releasing the memos would set a dangerous precedent, threaten to reveal intelligence sources and methods, and deter government officials from acting aggressively to fight terrorism in the future for fear that their actions would be revealed publicly, damaging the officials' professional reputation and raising the potential for criminal prosecution.

In 2009, President Obama ordered four memos released. The president was lauded in some circles for his commitment to transparency and for providing the public with access to these important documents. The intelligence community, however, decried the release of the memos, and the president's decision to proceed reportedly undermined his authority within the intelligence community and arguably limited his ability to insist on future disclosures for fear of open rebellion.

Decisions regarding what information should be made public are complicated, in part because they are not merely based on making the difficult determination of whether the value of the information at issue outweighs any costs it might have to America's security or intelligence-gathering capacity. Considering whether information should be made public also raises equally difficult questions regarding who should make that decision and on what basis. Should members of the national security establishment have the final word—individuals who are more familiar with the information and its implications—or should the president make his own determination regarding the costs and benefits of release? Should the ultimate decision about disclosure be left in the hands of the president? The military and intelligence agencies? The courts?

Even relatively non-contentious or politically charged circumstances where access to information and concerns over national security collide present these formidable challenges. For example, on taking office, President Obama tasked the National Declassification Center to review for declassification a 371-million-page backlog of sensitive national security records by December 2013. As of June 30, 2012, only 51.1 million pages had been reviewed, 41.8 million pages of which had been released to the public. Those numbers indicate some progress, to be sure. But at this pace, the December 2013 goal for completion of the review could not be met, and tens of millions of pages that might safely be made public nevertheless remain classified.

The level of transparency actually achieved by the Obama administration has been hotly debated. Some argue that the highly secretive approach adopted by the George W. Bush administration has merely continued. Others see a liberalization of access to information, which is lauded in some circles and denounced in others. But whatever one's opinion of President Obama's policies, these brief examples illustrate the inevitable tension between broad access to information and national security.

A Tension as Old as the Republic

President Obama may be the latest president to discover the challenges that providing access to information present in the national security context, but he is certainly not the first. In 1792, President George Washington convened the first ever cabinet meeting, seeking advice from Secretary of War Henry Knox, Secretary of State Thomas Jefferson, Secretary of the Treasury Alexander Hamilton, and Attorney General Edmund Randolph regarding whether he was obligated to share with Congress information about military losses suffered by General St. Clair in a battle with Native Americans in which hundreds of U.S. soldiers lost their lives. The cabinet's opinion was that "the Executive ought to communicate such papers as the public good would permit, and ought to refuse those, the disclosure of which would injure the public." In the end, President Washington decided to produce all the requested documents. But at the same time he recognized that there might be instances in which the disclosure of certain information would cause harm.

Over 220 years later, even the most avid advocate for government transparency acknowledges the necessity of keeping some national security information secret in order to keep sensitive information out of the hands of those that would do us harm. The most common examples are the position and movements of U.S. troops and sources and methods of intelligence collection, such as the identities of undercover intelligence agents.

Despite the value of cloaking some national security information in secrecy on occasion, failure to limit that secrecy can also have catastrophic consequences. Information is the lifeblood of democracy. As James Madison said in 1788, "A popular government without popular information or the means of acquiring it is but a prologue to Farce or Tragedy or perhaps both. Knowledge will forever govern ignorance, and a people who mean to be their own Governors must arm themselves with the power knowledge gives." Absent information about government policies, citizens cannot debate and evaluate the wisdom of the actions being taken in their name, hold officials accountable for their decisions, or participate meaningfully in the democratic process. Deliberative government is based on the premise that well-informed, carefully considered policy decisions—decisions that can only emerge from broad debate—are more likely to be wise decisions.

But there are other reasons to remain vigilant with respect to what information the government shields from view. Insisting on secrecy to protect the identity of an undercover agent in hostile territory is eminently reasonable. But from an individual government official's perspective, it might also be tempting to use secrecy in ways that are less productive. An official hoping to escape embarrassment or accountability might limit access to information not to protect the national security but instead to hide foolish, wasteful, or unlawful government action. Or she might operate in secrecy because she does not want to (or cannot) justify her policy decisions to colleagues, supervisors, or the public. Finally, it is human nature to alter behavior when we are observed by others. Government action immune from scrutiny can result in carelessness, laziness, corruption, or other abuses of power.

American history is replete with examples of the risk posed by invoking national security concerns to shield information from public disclosure. Four canonical incidents from the last half-century are commonly invoked illustrations of the potential danger of secrecy undertaken in the name of national security:

- **The Pentagon Papers**: In 1971, a Harvard-educated former Marine named Daniel Ellsberg turned over to the *New York Times* a set of top-secret Defense Department documents—known as the Pentagon Papers—regarding the history of America's political and military activities in Vietnam. The papers were disclosed at the height of the bitter controversy over U.S. involvement in the Vietnam War and revealed that the United States had expanded its military actions in ways that remained undisclosed to the American public—including U.S. bombing of the neighboring countries of Cambodia and Laos. Moreover, the papers showed that four presidential administrations, from Truman to Johnson, had made public declarations regarding their intentions in the conflict that were at odds with their actual decisions. Had the events described in the Pentagon Papers been available publicly at the time they took place, it is likely that public support for continuing the war effort would have flagged much earlier than it did, and possibly forced an end to the conflict years before it actually came about.

- **The Church Committee investigation:** A 1975 Senate committee, officially titled the United States Senate Select Committee to Study Governmental Operations with Respect to Intelligence Activities but known as the Church Committee for its chair, Senator Frank Church of Idaho, conducted an in-depth study of the activities of the U.S. intelligence community. The study revealed a variety of troubling government activities, conducted in secret over the preceding several decades. These included covert CIA operations to assassinate foreign leaders and to subvert foreign governments, FBI programs to conduct extensive surveillance of the political activities of domestic civil rights and antiwar organizations, and the National Security Agency's habit of intercepting and reading all international telegrams sent either to or from individuals in the United States.
- **The Iran-Contra affair:** During the presidency of Ronald Reagan in the early 1980s, under the direction of Colonel Oliver North, senior administration officials secretly facilitated the sale of arms to Iran, a country to which arms sales were prohibited, and diverted part of the payment for those arms to the anticommunist Nicaraguan Contras. The Contras were a guerrilla group whose aim was to unseat the Communist government of Nicaragua, a goal strongly supported by the Reagan administration. Funding of the Contras had, however, been explicitly prohibited by Congress. Both the arms sales themselves and the use of the proceeds were therefore explicitly barred by U.S. law. Despite several investigations into the episode, no evidence that President Reagan himself knew of the operation emerged, but fourteen Reagan administration officials were indicted for their role in the operation, including the secretary of defense. When George H. W. Bush, who had been vice president at the time of the affair, was president, he pardoned all officials who were indicted or convicted in connection with the scandal.
- **The Second Gulf War:** In early 2003, the George W. Bush administration sought domestic and international support for an invasion of Iraq to depose dictator Saddam Hussein and replace him with a democratic government. Support for the war was based on two assertions made by the Bush administration that later were revealed to be inaccurate. The first assertion was that Iraq was in possession of weapons of mass destruction. In making this assertion, the administration failed to reveal the existing dispute within the intelligence community regarding that conclusion. The second assertion was that Saddam Hussein had ties to those responsible for the 9/11 attacks. What was not publicly disclosed

was the fact that the only support for this assertion came from the brutal interrogation of a Libyan man who multiple U.S. intelligence agencies strongly suggested was intentionally misleading interrogators. Both assertions turned out to be false. In addition to relying on the threats of weapons of mass destruction and Iraqi links to the 9/11 attackers to build up support for the war, the administration also downplayed or ignored the challenges it would face in the post-invasion phase. The result was a war against a nation with no weapons of mass destruction and no ties to al Qaeda, and a post-invasion operation that cost thousands of lives and billions of dollars.

In each of these cases, the fact that Congress and the public were denied access to national security information enabled government officials to engage in activity that was unknown to the American people, who may not have supported it, and which resulted in loss of American standing in the world, and public faith in government.

The American people have not sat idly by in the wake of these incidents. Revelations of such secrecy have at times inspired attempts to pull back that veil. The most significant example came in the mid-1970s. In response to the Church Committee's findings, the Pentagon Papers, and the Watergate scandal that ended the Nixon presidency, there was a concerted effort to render government policy, and in particular national security policy, more transparent. One prong of those efforts was to enhance Congress's access to national security information. Congress established committees on intelligence in both the House and the Senate to oversee the activities of the agencies that make up the intelligence community, and imposed statutory limits on executive surveillance powers. Congress also enacted a statutory obligation for the executive branch to keep the oversight committees fully and currently informed of U.S. intelligence activities and expanded the scope of the public's access to information guaranteed by the Freedom of Information Act—a federal law that requires the disclosure of certain types of previously unreleased government information.

THE POST-9/11 ERA

The press toward access to information fueled by the scandals of the 1970s did not last. The conventional wisdom is that the events of September 11, 2001, "changed everything," and the balance between national security and the access to information is no exception. After 9/11, the government—and in particular the executive branch—embarked on an era of unprecedented secrecy that in many ways persists more than a decade later. The policies implemented in the wake of those attacks, and the government's response to challenges to those policies, illustrate the contemporary executive's expansive conception of the power of national security to limit both public and congressional access to information. They also form the background of today's debate over the proper scope of access to information.

One example of this post-9/11 secrecy comes from the practice of not disclosing Office of Legal Counsel memos setting out the legal justifications for significant security policy programs. While, as we have seen, President Obama eventually did reveal the contents of several of the memos about detainee interrogation, many remain secret. Government documents that have been made public refer to the existence of memos justifying warrantless wiretapping of U.S. citizens, lethal targeting of U.S. citizens by armed unmanned aerial vehicles, or drones, and several other government policies. Yet these memos themselves remain classified. As a result, not only the sources and methods of intelligence gathering or the logistical details of military actions are being protected—the very scope of the executive's authority to engage in military or intelligence activities and the rules about what the executive branch may or may not do are themselves undisclosed. In a political system where the laws governing the actions of the citizenry are meant to be publicly debated and codified in public records, this "secret law" governing the executive branch is an anomaly largely unheard of before 9/11.

Keeping these rules secret has enabled the government to keep secret entire programs implemented to protect the national security. In 2002 President Bush implemented a domestic surveillance program that bypassed existing laws and regulations and was revealed only because of the efforts of investigative journalists, who reported on the program in 2005. Similarly, the CIA for years detained and interrogated suspected terrorists in so-called black sites, prisons whose location and indeed very existence were concealed for years from the American people. And in the summer of 2013 we learned that in 2006 the executive branch adopted a secret (and controversial) interpretation of Section 215 of the USA PATRIOT Act—a post-9/11 statute that expanded the government's counterterrorism powers—to permit the National Security Agency to collect from telecommunications companies bulk data regarding domestic and international telephone calls.

One important tool the government has invoked to shield post-9/11 national security policies from disclosure is the state secrets privilege. This is an evidentiary privilege that the government may invoke in court to prevent the disclosure through judicial proceedings of information that could harm the national security. The privilege itself dates back to at least the 1950s, but it has been invoked aggressively in the wake of 9/11, not only to shield particular information but also to demand that certain suits be dismissed altogether, preventing the judiciary from ruling on the lawfulness of the government action that those suits challenge. State secrets has been invoked to block suits regarding the alleged rendition of terror suspects to other countries for the purposes of interrogating them through torture, to prevent telecommunications customers from determining whether the privacy of their phone calls and emails have been compromised in violation of law and policy, and to dismiss claims by American Muslims that FBI intelligence investigations have unlawfully targeted individuals on the basis of their religious beliefs and practices in violation of the First and Fourth Amendments to the United States Constitution.

One final post-9/11 challenge to the access to information maintained in the name of national security bears mentioning—the unprecedented pursuit of individuals suspected of leaking classified information. One consequence of government efforts to shield major policy from public scrutiny is an increased likelihood that the policy's existence will become known through unofficial channels. After all, it is part of the news media's job to play a watchdog role, investigating government actions and reporting to the public on issues of public concern. And the more secretive the government becomes, the more likely it will be that some government official will become a "whistle-blower"—someone who determines on his or her own that certain information should not be concealed and therefore shares it with congressional overseers or the news media. This is how the Pentagon Papers, for example, ended up being published in the *New York Times*. And more recently, it is thanks to such leaks that we know about, among other things, the extent of the National Security Agency's telephone and Internet surveillance, the Office of Legal Counsel's "torture" memos, President George W. Bush's domestic warrantless wiretapping program, and the CIA's network of black-site prisons.

The Espionage Act of 1917 criminalizes in certain circumstances the unauthorized release of information to someone who lacks the authority to receive it. As its name implies, the statute is aimed at preventing and punishing espionage—the practice of government officials sharing sensitive information with foreign governments or others who wish to do harm to the United States. But the statutory language of the Espionage Act is sufficiently vague that it arguably empowers the government to prosecute officials who leak information to the media, and possibly even to prosecute media outlets that publish the information. The Obama administration has been particularly aggressive in investigating and prosecuting individuals suspected of leaking national security information. Since President Obama came into office, the Justice Department has brought seven such prosecutions of leakers or whistle-blowers, as compared to three prosecutions in all previous administrations combined.

These prosecutions have drawn vocal criticism. On the one hand, leakers have violated their terms of employment and potentially placed the country's national security at risk. On the other hand, such individuals are sometimes the only means through which the nation learns of unwise, wasteful, or unlawful government action. Aggressive prosecution of such leaks risks deterring whistle-blowing and placing significant impediments on effective news reporting.

While efforts to balance the interests of national security and access to information are far from new, the twenty-first century has brought with it new challenges—and opportunities. Technological changes mean that vast amounts of information are readily available, can be stored cheaply, and may be disseminated around the globe with the click of a button. These changes permit the government to more effectively communicate with the citizenry, but they also make it much more difficult for the government to maintain the secrecy of sensitive information. The challenge of guarding secret information is best illustrated by Army Private Bradley Manning's 2010 leak of a trove of classified diplomatic cables and Edward Snowden's 2013 revelations about the National Security Agency's surveillance programs. WikiLeaks published the cables that Manning provided, in their entirety. WikiLeaks even failed in some instances to redact the names of confidential informants working with the U.S. government, putting those individuals' lives in danger. And Snowden has shared an enormous amount of information about highly classified surveillance programs with media entities around the world, which have reported on those programs extensively. So it is easier than ever before to leak secret information and ensure that information has a broad audience. At the same time, the pervasiveness of records of telephone calls and Internet traffic not only facilitates government efforts to protect against threats to the national security but also enables aggressive efforts to identify and prosecute the source of leaks.

Striking a Balance

Whether in the time of George Washington or in the era of modern terrorism, the tension between national security and access to information poses difficult questions. This is due in part to the fact that there are no absolutes—nobody proposes that all national security information be kept secret or that it all be disclosed publicly. Addressing the tension necessarily demands that we strike a balance between, on the one hand, promoting access to information and its critical role in our democracy, while on the other hand guarding the secrets that keep us safe. Complicating this balancing act is the fact that it is not a straightforward tradeoff. More secrecy does not necessarily mean more safety, and vice versa. Recall that secrecy can have costs as well as benefits—by enabling government officials to implement unwise or unlawful policy and to evade accountability for those decisions, by allowing the government to determine policy without input from all sides of the issue, and by undermining the democratic nature of our government.

Given the contingent nature of the question regarding what information must be kept secret in the interests of national security, reasonable people can disagree on its answer. The critical questions therefore turn out to be not *whether* national security information should be kept secret, but exactly *what types* of national security information should be kept secret and, just as critically, *who decides* the answer to that question, *what values* should drive those decisions, and *who should have access* to information whose dissemination is limited. In close cases, for example, should we err on the side of secrecy or access to information? If the disclosure of certain information is concededly likely to damage national security, are there any benefits to making the information available that justify disclosure nonetheless?

Currently, we have a relatively elaborate legal regime designed to try to answer some of these questions and to strike a balance between access and national-security-related secrecy. But like all human creations, it is imperfect. At the heart of the system are the rules governing the classification of information, which are set out by the president—as of this writing, the current policy is contained in Executive Order 13526, issued by President Obama in December 2009. Information may be classified if it meets two criteria: First, it must fall within a category of information eligible for classification—such categories include military plans, weapons systems, intelligence activities, cryptology, etc. And second, an official with classification authority must determine that "the unauthorized disclosure of the information reasonably could be expected to result in damage to the national security." The more potential damage to national security the information could cause, the higher the level of classification it receives. Information whose disclosure reasonably could be expected to "cause damage to the national security" may be classified as "Confidential." If disclosure reasonably could be expected to "cause *serious* damage to the national security," it may be classified as "Secret." And "Top Secret" classification is reserved for information whose disclosure reasonably could be expected to "cause *exceptionally grave* damage to the national security."

There are also several legal regimes supporting the access to information. The first comes from the Constitution itself. The First Amendment guarantees of freedom of speech and of the press, for example, suggest a constitutional preference for the free flow of information. These guarantees prevent the government from barring access to information properly in the public sphere and are premised on the principle that openness should be the norm, that policy choices should be based on ideas that prevail in public debates, rather than by denying access to information that does not promote government officials' policy preferences. The Supreme Court has recognized the role that free speech plays in facilitating government accountability by determining that the First Amendment includes the right to certain government information. And the very deliberative nature of the legislative process required by the Constitution assumes a culture of public dialogue and consensus building that cannot take place in the absence of information.

Second, the 1966 Freedom of Information Act's statutory regime provides researchers, journalists, and private citizens a mechanism to demand large amounts of information from the government. The act establishes mandatory disclosure procedures for most agencies within the executive branch, from the Environmental Protection Agency to the Department of Defense.

Congressional oversight is another potential window into the world of national security policy. As the entity that controls the budget for the entire federal government, including the military and the intelligence agencies, Congress can use the leverage of that power by denying or conditioning funding on certain information disclosures. Moreover, the president and the director of national intelligence are statutorily required to convey certain types of information to congressional oversight committees. They must keep the congressional intelligence committees "fully and currently informed of . . . intelligence activities . . . including any significant anticipated intelligence activity." Similarly, the law requires "presidential . . . reporting of covert actions," which are "activities of the United States Government to influence political, economic, or military conditions abroad, where it is intended that the role of the United States Government will not be apparent or acknowledged publicly."

And then there is the highly informal regime of communications between government officials and the news media. These relationships play a significant role in disseminating information to the public. Such dissemination is not limited to unlawful leaks of highly classified programs such as the NSA's surveillance activities. Government officials regularly provide information to reporters, who then convey it to the public. Sometimes these communications are authorized at the highest levels because they shine a positive light on government actions. Sometimes they are the result of bureaucratic infighting, where one side hopes to use public opinion to help its position to prevail. And sometimes they result from the hard work of investigative journalists, who are able to piece together a story from multiple forms of publicly available information and to get confirmation of their theory from a government source.

In theory, these regimes work together to operate as a sorting mechanism, preserving the secrecy of information whose disclosure would do harm to America's national security, but providing for the disclosure of information that both safely can be disseminated and that has value in the democratic process. In practice, however, each of them includes important concessions to the tension between information access and secrecy. The Constitution itself actually references secrecy just once, specifying that Congress may decide at times to keep the records of its proceedings secret: Article I, Section 5, clause 3 reads, "Each House shall keep a Journal of its Proceedings, and from time to time publish the same, excepting such Parts as may in their Judgment require Secrecy." But despite the absence of any textual basis for executive secrecy, statements from America's founding fathers indicate that they envisioned a president who could act with "secrecy . . . dispatch . . . vigor and energy." The Constitution gives no hints, however, to the scope of the secrecy the framers foresaw.

Similarly, the Freedom of Information Act includes nine exemptions to its disclosure requirements, the first of which states that information "properly classified as secret in the interest of national defense or foreign policy" is exempt from the statute's mandatory disclosure rules. This exemption is particularly relevant given the widespread, bipartisan agreement that up to 50 percent of information that is classified need not be. Despite decades of efforts and multiple blue ribbon commissions urging reform, this overclassification—and thus unjustified withholding of information from the American people—persists.

Congressional oversight also makes accommodations when it comes to accessing information regarding national security. While the intelligence committees must be provided notice of covert actions, that notice can be limited to the so-called Gang of Eight—the leaders of both the Democratic and Republican parties from both the House and Senate, and the chairs and ranking minority members of both intelligence committees. Presidents have often used the Gang of Eight notification procedures for intelligence activities as well. Thus much of what the executive branch is doing when it comes to intelligence operations is known to just eight members of Congress who are not permitted to share what they learn with their colleagues or staff. Congressional access to information is therefore often quite limited when it comes to national security policy.

Thus each of the regimes implemented to govern access to information raises the same basic debates about how and where to strike the balance between openness and secrecy.

ISSUES FOR DEBATE

This book explores five aspects of the conflict between national security and access to information. It begins by asking the fundamental question whether national security policy, much of which is by necessity secret, is compatible with democracy and, if so, where the line between acceptable and excessive secrecy lies. Part 2 explores some of the potential costs and benefits of limiting access to information and asks whether we have struck the proper balance between secrecy and openness in our current legal and regulatory regime. Part 3 takes the debate to the legislative branch and considers what the rules should be regarding legislators' access to sensitive national security information. In Part 4, we move to the third branch of government—the courts—and ask whether and when the government should be permitted to invoke the controversial state secrets privilege to have suits against it dismissed and what the judicial role should be in making decisions about disclosure. Finally, Part 5 moves beyond government actors to ask how we should handle unauthorized disclosures of national security information: Should leakers or the news media (however that is defined) be criminally liable for disclosing or publishing classified national security information? Under what circumstances should executive branch officials be permitted to report suspected fraud, waste, or abuse to Congress or the media?

The debates explored in this book will not go away. Instead, we will continue to ask ourselves the same questions again and again: How do we define the universe of information that is shielded from disclosure? Who has access to that information? Who decides the answers to both of those questions? And how are those answers enforced? These questions are never truly settled. Instead, our political process includes a constant tug-of-war involving efforts by legislators, journalists, and the public to access information opposed by executive efforts to shield information from disclosure. The result is a constantly evolving landscape in which We the People struggle collectively to reach the proper balance.

Part 1: The Tension between Secrecy and Democracy

The materials in this section tackle the conflict between national security and access to information at its most essential level, asking whether secrecy and self-government are fundamentally incompatible. Should we abandon secrecy in the name of democracy? Are there areas of policy in which true democratic governance is impossible? If, on the other hand, we acknowledge that both secrecy and access to information are necessary to effective democracy, how can we take a more nuanced look at this relationship and seek ways to reconcile one with the other?

In his essay "Democratic Secrecy," Dennis Thompson first argues that any secrecy within a democratic society should be structured with an eye toward promoting accountable government. He then sketches out what this approach might look like, and acknowledges the challenges that it poses. In an essay originally published in 1976, former CIA director William Colby suggests approaching the problem from a different angle, positing that the central question should be not what needs to be kept secret, but instead what needs to be exposed. Colby's concerns and suggested reforms provide perhaps the best evidence of the stubborn and persistent nature of the struggle for optimal government secrecy practices—40 years later, we continue to ask the questions he raised. Finally, regardless of which approach one adopts—whether one determines what information remains secret by identifying necessary *secrets* or necessary *disclosures*—former Sen. Russell Feingold, transparency advocate Steven Aftergood, and law professor Heidi Kitrosser, at a hearing before the Senate Judiciary Committee's Subcommittee on the Constitution, insist that there is no legitimate justification in a democracy to keep secret the very content of the law itself.

As you read the selections, consider the following questions:
- What information should the government be permitted to keep secret? How should we as a society make that decision? Who should have access to "secret" information?
- What values does access to information promote? What about the values furthered by restricting access to information? When the two are in conflict, should the former or the latter be given priority?

- Imagine that after a robust public debate, Congress passes legislation requiring the executive branch to keep secret any national security policy that does not involve the actual use of force. Is that secrecy less problematic from a democratic perspective than it would be without such a legislative mandate? If so, why?
- How should government officials determine whether to implement policies whose success depends upon secrecy? And if those officials rely upon their own judgment in making those decisions, how can they be held accountable for the legality and effectiveness of those policies?
- If each of these challenges has persisted since at least 1976, how likely are we to arrive at definitive answers? In the absence of definitive answers, how should these questions be resolved?

Democratic Secrecy

*by Dennis F. Thompson**

Sunshine laws, the Freedom of Information Act, investigative journalism, and a robust First Amendment ensure that U.S. citizens have access to more information about public officials and public agencies than ever before in history. Yet even in what may be the most open national government in the world, secrecy persists. According to the Information Security Oversight Office, which keeps watch over the U.S. government's secrets, more than 3½ million new secrets are created each year.[1] That works out to almost 10,000 new secrets a day. No doubt many more secrets were not even recorded. Until recently, even the rules and criteria for classifying and declassifying secret information were themselves secret. There are now two million officials in government and another one million in private industry with the authority to classify documents. Many of these are what are called derivative classifiers, who without signing their own names can declare their own document classified just because it quotes from another originally classified document.[2]

Government secrecy certainly has not been ignored. Many scholars and reformers have examined it critically, and government bodies have investigated the problem. A bipartisan national Commission on Government Secrecy headed by Senator Daniel Patrick Moynihan recently concluded that a massive "culture of secrecy" has spread with little oversight throughout the government during the past eighty years, and has seriously eroded our democratic process.[3] Nevertheless, most of the literature on government secrecy neglects the fundamental democratic values underlying the problem and focuses instead on the laws and policies that regulate secrecy, patterns of abuses by individual officials, or particular practices such as executive privilege and national security.[4] When writers examine fundamental values, they usually pose the problem as a conflict between secrecy and democracy.[5]

This article seeks to show that for a limited but significant class of public policies there is a fundamental conflict of values that is not readily resolvable and that creates a continuing problem for government secrecy in a democracy. The conflict is not primarily between secrecy and democracy but arises within the idea of the democratic process itself. Some of the best reasons for secrecy rest on the very same democratic values that argue against secrecy. The demo-

Reprinted by permission from *Political Science Quarterly*, 114 (Summer 1999): 181–193.

cratic presumption against secrecy (and in favor of publicity) can be defended, but not so simply as is usually supposed.

The conflict involves this basic dilemma of accountability: democracy requires publicity, but some democratic policies require secrecy. The first horn is familiar enough: the policies and processes of government must be public in order to secure the consent of the governed. At a minimum, democracy requires that citizens be able to hold officials accountable, and to do that citizens must know what officials are doing, and why. But the second horn points to the fact that some policies and processes, if they were made public, could not be carried out as effectively or at all. These policies and processes may well be ones to which citizens would consent if they had the opportunity. The most familiar examples are in foreign policy and law enforcement. If the Dayton negotiations on Bosnia had been open to the press and all the terms of the final agreement fully disclosed, the leaders would almost certainly not have been able to reach an agreement. Or if the plans for a sting operation to catch drug dealers were revealed even after it took place, the safety of informers and future operations of a similar kind would be jeopardized.

The dilemma of accountability may be thought of as a political version of the Heisenberg uncertainty principle. Just as physicists can't measure a particle's position and momentum at the same time (because the process of measuring the position disturbs the momentum), so citizens cannot evaluate some policies and processes because the act of evaluating defeats the policy or undermines the process.

Faced with this dilemma, democrats might seem to have only two alternatives: abandon the policy or sacrifice democratic accountability. The first alternative is sometimes the right one. In the Iran-contra affair during the mid-1980s, Lt. Col. Oliver North kept his actions and the policy of trading arms for hostages secret by giving misleading answers to Congress. A congressional counsel later challenged him by asking, "But these operations were designed to be secrets from the American people?" North responded: "I'm at a loss as to how we could announce it to the American people and not have the Soviets know about it. . . ."[6] But the trouble was that it was not only the Soviets who would have undermined the policy but also many Americans, including a majority in Congress. If one of the reasons that a policy cannot be made public is that it would be defeated in the democratic process, then the policy should be abandoned.

Even the second alternative—sacrifice the accountability—may be appropriate in exceptional circumstances. President John Kennedy did not tell the

American people during the Cuban missile crisis that in order to get Nikita Khrushchev to withdraw Soviet missiles from Cuba, he agreed to remove American missiles from Turkey.[7] Nor through most of the nuclear era did most Americans, including most members of Congress, know much about critical elements of nuclear strategy; moral not only technical choices were made without public accountability.

But many policies that require secrecy to be effective do not lend themselves to either of these alternative strategies; we usually do not want to give up either the policy or the accountability. So in practice, we try to compromise by moderating the secrecy—by lifting the veil of secrecy just enough to allow for some degree of democratic accountability. In general, this strategy is more difficult and should be employed with more caution than is usually assumed. The dilemma of accountability is often inescapable, and in any choice between secrecy and publicity, publicity should have ultimate priority. The basic reason is that in any balancing of these values, there should be enough publicity about the policy in question so that citizens can judge whether the right balance has been struck. Publicity is the precondition of deciding democratically to what extent (if at all) publicity itself should be sacrificed.[8]

This dilemma can be seen more clearly by considering two general ways in which secrecy may be moderated—ways in which the veil of secrecy may be penetrated. In each case we need to ask what kind of democratic accountability this makes possible and whether it is sufficient. This approach is intended to broaden the discussion of government secrecy to include some forms that are common enough in the life of public officials but neglected in the literature.

TEMPORALITY: WHEN IS THE VEIL LIFTED?

The first way in which secrecy may be moderated involves its temporal dimension. We moderate the secrecy by making it temporary: lift the veil in time for citizens to judge the policy or process. The main question we should ask is: What if any democratic accountability is lost by the delay?

Consider the case of the ill-fated Clinton administration's Task Force on National Health Care Reform, which in early 1993 brought some 500 experts together in four months of meetings to design a comprehensive plan to guarantee health care. For much of that time, the meetings were closed, and even the identities of the experts were kept secret. The administration argued that this kind of process allowed participants to take more risks at the earlier stages of the formulation of policy and that it reduced the chance that a well-grounded policy (which could later win public approval) would be rejected early simply because it was unpopular with special interests.[9] The courts eventually disallowed the secrecy.[10]

But the administration did not ask citizens or their representatives to consider whether the secrecy was justified for this purpose. It is difficult to argue that the secrecy served the overall cause of health care reform very well. In the end, the health care plan failed—no doubt for many reasons. But it should have been clear that public support for any plan would ultimately be harder to achieve if the policy makers did not show that they were responding to criticisms and taking into account diverse interests in the process of formulating the plan.

This is not only a political but also a moral point: the less that citizens know about a policy, the less accountable the government is for the policy. Further, the less meaningful is the consent citizens give to it, the less justifiable is the use of state power to enforce it. Thus even temporary secrecy can block citizens from knowing about critical phases of the process in which the policy is adopted and thereby diminish both accountability and consent.

Temporary secrecy does not of course always diminish accountability. Sometimes it can enhance the democratic process, and there is even some information that is made public but that should be kept temporarily secret. For example, the exit polls conducted by the news media during an election reveal the likely results before some citizens have had a chance to vote and thereby may influence their decisions in ways that seem inappropriate. This kind of publicity distorts the process of accountability.

So how should we decide whether temporary secrecy is justified or not? Is there a general principle that might help officials and citizens focus their inevitable arguments about particular cases? Any such principle should have two parts: a secret is justified only if it promotes the democratic discussion of the merits of a public policy; and if citizens and their accountable representatives are able to deliberate about whether it does so.

The first part of the principle is simply a restatement of the value of accountability. The second part is more likely to be overlooked but is no less essential. Secrecy is justifiable only if it is actually justified in a process that itself is not secret. First-order secrecy (in a process or about a policy) requires second-order publicity (about the decision to make the process or policy secret).

The requirement of second-order publicity is a sensible resolution of the dilemma of accountability for many cases, but there are some kinds of cases it does not handle well. The first are policies or practices in which the accountability is essentially context-sensitive. These are cases in which the controversial element of the policy is specific to the case, cannot be revealed without undermining the policy, and has irreversible effects. In such cases, giving advance approval of the general type of the policy or counting on retrospective review are not adequate forms of accountability.[11]

It seems perfectly acceptable for a city council to approve the use of unmarked police cars while keeping the specific times and locations secret. But consider the case of a covert operation run by the Drug Enforcement Administration (DEA) in Texas in the late 1980s. The DEA routinely allowed local police officials to claim that they had seized illegal drug shipments, even though the shipments were brought into the country by DEA's own undercover agents.[12] The practice was designed to protect the identity of the agents who were acting as middlemen for South American drug traffickers and to allow the investigations to continue, but to stop the drugs from reaching distributors in the United States. The practice was evidently effective and became public only after reporters began to have suspicions about the inflated numbers of drug arrests. DEA officials argued that the practice was carefully limited and had been effective in serving an important goal that Congress had approved in general terms. But the absence of any prospective accountability for the method (as distinct from the goal) of the policy is still troubling. If we believe that this and similar undercover operations are necessary, we have an unresolved conflict between secrecy and accountability in all cases of this kind.

Transparency: How Thick Is the Veil?

The other general type of case that the proviso of requiring second-order publicity does not handle takes us to the other dimension of secrecy—transparency (how thick the veil is). Here the problem is that publicizing the practice or policy, making it explicit even in general terms, tends to undermine it. These are cases in which second-order publicity about a policy would destroy its first-order efficacy. Democratic accountability requires transparency, but some policies and process require obscurity.

The form of secrecy at issue here, rarely discussed in the literature, is partial: it lies somewhere between deep concealment and full disclosure. Such secrets are not completely concealed because their content may be widely known or could be widely known. But their content is not made explicit, and its not being made explicit is necessary for the policy's being effective. We might think of such partial secrets as tacit silences: things that are better left unsaid. There are at least three kinds.

Excuses and Nonenforcement

The first kind of partial secret or tacit silence can be illustrated by the feature of the administration of the criminal law. Jeremy Bentham once proposed a scheme that he thought would maximize both the deterrence and humanitarian aims of the criminal justice system.[13] As a good utilitarian, he did not like capital punishment, but he thought that the threat of capital punishment was sometimes necessary to deter serious crimes. His solution: the law should prescribe death by poison for certain crimes; the poison would be given to the convicted criminal in public, and after he collapsed and was carried away, he would be given an antidote. The criminal would of course have to be told that the penalty for revealing this secret was death by poison—without any antidote. The same would go for the officials who were in on the secret.

Like many of Bentham's schemes, this is not the most sensible solution to the problem, but it reveals in an only slightly more extreme form some features in the administration of our contemporary criminal justice system that many legal scholars and jurists defend. This is the phenomenon of what is called "acoustic separation"[14] (or in terms of the metaphor here it could be called "differential transparency").

On this view, most particular laws imply two kinds of rules: conduct rules, which tell citizens that if they engage in certain conduct, they will be punished in certain ways; and decision rules, which tell officials how to apply the conduct rules. In a system that is purely transparent, one that completely satisfies the publicity principle, the decision rules as well as the conduct rules would be known to all citizens. But in our current system, there is an acoustic separation between the citizens and officials: citizens hear only the conduct rules, not the decision rules. Following the metaphor of transparency, we could say: they can see through only the part of the veil that covers the conduct rules.

An example comes from the law of excuse—the excusing or mitigating factors that are considered in applying a law to a particular individual. "Ignorance of the law is no excuse." Most people (and many officials) evidently believe that this is a prevailing rule in our legal system. They believe that the court decisions and statutes do not allow ignorance of the law as an excuse for breaking the law. But that does not seem to be the case. According to certain authoritative, though not widely publicized, commentaries, there are so many exceptions to the excuse that it hardly expresses a rule at all. Ignorance of the law is in fact quite often accepted as a legitimate excuse. You may be excused, for example, if the charge is based on a regulation instead of a statute, if the charge is based on an omission rather than an action, or if you relied on an authoritative source for your information even if the source was mistaken.[15]

These exceptions have developed because in many cases it is clearly unfair to punish someone who really did not know that he was breaking a law. We usually hold people morally responsible only for their intentional actions and therefore think that punishment is justified only if they knowingly or at least negligently commit an offense. But if it were generally known that one could avoid punishment by claiming ignorance of the law, some people would not only try to feign ignorance of the law, but also would have an incentive to cultivate legal ignorance.

Similar considerations apply to imposing penalties of many different kinds in administrative proceedings, whether the parties are citizens outside government or civil servants inside the agency. The Environmental Protection Agency (EPA) and the Internal Revenue Service (IRS) do not reveal exactly what kinds of excuses have worked well in the past. In many cases, the agencies simply do not enforce the rules when the violations fall beyond a certain (unpublicized) threshold. Complete transparency would require publicizing these thresholds, and other facts such as that the agency usually gives a warning, perhaps even two warnings, to violators of a particular rule before taking any further action. But both citizens and employees would be less likely to violate the rules in the first place if this fact were left somewhat unspecified.

Thus, publicizing the stricter conduct rule while obscuring the more lenient decision rule resolves what would otherwise be a difficult dilemma. It mitigates the conflict between two important values—deterrence and fairness. Although the acoustic separation is not complete—the veil does not totally obscure the decision rules to citizens—we should be glad (the proponents of acoustic separation say) that the decision rule is not more generally known. It is fortunate that the exceptions to the conduct rule that ignorance of the law is no excuse are not more widely publicized.

But if this concession to obscurity—this sacrifice of transparency—mitigates this conflict in the law, it exacerbates the more general democratic conflict in the dilemma of accountability. Differential transparency is not a desirable practice in a democracy, and should not be encouraged even if it is to some extent inescapable. It is undesirable for at least three reasons.

One problem with acoustic separation is that it tends to be self-defeating over time. The rationale for the exceptions to general rules (like "ignorance of the law is no excuse") is that they make the law conform more closely to our ordinary notions of morality (in this case the principle that people should be punished only for intentional wrongdoing). But if the exceptions are developed over time in unpublicized cases by administrators and judges, they may begin to diverge from common morality, or at least citizens will have no assurance that they conform to it. Public deliberation seems to be a precondition for keeping the exceptions secret in the first place.

A second problem with acoustic separation is that because in practice it can never be complete, some citizens will penetrate the barrier and use the information, while other citizens cannot. Large corporations and individuals who can afford regularly to consult lawyers can use their inside knowledge of the decision rules to their advantage. The unfairness of this advantage is especially evident in the areas of tax and environmental law: the internal enforcement guidelines of the IRS or the EPA (what excuses are accepted, what levels of violation are ignored, what conduct triggers investigations) may not always be publicized; but some corporations and individuals can still find out what they are and use their knowledge to their own advantage.

Finally and more generally, any attempt in a democracy to send differential messages to different publics about general policies as fundamental as criminal justice is likely to miscarry. The audience with the most to lose or the most to gain usually gets the real message first, and the general public is the last to know. The American criminal justice system sends a different message to the public than it does to criminals, but with just the opposite effect from what Bentham or the advocates of acoustic separation intend. Similarly, the administrative law system may send a different message to well financed and well connected lobbyists than it does to ordinary citizens.

To convince the public that they are vigorously fighting crime, politicians enact popular get-tough measures on crime—longer prison terms, mandatory sentences, and capital punishment for more crimes. But without adequate institutional support for these measures (such as police and prosecutors to enforce the laws, judges and juries prepared to impose the sentences, and prisons to house adequately the convicted criminals), the measures are not likely to reduce crime and may even merely result in more plea bargains, more parole, and fewer convictions. The system tells the criminal on the street that, despite the public rhetoric, the actual risk of getting caught, let alone serving a long term, is not high. Acoustic separation—differential transparency—of this variety not only fails to promote genuine accountability but also defeats its own policy aims.

Compelled Silence

The second kind of case in which transparency is transgressed carries the partial secrecy of excuses and nonenforcement a step further. In those cases just examined, the discrepancy between what the law says and how it is enforced is partially secret or at least obscure, and therefore the prohibited practice is indirectly kept secret too. In the kind of case to be considered next, the law explicitly requires that the practice be secret, and the prohibited conduct becomes illegal only if it is revealed.

This is the current policy on gays in the military: the so-called "don't ask— don't tell" regulations proposed by the Clinton administration in 1993, endorsed by Congress, and upheld by the courts.[16] The military is no longer permitted to ask applicants for military service their sexual orientation and cannot investigate their sexual orientation unless they receive "credible information" about it from other sources. At the same time, gays are not permitted to disclose their orientation. They may go to gay bars, designate their partners on insurance forms, and take other similar actions; but they may not announce to anyone that they are gay. If they do, they are subject to discharge and other penalties.

Notice that this is different from laws that protect rights of privacy. In the policy on gays, the conduct is prohibited even if it takes place in private and even off-duty. To make clear that the law is not neutral on the question of the legitimacy of the conduct itself, the House added to the Pentagon order the statement "homosexual conduct in the military is unacceptable."[17]

Defenders of the policy describe it as a compromise between the needs of the military and the rights of a disadvantaged minority. Most if not all of the dangers that the military says homosexuality causes can be avoided if gays keep their orientation secret. The military presumably is worried that the presence of openly gay soldiers will make close-quarter living as on shipboard more difficult and create some ambivalence in the camaraderie that fighting units require. The rights of gays are also partially protected: they can serve in the military if they are discreet about what they say and what they do. Gays now serving in the military are better off than they were under the previous policy; and according to one report, most were indeed pleased by the new policy, though of course "their joy [had to be] savored quietly" in private.[18]

But as with many compromises, this one does not please most people on either side of the controversy. Those sympathetic to the military think that it undermines combat readiness, and those sympathetic to gays still find it discriminatory. Much could be said against the policy, but the relevant points here relate specifically to its lack of transparency.

Notice first, however, that the policy is not vulnerable to the objection that it breaches democratic accountability in the way that some similar policies might. For example, many government-financed hospitals and HMOs implicitly allow physician-assisted suicide, presumably with the tacit approval of their doctors and most citizens of the community but contrary to existing law. The practice is tacitly permitted as long as no one talks about it openly, which means that most citizens or their representatives have not had a chance to vote for or against permitting the practice. In contrast, the "don't ask—don't tell" policy on gays in the military has been the subject of ample deliberation and has been openly endorsed in a democratic process. This was possible because the policy itself is public. The policy does not require that any of its essential features be secret, only the specific conduct of certain individuals. The policy thus seems to be an example of partial secrecy or nontransparency that is consistent with democratic accountability.

But the lack of transparency still creates problems for accountability. The policy inevitably leaves a great deal to the discretion of individual military officers to decide what is to count as "telling" and what is to count as "credible information" sufficient to launch an investigation. Given the nature of the policy, this discretion is likely to be exercised in private at least in the initial stages. But there have been accusations that some officers have abused this discretion by undertaking investigations without sufficient evidence. It would seem then that greater accountability, a degree of publicity at least within the government, is necessary. Yet the more public this process becomes (even within the military), the consequence is the same as if the accused himself did in fact "tell." He is now known to be gay. The lack of transparency brings about a deficiency in accountability—not for the policy itself but for its application.

The policy has further problems of accountability. The pressure toward silence drives not only homosexual activity underground but also activities and discussion about the effects of the policy. The secrecy the policy requires makes it harder to find out how the policy is actually working: whether for example it is discouraging gays from entering the military, how unpleasant it is making their life once in service, whether the suppression of gay identity is worse for military effectiveness than open toleration would be. Much of what citizens and legislators need to know in order to judge whether to continue the policy or to change it over time is not easily accessible, because so much of the operation of the policy lies behind a less than transparent veil.

Political Hypocrisy

One of the most common charges in contemporary political debate is hypocrisy, the alleged contradiction between what officials try to make the public believe about how they act and how they actually act. Hypocrisy involves pretending that one's "motives and intentions and character are irreproachable when [one] knows that they are blameworthy."[19] The force of the charge thus depends on the private conduct being less known, or at least less acknowledged, than the public conduct. Otherwise, the pretense would be obvious, and the charge would be one of simple inconsistency.

Accountability might seem to require exposure of hypocrisy, and under some conditions and to some extent it does. When an official is in charge of enforcement of drug policy but is addicted to crack, or when a politician opposes legislation to protect gays against discrimination but engages in homosexual activity, the exposure helps make a point that is relevant to citizens' judgment about how well the official is doing his or her job. But as the most astute analysts of hypocrisy have emphasized, anti-hypocrisy can often do more damage to the democratic process than the hypocrites do.[20] It focuses political debate too much on motives instead of actions, makes compromise more difficult, and can intensify class and racial antagonism. Some of these effects also undermine accountability itself.

If the partial secrecy that supports this individual hypocrisy is sometimes desirable, it is much less justified in the case of a more insidious form—institutional hypocrisy.[21] This form involves a disparity between the publicly avowed purposes of an institution and its actual performance or function. This disparity often develops over time as an institution comes to serve purposes other than those for which it was established. In some cases, no one is deceived and no harm is done to the democratic process. The Electoral College may have once been supposed to provide an additional forum for democratic deliberation, but most citizens today would be more than surprised if the electors decided to conduct a serious debate about the merits of the candidates and cast their votes according to their own best judgment.

But in other cases the divergence between the official purpose and the actual function is not so open and the consequences not so benign. In some—especially those involving almost any agency that can claim to be protecting national security—the institutional hypocrisy is often deeply deceptive. The National Security Council (NSC) is supposed to provide the president with an independent source of advice and control over the conduct of foreign policy. When it becomes a tool for evading congressional oversight, as it did in the Iran-contra affair, an appeal to its official purpose constitutes institutional hypocrisy that has serious consequences for the democratic process. Lt. Col. Oliver North and Admiral John Poindexter tried to justify their congressionally unauthorized use of the NSC by arguing that the Boland amendment banned only operational agencies from intervening in the conflict in Nicaragua. The NSC, they said, is merely a planning and advisory agency.[22] They thus exploited the official purpose of the institution while using it for illegitimate purposes. The disparity was part of the cause as well as the consequence of the damage to the democratic process.

In the case of institutional hypocrisy, we should generally resolve the dilemma in favor of accountability and expose the partial secrets. Criticisms of systematic discrepancies between intention and action in governmental agencies can help set the agenda for institutional reform. The critics who charge a federal regulatory agency with serving the interests of the industries it is supposed to regulate more than the interests of the citizens it is supposed to serve can not only identify the need for reform but can indicate the form it should take. The long-term legitimacy of these and other such institutions depends on establishing more coherence between their official purposes and their actual practices.

But notice that the demand for exposure of institutional hypocrisy is not always consistent with the exposure of individual hypocrisy. Not only does the preoccupation with individual hypocrisy distract attention from the institutional form, it also may interfere with its exposure. Institutional hypocrisy and individual hypocrisy are not only distinct but often opposed. Institutional hypocrisy is sometimes made possible by the absence of individual hypocrisy.

Oliver North was not a hypocrite in any conventional sense. He did not believe that his motives or intentions were reproachable. He could not be accused of acting out of self-interest in any of its usual disreputable forms. He believed in his cause and believed that he was serving both his president and his nation in carrying out his scheme to trade hostages for arms to Iran and divert some of the proceeds to the contras in Nicaragua. He was not even trying to make himself appear better than he thought he was, since he believed that if most citizens fully understood what he was doing they would consider him a hero. Had North been a conventional hypocrite, he would not have been so successful in enlisting others in support of his cause and thereby in effecting the institutional hypocrisy that should count as his gravest wrong. His main moral fault was not that he failed to be true to himself, but that he failed to be true to those to whom he was accountable. In his individual sincerity, he created and sustained an institutional hypocrisy.

Thus, democratic accountability may be better served by paying less attention to the individual and more to the institutional form of hypocrisy. Both are in a sense partial secrets, and thus both create a potential dilemma of accountability; but the moral discrepancies in their individual conduct that officials refuse to acknowledge are often not so damaging as the functional divergences in institutional goals that they try to obscure.

CONCLUSION

Democratic accountability does not require unconditional publicity in the conduct of democratic government. Secrecy of various kinds is sometimes justified and even desirable in a democracy. But it is justified only under carefully specified conditions, which ensure that the secrecy itself is subject to democratic accountability.

The first part of any justification requires second-order publicity: the decision to keep a decision or policy secret should be made publicly. Further, it may not be sufficient to have procedures for deciding whether particular decisions or practices should be public. It may also be necessary to design procedures for deciding whether decisions about these decisions should be public. (It is usually not necessary or desirable to carry this logic to some n^{th} order publicity.)

The requirement of second-order publicity takes care of most cases of temporary secrecy, but it does not handle so well the important but neglected cases of partial secrecy. The challenge here is to provide procedures for acknowledging partial secrets without undermining the policies they support. The only feasible solutions seem to be either to rely on representatives who can be trusted to review in private the policy and its application, or to conduct public debates in general terms without revealing the specific nature of the policy. That neither of these alternatives usually provides adequate democratic accountability is a further reason to seek ways to promote transparency in the design of the government institutions and the making of public policies.

The dilemma of accountability poses a choice between either abandoning a policy or weakening responsibility for it. The dilemma cannot always be resolved because it is inherent in the theory and practice of democratic government itself, or at least any democratic government in which citizens would wish to adopt policies that cannot be promptly disclosed or processes that are not fully transparent. But public officials and political institutions can diminish the damage to democratic accountability by making sure that temporary secrets do not become permanent and that partial secrets do not become total.*

NOTES

*An earlier version of this article was presented at Rice University in April 1997, and I am grateful to Larry Temkin and his colleagues there for their valuable comments. I have also benefited from discussion of some of the arguments in this paper with Arthur Applbaum, Amy Gutmann, Larry Lesig, and the late Judith Shklar.

1. Information Security Oversight Office, *Report to the President*, 1995 (Washington, DC: U.S. Government Printing Office [hereafter GPO], 1996), ii.

2. *Report of the Commission on Protecting and Reducing Government Secrecy*, Pursuant to Public Law 236, 103rd Congress (Washington, DC: GPO, 1997).

3. Ibid.

4. Itzhak Galnoor, ed., *Government Secrecy in Democracies* (New York: Harper & Row, 1977); Donald C. Rowat, ed., *Administrative Secrecy in Developed Countries* (New York: Columbia University Press, 1979); Kenneth G. Robertson, *Public Secrets: A Study of the Development of Government Secrecy* (New York: St. Martin's Press, 1982); Mark J. Rozell, Executive Privilege: *The Dilemma of Secrecy and Democratic Accountability* (Baltimore: Johns Hopkins Press, 1994); Daniel P. Moynihan, *Secrecy: The American Experience* (New Haven: Yale University Press, 1998); and David Vincent, *The Culture of Secrecy in Britain, 1832–1998* (New York: Oxford University Press, 1998).

5. Francis E. Rourke, *Secrecy and Publicity: Dilemmas of Democracy* (Baltimore: Johns Hopkins Press, 1966). But see Sissela Bok, *Secrets: On the Ethics of Concealment and Revelation* (New York: Pantheon Books, 1982), 102–115, 171–190.

6. David Nacht, "The Iran-Contra Affair" in Amy Gutmann and Dennis Thompson, eds., *Ethics and Politics*, 3rd ed. (Chicago: Nelson-Hall, 1997), 57–66.

7. Graham T. Allison and Lance M. Liebman, "Lying in Office" in ibid., 49–53.

8. For discussions of the publicity principle, Amy Gutmann and Dennis Thompson, *Democracy and Disagreement* (Cambridge, MA: Harvard University Press, 1996), 95–127; and David Luban, "The Publicity Principle" in Robert E. Goodin, ed., *The Theory of Institutional Design* (Cambridge, UK: Cambridge University Press, 1996), 154–198.

9. For contemporaneous editorial comments on the secret deliberations, see "Health Team Needs Breathing Room," *St. Louis Post-Dispatch*, 31 March 1993; and "Let's All Be Health Care Insiders," *New York Times*, 13 March 1993.

10. The first federal court ruling was *American Association of Physicians and Surgeons, Inc., v. Clinton*, Civil Action No. 93-0399, 11 March 1993, 813 F. Supp. 82, 1993 U.S. Dist.

11. On the difficulties with these forms of accountability, see Dennis F. Thompson, *Political Ethics and Public Office* (Cambridge, MA: Harvard University Press, 1987), 22–31.

12. Associated Press, "U.S. Looking Into Undercover Drug Manipulation," *New York Times*, 29 November 1988.

13. Shirley Letwin, *The Pursuit of Certainty* (Cambridge, UK: Cambridge University Press, 1965), 173.

14. Meir Dan-Cohen, "Decision Rules and Conduct Rules: On Acoustic Separation in Criminal Law," *Harvard Law Review* 97 (January 1984): 625–677.

15. Ibid., 645–48.

16. "Gay Rights in the Military: The Pentagon's New Policy Guidelines on Homosexuals in the Military," *New York Times*, 20 July 1993.

17. Clifford Krauss, "With Caveat, House Approves Gay-Troops Policy," *New York Times*, 29 September 1993.

18. Thomas L. Friedman, "Gay Rights in the Military," *New York Times*, 21 July 1993.

19. Judith Shklar, *Ordinary Vices* (Cambridge, MA: Harvard University Press, 1984), 47.

20. Ibid.

21. Dennis F. Thompson, "Hypocrisy and Democracy" in Bernard Yack, ed., *Liberalism Without Illusions* (Chicago: University of Chicago Press, 1995), 173–90.

22. Theodore Draper, *A Very Thin Line: The Iran-Contra Affairs* (New York: Hill and Wang, 1991), 25–26, 33–37, 344.

*Dennis F. Thompson is Alfred North Whitehead Professor of Political Philosophy in the Department of Government and the Kennedy School of Government at Harvard University.

Thompson, Dennis F. "Democratic Secrecy." *Political Science Quarterly* 114 (Summer 1999): 181–193.

Intelligence Secrecy and Security in a Free Society

*by William E. Colby**

Knowledge is power, giving strength to one who possesses it, weakening him deprived of it. On this concept secret intelligence arose over the centuries, justified by the sovereign state system in which a nation's independence and welfare depended on its strength.

But in recent years a new concept of national strength has arisen. The active political involvement of a nation's population was seen necessary to national survival and progress. This development led to the necessity of informing and even "indoctrinating" the nation in its government's policies in order to inspire the population to sacrifice for the nation's goals. As universal suffrage, education, and communications improved and spread, so did the need to inform the people of the challenges their nation faced.

In nations with authoritarian discipline or ones amenable to direction by an "establishment," the reserve power of the secret was accepted, and preserved. But free societies and their free press strove for the revelation of the secret, creating a contest between how much should be revealed to produce an informed public and how much should be withheld in the nation's interest. In times of great challenge, national allegiance prevailed over curiosity, and secrets were respected. In other periods, the public and the press were less acquiescent, and exposures proliferated.

In the United States, Vietnam and Watergate marked a turning point in this relationship. The media penetrated the deepest recesses of government. These revelations convinced many citizens that the leadership was manipulating access to fact in order to mislead the public and that it was violating the trust which justified any claim to secrecy. Sensational charges of intelligence abuses then cast doubt on the propriety of any secrets, as it seemed that wrongdoing could be concealed behind even the most justifiable of secrets.

Is secrecy incompatible with a free society? Should we forswear secret intelligence in order to protect our freedoms, and look to a resulting moral strength to save us from threats from the world around us? Or must we accept limits on our freedoms in order to preserve our community in a dangerous world?

We are not faced with such cataclysmic choices. Both exposure and secrecy are essential to a truly free society. But we must achieve a new theory of secrecy appropriate to our new society of instant communication, universal education, and mass opinion.

THE LEGITIMACY OF SECRECY

Secrets are necessary to a free society. A fundamental of our democracy operates in secret—the ballot box, and its secrecy is essential to the workings of our democratic system. A number of other secrets are protected by our laws and legal procedures—the attorney-client and doctor-patient relationship, crop statistics compiled by the Agriculture Department which might upset the free market if prematurely revealed, and income tax returns which may be less forthcoming unless protected from improper exposure to public curiosity.

These and other secrets are accepted and protected in order to make our democracy work. We even see a trend toward greater concern for personal secrecy in the growth of privacy legislation, designed to protect the citizen from exposure and control by the improvements in information acquisition and processing in the modern world. Also, many of our journalists look for more specific, legal recognition of the importance of protecting their sources who do not wish to be disclosed.

If "national security" is discredited as a catch-all justification for total secrecy, a new theory of legitimate secrecy must replace it. The "troopship sailing order" still anachronistically cited by the courts as the justifiable secret must be translated into its modern counterpart. But if the dispatch of troops and their continued employment depends on Congressional and public acquiescence under the War Powers Act, then the rationale for their use must be exposed to our public, and not hidden behind statements claiming to protect intelligence sources or to avoid national diplomatic embarrassment.

One of the best statements of the dilemma of secrecy in our free society was made by President Ford when he said that he would be glad to share our secrets with 214,000,000 Americans if no further exposure would occur. In his statement, he reflected the positive need to inform our citizens of their government's activities but noted also the fact that the world reads our press avidly. Other Presidents have experienced this paradox of secrecy and the free society. President Eisenhower took full responsibility for the 1960 U-2 mission that was shot down over the Soviet Union; he intended to demonstrate that he was fully carrying out his Constitutional responsibilities to direct the executive branch. Yet, as former Soviet Premier Khrushchev explained in his memoirs, Eisenhower's acknowledgment of responsibility raised an intelligence problem to a chief-of-state challenge, and led Khrushchev to cancel the Paris Summit in reprisal. The requirements of public responsibility in our free society conflicted with the mores of international life, which called for secrecy or at least a disclaimer of intelligence problems. President Kennedy followed Eisenhower's path by accepting full responsibility for the "covert" Bay of Pigs operation in 1961 despite the tenuous prior arrangements made for its "plausible denial."

But if American political life operates on a new theory of secrecy, its legal and bureaucratic directives do not reflect it. The language of such directives clings to the outmoded concepts of sovereign secrecy. Valves through which the pressures of the real world can be relieved exist in backgrounders by "senior American officials," in "whistle blowers," and in congressional exposure—all of which contradict the concept of "national security" on which the structure of secrecy is built. Two key documents in recent years have attempted to update basic concepts of secrecy: President Nixon's Executive Order 11652 of March 1972, and the Freedom of Information Act amendments of November 1974. Each has made a step toward a new structure of secrecy, but each contains major weaknesses which will limit its effect.

The Executive Order starts with a call for greater openness in American government, but continues to recognize the propriety of secrecy "in the interest of the national defense or foreign relations of the United States." It sets out three degrees of classification—Top Secret, Secret, and Confidential. The Order includes several innovations, however. It attempts to impose individual responsibility for the decision that a matter should be secret, requiring that individuals be formally authorized to classify. It sets out a procedure for declassification, either by the passage of specific time limits or by review following a request. And it establishes a review committee to monitor the system and to receive and act on complaints.

In fact, however, the Order made little change in the traditional climate and processes of secrecy in intelligence. Instead, it spawned a large bureaucratic exercise of stamping each of thousands of pieces of paper with a notation that it fell within one of the provisions whereby automatic declassification could be deferred. The quantitative requirements of bureaucratic life made it impossible to apply the Order's call for a careful and independent judgment on each piece of paper. Thus the process became mechanical, was handled in large part by the secretarial staff, and concentrated on avoiding chance exposure by error at the cost of extra classification. It did however lead to the release of a number of World War II documents and speeded access to other historical source material in some small degree.

The Freedom of Information Act amendments of November 1974 had a more substantial effect, although their major impact has been on the release of historical documents rather than the revelation of current ones. The amendments' major feature gives any citizen the ability to secure documents that he can reasonably describe unless they fall within one of several exceptions; if the government agency and the citizen disagree, a court is to decide.

This last provision was passed over President Ford's veto; he maintained that a court is not the appropriate body to determine whether documents need protection in the interest of the national defense or foreign policy of the United States. He did concede that a court could properly review whether the government classification officer had acted reasonably. The President may have nevertheless won his point. Congressman Morehead, House manager and conferee for the Act, stated before the vote overriding the veto that the President's procedure would still be "exactly the way the courts would conduct their proceedings."[1]

The Act and its amendments have had a substantial effect in opening to the public view many documents which might never have seen the light of day without it. Its impact was increased by the congressional intelligence investigations of 1975, stimulating many requests for material which had been adverted to in official reports or leaks.

Exciting as some of the revelations under these new rules have been, they have not really solved the dilemma of secrecy in a free society. The revelations may even have been harmful, since it was the sensational quality surrounding past events or activities that captured public attention. The public thus formed an outdated image of a government agency which had already changed its rules and procedures to forswear the activities revealed. The purpose of free information is to encourage debate about our current programs and policies, not to support mere exercises in historical revisionism.

A NEW THEORY OF SECRECY

A new theory of secrecy can begin by approaching the question from its other side, defining what needs to be exposed rather than what needs to be kept secret. It is too easy, to say that "everything" should be known unless there is a good reason for its secrecy, as spelled out by the "exemptions" of allowable secrets in the 1972 Executive Order and under the Freedom of Information Act. Bureaucratic attention then focuses on the exemptions.

Instead, a new theory of secrecy can start with a reversal of the old rule of discipline within the intelligence agencies—the "need to know." This rule provided that secret information would be made available to those who needed it for their duties—and only to them. In the American constitutional system and with modern communications, this rule calls for commitments and procedures to make information available to all participants in American decision making so that they can fully play their roles. The executive branch thus must *inform* the Congress and the public. Intelligence must serve as well as abide by the Constitution. In most cases, "need to know" would also provide the basis for a sharp delineation between the politically significant information needed for public decision-making and the technical detail not essential to such decisions. The latter generally constitutes the data which would be of value to our nation's adversaries.

THE ANGOLAN EXPERIENCE

The recent American experience in Angola provides an example of the need for this new approach. Classified intelligence provided warnings as early as late 1974 that Soviet arms were being provided to the Popular Movement for the Liberation of Angola (MPLA). The Soviet intent was clearly to strengthen this Movement, not in its liberation efforts, but rather against its rivals for control of the country in a post-independence struggle. Liberation was no longer a goal once the Portuguese had announced their intent to free Angola by November 11, 1975. This intelligence was viewed by the executive branch officials privy to it as ominous, in the light of the Soviet Union's growing position in Somalia, the Indian Ocean, and Guinea, and against the backdrop of its mid-1960s aborted attempt to establish a position in the Belgian Congo, now Zaire. The black nations bordering Angola were also concerned about the Soviet aid and suspected it as bearing the seeds of radical challenge to their security. It also raised the likelihood of violence in black-white relations in Southern Africa, to the detriment of hopes that these relations might be improved through negotiations. But the intelligence reports and assessments remained within classified channels and were not shared with the public.

In early 1975, the Forty Committee of the National Security Council approved a secret program of political, non-military assistance for the National Front for the Liberation of Angola (NFLA). For many years the Front had operated against the Portuguese from neighboring Zaire. In compliance with a little noticed amendment to the Foreign Assistance Act passed in December 1974, this assistance was found by President Ford to be important to the national security of the United States and was reported in closed sessions to the Foreign

Relations, Armed Services, and Appropriations Committees of the Senate and the House, in which no particular objections were raised.

By June of 1975, the Soviet assistance was proving effective. Several efforts by African nations failed to arrange a coalition or other compromise among the three groups vying for post-liberation power. The MPLA used the Soviet military aid to push the National Front and the National Union for the Independence of Angola (UNITA) towards their traditional tribal sectors. It was clear that independence in November would find the MPLA in full control of Angola unless the resistance of its two rival groups could be strengthened.

The National Security Council thus approved additional assistance, including military hardware, for these two groups. Again, in conformance with the 1974 law, I briefed the six committees of the Congress, plus the two select committees investigating intelligence, in secret sessions. In response to a request to summarize one committee's reaction to the briefing, I said that I thought the members of the committee were not very much "fur it" nor very much "agin it." Under the existing law, I said this left the executive branch free to proceed, which the committee accepted. Only two or three members noted objections to the activity.

American assistance proved effective. Within two months, the tide of the struggle had reversed. The two opposing groups not only cleared their own areas but began to threaten the MPLA's base in Luanda. The Soviets responded with an escalated large-scale airlift of modern weaponry, including tanks, artillery, and rockets, and the rapid movement of some 12,000 Cuban military personnel to join directly in the battle. The tide reversed again. In October calls were made for additional military equipment and support for the National Front and UNITA. UNITA also, in desperation, accepted assistance from South Africa, thus causing its immediate rejection by a number of black African nations.

The National Security Council supported the increase in assistance, hoping that frustration of the Communist drive could lead to a compromise settlement through the good offices of the nations of black Africa. But available funds had been exhausted, and positive congressional approval was needed to obtain additional funds. While the request was being discussed with the various committees, the secret American assistance in Angola leaked into the press.

Three elements combined to produce a storm of protest. The fall of Vietnam had solidified public opinion against what appeared to be faraway involvement. The intelligence investigations and their sensational revelations produced distrust of secret activity. And there was no preparation of the public for the disclosure of American assistance through a clearly defined over-all United

States policy toward Angola, within which secret assistance might have been understood. That America's assistance went to anti-Portuguese nationalists struggling against a faction favored by the then left-leaning Portuguese colonial authorities, that our assistance came after consultation with neighboring black nations, and that it in no way contemplated Vietnam-style American military involvement, were facts that were lost in the attack against a "covert" policy and program.

The Congress voted against further aid to Angola, and within a few weeks the MPLA's victory over its opponents, with the aid of Soviet airlifted arms and Cuban soldiers, was complete. America's assistance to black nationalist groups resisting Soviet and Cuban supported factions stopped.

There are arguments for and against the Angolan experience. But I describe it here for another purpose, to show that even if American aid was assumed to have been desirable, those Americans who "needed to know" about it, did not. Since much of the intelligence about Soviet and Cuban involvement was initially classified, it was shared only with decision makers in the Executive Branch and with the congressional committees that were briefed in compliance with the 1974 law. Since many of the diplomatic discussions with black African nations were in confidence, their concern over Soviet and Cuban support of the extremist MPLA was kept within Executive Branch policy councils. The assistance given to the National Front and the National Union was not contained within a policy envelope that was debated and agreed upon publicly. Yet the congressional vote revealed clearly that under the Constitution the public had a "need to know" the facts and assessments about Southern Africa if it was to support an American decision to limit the extension of Soviet and Cuban power there.

"Need to Know" and Secrets

"Need to know" can also solve some of the subsidiary questions about how much information should be disseminated. The identity of a secret intermediary whose role, livelihood and even life might be endangered if his identity were exposed need only be known to those actually dealing with him and the staffs who must warrant his reliability by their independent investigations. "Need to know" may require that the substance of the information he reports be made available to those who must use it to make American policy decisions, but none of these policy levels need to know his actual identity. His professional intelligence contacts could thus produce his information in a form appropriate for broad circulation without divulging his identity.

This new concept will place unaccustomed responsibilities on intelligence officers, who have justified the restricted and comfortable circulation of their substantive intelligence reports by the need to protect their sources. With the obligation to disseminate the intelligence equal to the responsibility of acquiring it, new forms of reports and finished assessments must be developed in which the sources do not appear but the information does. In some such cases the source can be generically described when he or it cannot be pinpointed; in others the journalist's convention of a "reliable source" must be used; in others the information or assessment must merely be stated on the intelligence officer's or service's own authority. Close collaboration between collector and analyst would be required because the analyst must have a clear understanding of the reliability of the source. And the reputation of the final product of the service will be built upon its cumulative value and accuracy over time, not by the fascination of an inside look.

The line between dissemination and secrecy is somewhat more difficult to draw in the world of diplomacy, but again the "need to know" approach can provide a guide better than those applied today. The suggestion in the 1920s of "open covenants openly arrived at" proved unrealistic in a world in which national pride rejected any public compromise of initial bargaining positions in diplomatic negotiations. But we have found equal loss of credibility and popular acceptance from attempts to manipulate public opinion and support through selective release of positive news by the government, especially when matched by exposure of negative material through leaks by unhappy line officers.

With recognition that the American public "needs to know" the essential structure of negotiations or other foreign policy problems, these can be briefed in broad terms without exposing the confidences which are essential to the process. The successful example of the statements by "a senior American official" travelling on Secretary Kissinger's aircraft during his Middle East negotiations demonstrates this approach best. Formalized, the approach could lead to a security system appropriate to diplomacy, marking position papers as "protected while under negotiation," identifying confidences provided by foreign friends as not to be associated with them, and limiting the circulation of criticism of foreigners and foreign situations which would cause insult or retribution if revealed. It would certainly be an improvement over current procedures requiring such real justifications to be phrased in the terms of the 1972 Executive Order (i.e., exposure would cause "exceptionally grave," "serious," or mere "damage" to the "national security"). Despite the flood of leaks and other exposures of such material over the past several years, it has been difficult to specify such "damage to the national security" in any but general terms.

In the military field, the approach is just as applicable, and the distinctions reasonably easy to draw. In fact, the Defense Department and the military services to a large degree appreciate the public's and the Congress's "need to know" and are carrying on an extensive program of public information and Congressional briefings, including the content of many documents which still bear secrecy markings threatening doom to any exposer.

This new approach to secrecy is subject to the challenge that it might result in the selective exposure of *favorable* information only, on the thesis that the Congress or the public needs to be "convinced" of a preferred solution rather than to "know" the full spectrum of information and assessment about a problem. But attempts to use this approach only to that limited degree would fall of their own weight. The critic within the system would press the public's need to know his side of the case with its supporting information and rationale. In very little time the record would clearly reveal a bias in the matters exposed, or error in the assessments or data distributed. Any failure of integrity in applying the system would be more identifiable than the present process of throwing the blanket of "national security" over a host of matters which deserve confidential handling but whose exposure certainly would not collapse the Capitol.

Another dilemma has complicated our security system, that of including in it material which may be generally known but which should not be asserted or admitted officially. As a centuries-old rule of international relations the spy has been disowned when caught. In more recent years, this rule has been both violated and respected. President Eisenhower, we recall, assumed responsibility for the U-2. On the other hand, after many detailed journalistic accounts of intelligence operations obtained from leaks, the Executive Branch has refused comment. The first case caused, while the second cases avoided, international confrontations.

An executive branch claim that official admission of such an event would cause "damage to national security" is usually rejected by Congress and the press who point to wide public knowledge of it. With a general acceptance of the public's "need to know," release of such information can be made by a congressional committee or the press without attribution while the executive officially remains silent. This in fact took place with respect to several matters reviewed by the select committees investigating intelligence—in a typical, pragmatic, American constitutional solution to a theoretical dilemma.

Who Is to Decide

A problem inherent in any system of secrecy arises over who is to decide what is to remain secret. The present structure based on the 1972 Executive Order requires the individual appointment of classification officers and gives them the concomitant authority to declassify. As mentioned earlier, it calls for automatic declassification at certain time limits unless the material is exempted, and in such cases provides that the validity of the exemption may be reviewed. The decision in all cases, however, essentially remains with the originating department or agency. The 1974 amendments to the Freedom of Information Act provided an additional locus of decision in court review of the agency's decision that material be withheld. The major unsettled question, though, revolves around the Congress's role and authority in this field.

The present classification system rests on executive branch authority, in Executive Order 11652. Congress has recognized the legitimacy of such a category of information in many statutes, such as the Freedom of Information Act with its exemption of matters "specifically required by Executive Order to be kept secret in the interest of national defense or foreign policy." At the same time, the Congress again in many statutes such as the Freedom of Information Act, has clearly stated that no authority is granted to withhold information from the Congress. With the exception of the sharply limited but still somewhat imprecise area of so-called "executive privilege," the Congress asserts full access to executive department or agency information as an aspect of its constitutionally-provided legislating and appropriating functions.

Sharing secret information with Congress removes the information from executive branch administrative authority, however, and subjects it to possible exposure on the floor, since members are protected by the "speech and debate" clause of the Constitution. In recent times this regrettably has increased its vulnerability to being leaked.[2] A series of confrontations has thus occurred over whether secret information should be shared with a Congress asserting a right to reveal it. Preliminary steps were taken recently to cite Secretary Kissinger and myself for contempt of Congress over this issue. The resolution of those cases, and of many more, eventually occurred through mutual compromise, leaving the ultimate constitutional question unanswered—in the best tradition of the separation of powers.

It is probably best not to decide between the respective and contradictory claims of full access and authority made by each branch, and instead resolve conflicts on a case by case basis. The alternative could be an unrealistic "victory" by one branch over the other or a complex and unworkable over-all arrangement leading to interminable bickering about its interpretation. However, commitment on both sides to the Congress's and the public's "need to know" with recognition that some categories of detail are not "needed," would reduce the occasions of conflict.

PROTECTION OF SECRECY

Any review of the status of secrecy in America must also look at the protection of secrecy. A recent study summarizes its status starkly by saying, "The basic espionage statutes are totally inadequate."[3] The flood of secrets which has marked the past two years has called into question the nation's ability to keep any secrets, has worried many nations dependent on America's support, and has provided our foreign adversaries with a cornucopia of specific material to use against us.

A principal failing of the present secrecy system is that essentially it protects only against foreign espionage. In fact, in today's world, information published becomes available to adversary and ally, as well as citizen, and the intelligence profession in many countries now includes many students and researchers of our open literature. Resultant government attempts to bar publication through injunction have run into the Supreme Court's position that "prior restraints on speech and publication are the most serious and the least tolerable infringement on First Amendment rights."[4] In one case involving a former CIA employee threatening to reveal secrets learned during his employment, an agreement that he made when he began work to keep those secrets was enforced by injunction. However, the government's success in that case depended more on contract law and its fortuitous discovery of the employee's publishing plans before he implemented them than on secrecy law, and punishment after the fact might have been considerably more difficult.

On various occasions, the executive branch has raised with Congress the need for clear legal punishment for the unauthorized publication of the nation's defense and foreign policy secrets. Congress has consistently seen broad dangers to free speech, the free press and executive responsibility in such proposals. The broad restrictions of the British Official Secrets Act were seen as incompatible with the protections of the Bill of Rights. The price of protection of the executive's secrets was seen as too high and the exposure of some of the nation's secrets was accepted as a reasonable cost of a free society. In many cases, such exposure was viewed as a positive contribution to the revelation and correction of governmental wrongdoing.

In the past year, however, two developments make another look at this problem mandatory. First, the flow of legitimate secrets has increased manyfold, with adverse effects on the government's ability to act and to maintain a reasonable discipline among its employees. Serious Americans, including some in the press, are wondering aloud if reasonable limits have not been passed on undisciplined exposure.

The second development is President Ford's recommendation of legislation to punish the unauthorized disclosure of intelligence sources and methods. Following considerable study and debate within the executive branch, he submitted a sharply limited bill. The bill would apply only to those in authorized possession of such secrets and would impose penalties on them for any unauthorized disclosure of the secrets that they had promised to keep. However, it would shield the recipient of the information—whether a journalist or any other citizen—from penalty. It also provides that a court *in camera* can review whether the revealed information was lawfully classified. This provides judicial review of the executive decision that the matter be held secret and protects against capricious over-classification or cover-up of wrongdoing. The modified bill would thus give full recognition to the essentials of our free society and would protect the intelligence sources necessary to its continued existence in a world which has not yet become safe for democracy.

One objection raised against the bill can be easily solved. Journalists have been concerned that they might be subpoenaed as witnesses and asked to divulge sources of leaked information, even though they themselves would be immune from prosecution. A "shield law" provision could be added that any user of the exposed information under the Bill of Rights could not be compelled to testify against his source. This could still permit punishment of the violation based on other evidence.

Within the framework of a new commitment by the executive to the Congress's and the public's "need to know," this better protection of what they do not need to know should gain the Congressional votes and the public support for passage into law. This policy of "need to know" would constitute a new and uniquely American theory of intelligence secrecy which conforms to American values. Indeed, the practice of such a theory could lead to a freer exchange with other nations and peoples of what they too "need to know" about the difficult economic, sociological, political and security problems of the world in the 1980s and 1990s. These then might be negotiated and resolved by cooperation based on knowledge obtained through intelligence.

NOTES

1. *Congressional Record* Nov. 20, 1974, P.H-10865.

2. The Committee of Secret Correspondence of the Continental Congress in 1776 first identified this problem when it refused to pass certain secret information to the Congress as it found "by fatal experience, that the Congress consists of too many members to keep secrets."

3. Harold Edgar and Benno C. Schmidt, Jr., The Basic Espionage Statutes and Publication of Defense Information, 73 *Columbia Law Review* 929, 1076 (1973).

4. *Nebraska Press Assn. v. Stuart*, June 30, 1976.

*William E. Colby was a career intelligence officer. He retired as director of the United States Central Intelligence Agency in 1976.

Colby, William E. "Intelligence Secrecy and Security in a Free Society." *International Security* 1, no. 2 (Autumn 1976): 3–14. © 1976 by the President and Fellows of Harvard College and the Massachusetts Institute of Technology.

Used by permission.

Statements of Senator Russell Feingold, Steven Aftergood, and Heidi Kitrosser

Statements of Senator Russell Feingold, Steven Aftergood, and Heidi Kitrosser*
Before the Subcommittee on the Constitution of the Committee on the Judiciary United States Senate
"Secret Law and the Threat to Democratic and Accountable Government"
April 30, 2008

Opening Statement of Hon. Russell D. Feingold, U.S. Senator from the State of Wisconsin

[...]

[T]here is a particularly sinister trend that has gone relatively unnoticed: the increasing prevalence in our country of secret law.

The notion of secret law has been described in court opinions and law treatises as "repugnant" and "an abomination." It is a basic tenet of democracy that the people have a right to know the law. In keeping with this principle, the laws passed by Congress and the case law of our courts have historically been matters of public record. When it became apparent in the middle of the 20th century that Federal agencies were increasingly creating a body of non-public administrative law, Congress passed several statutes requiring this law to be made public for the express purpose of preventing a regime of secret law.

That purpose today is being thwarted. Congressional enactments and agency regulations are, for the most part, still public. But the law that applies in this country is determined not only by statutes and regulations, but also by the controlling interpretations of courts and, in some cases, the executive branch. More and more, this body of executive and judicial law is being kept secret from Congress as well.

[...]

In a democracy, the government must be accountable to the people, and that means the people must know what the government is doing. Through the classification system and the common law, we have carved out limited exceptions for highly sensitive factual information about military operations, intelligence sources and methods, nuclear programs, and the like. That is entirely appropriate and important to protecting our national security. But even in these areas, Congress and the courts must maintain some access to the information to ensure that the President is acting in accordance with the law and the Constitution. And when it comes to the law that governs the executive branch's actions, Congress, the courts, and the public have the right and the need to know what law is in effect. An Executive that operates pursuant to secret law makes a mockery of the democratic principles and freedoms on which this country was based.

[...]

STATEMENT FOR THE RECORD OF STEVEN AFTERGOOD

My name is Steven Aftergood. I direct the Project on Government Secrecy at the Federation of American Scientists, a non-governmental policy research and advocacy organization. The Project seeks to promote public oversight and government accountability in intelligence and national security policy.

Summary

Secret law that is inaccessible to the public is inherently antithetical to democracy and foreign to the tradition of open publication that has characterized most of American legal history. Yet there has been a discernable [sic] increase in secret law and regulation in recent years. This testimony describes several of the major categories of secret law, including secret interpretations of the Foreign Intelligence Surveillance Act, secret opinions of the Office of Legal Counsel, secret Presidential directives, secret transportation security directives, and more. Legislative intervention may be required to reverse the growth of secret law.

Introduction: "The Idea of Secret Laws Is Repugnant"

To state the obvious, secret law is not consistent with democratic governance. If the rule of law is to prevail, the requirements of the law must be clear and discoverable. Secret law excludes the public from the deliberative process, promotes arbitrary and deviant government behavior, and shields official malefactors from accountability.

In short, as one federal appeals court put it, "The idea of secret laws is repugnant."[1]

From the beginning of the Republic, open publication of laws and directives was a defining characteristic. The first Congress of the United States mandated that every "law, order, resolution, and vote [shall] be published in at least three of the public newspapers printed within the United States."[2]

Secret law in the United States also has a history, but for most of the past two centuries it was attributable to inadvertence and poor record keeping, not deliberate choice or official policy. In 1935, for example, "Federal attorneys, to their great embarrassment, found they were pursuing a case before the Supreme Court under a revoked executive order."[3]

Confronted with the rise of the administrative state and its increasingly chaotic records management practices, Congress responded with a series of statutory requirements designed to regularize the publication of laws and regulations, and to prevent the growth of secret law. These included the Federal Register Act of 1935, the Administrative Procedures Act of 1946, and later the Freedom of Information Act. "The FOIA [Freedom of Information Act] was designed . . . as a means of deterring the development and application of a body of secret law."[4]

But with the start of the Cold War and the creation of the various institutions and instruments of national security decisionmaking, secret law, directives and regulations became a continuing part of American government.

Today, such secrecy not only persists, it is growing. Worse, it is implicated in fundamental political controversies over domestic surveillance, torture, and many other issues directly affecting the lives and interests of Americans.

FISA Court Opinions

Many of the concerns that arise from secret law are exemplified in the dispute over public access to judicial interpretations of the Foreign Intelligence Surveillance Act (FISA), the law that regulates domestic intelligence surveillance.

[...]

In August 2007, the American Civil Liberties Union petitioned the Foreign Intelligence Surveillance Court (FISC) on First Amendment grounds to publicly disclose those legal rulings, after redacting them to protect properly classified information.[5]

The ACLU noted that the contents of the requested rulings had been repeatedly referenced by Administration officials, including the Attorney General and the Director of National Intelligence, without identifiable harm to national security.

While the government contends to this Court that the sealed materials are properly classified and must remain secret in their entirety, administration officials continue publicly to reference, characterize, and discuss the materials in the service of a legislative and political agenda.

Given the many public statements made by government officials, it is plain that at least some of the sealed materials can be disclosed. . . . The administration's own public statements make clear that the materials can be discussed without reference to any particular investigation or surveillance target.[6]

And the requesters proposed a crucial distinction between the Court's legal interpretations, which they argued should be presumptively releasable, and operational intelligence material, which they admitted to be presumptively classified.

The material that the ACLU seeks consists not of factual information but legal analysis. . . . The ACLU seeks court records containing legal reasoning and legal rulings, and only to the extent they contain legal reasoning and legal rulings.[7]

Needless to say, the ACLU does not ask the Court to disclose information about specific investigations or information about intelligence sources or methods. However, this Court's legal interpretation of an important federal statute designed to protect civil liberties while permitting the government to gather foreign intelligence should be made public to the maximum extent possible.[8]

The Justice Department denied that such a distinction could be maintained:

Any legal discussion that may be contained in these materials would be inextricably intertwined with the operational details of the authorized surveillance.[9]

The Justice Department went on to assert, improbably in my opinion, that not even the "volume" of the materials at issue, let alone their contents, could be safely disclosed.[10]

The Court denied the ACLU motion and asserted, in any case, that it lacked the expertise to declassify the requested records without undue risk to national security. Nevertheless, in issuing its denial, the FIS Court endorsed some of the ACLU's major premises:

The ACLU is correct in asserting that certain benefits could be expected from public access to the requested materials. There might be greater understanding of the FISC's decisionmaking. Enhanced public scrutiny could provide an additional safeguard against mistakes, overreaching or abuse. And the public could participate in a better-informed manner in debates over legislative proposals relating to FISA.[11]

Perhaps most important, the Court decision confirmed that the FISA Court is not simply engaged in reviewing government applications for surveillance authorization to ensure that they conform with legal requirements. Rather, the Court has repeatedly generated binding new interpretations of the FISA statute. Thus, aside from the 2007 opinions sought by the ACLU,

> the FISC has in fact issued other legally significant decisions that remain classified and have not been released to the public (although in fairness to the ACLU it has no way of knowing this).[12]

In summary, it has become evident that there is a body of common law derived from the decisions of the Foreign Intelligence Surveillance Court that potentially implicates the privacy interests of all Americans. Yet knowledge of that law is deliberately withheld from the public. In this way, "secret law" has been normalized to a previously unknown extent and to the detriment, I believe, of American democracy.

Office of Legal Counsel Opinions

The Office of Legal Counsel [OLC] at the Justice Department produces opinions on legal questions that are generally binding on the executive branch. Many of these opinions may be properly confidential. But others interpret the law authoritatively and in ways that are reflected in government policy. Yet most of these opinions are secret, so that the legal standards under which the government is actually operating at any given moment may be unknown to the public.

Other witnesses today will address this category of "secret law" in detail. I would only note that there appears to be a precipitous decline in publication of OLC opinions in recent years, judging from the OLC website.[13] Thus, in 1995 there were 30 published opinions, but in 2005 there were 13. In 1996, there were 48 published opinions, but in 2006 only 1. And in 1997 there were 29 published opinions, but only 9 in 2007.

Other things being equal, OLC "publication policy and practice should not vary substantially from administration to administration," according to a statement issued by several former OLC employees. "The values of transparency and accountability remain constant, as do any existing legitimate rationales for secret executive branch law."[14]

But despite these constants, current OLC publication policy has varied substantially from the past Administration, in the direction of greater secrecy.

Reversible Executive Orders

One secret OLC opinion of particular significance, identified last year by Senator [Sheldon] Whitehouse, [D-RI,] holds that executive orders, which are binding on executive branch agencies and are published in the Federal Register, can be unilaterally abrogated by the President without public notice. Because many executive orders are partly rooted in statute or reflect statutory imperatives, this approach has the potential to subvert Congressional intent and to do so secretly.

Based on his review of the document, Sen. Whitehouse paraphrased the classified OLC opinion as follows:

> An Executive order cannot limit a President. There is no constitutional requirement for a President to issue a new Executive order whenever he wishes to depart from the terms of a previous Executive order. Rather than violate an Executive order, the President has instead modified or waived it.[15]

Sen. Whitehouse expressed particular concern about the status of Executive Order 12333, an order published in 1981 which governs the conduct of surveillance and other intelligence activities. The President's authority to issue the order was explicitly derived, in part, from the National Security Act of 1947.[16] Congress plainly has an interest in the exercise of the authority that it delegated by statute.

But if the terms of such an order can be modified or waived by the President "whenever he wishes" and without notice, Congress is left with no opportunity to respond to the change and to exercise its own authorities as it sees fit. Worse, the OLC policy disclosed by Sen. Whitehouse implies a right to actively mislead Congress and the public, who will mistakenly believe that a published order is still in effect even when it isn't.

Executive orders are used to define some of the most basic policy positions of the United States, on everything from assassination of foreign leaders to domestic intelligence activities to protection of human subjects in scientific research. But now it appears that none of these policies are securely established. In fact, any of them may already have been violated (or, rather, "waived") without notice. We just don't know.

Two additional points may be worth noting. First, following Senator White-house's disclosure, I requested a copy of the referenced opinion from OLC under the Freedom of Information Act. The request was denied, on grounds that the opinion is classified, that it would reveal intelligence sources and methods, and that it is protected by deliberative process and attorney-client privileges. Not even the language cited by Sen. Whitehouse could be released.[17] Thus the legal opinion that places the status of thousands of executive orders in doubt itself remains classified.

Secondly, the idea that a President can simply waive an executive order "whenever he wishes" without notice (as opposed to formally rescinding or re-placing it, which he is entitled to do) appears to be a novel interpretation. OLC opinions, as far as I can tell, do not simply restate well-established legal posi-tions; rather, they address new issues and new circumstances. So once again, this classified OLC opinion appears to represent a new departure and a secret new expansion of unchecked executive authority.

Secret Presidential Directives

By late January 2008, the Bush Administration had issued 56 National Secu-rity Presidential Directives (NSPDs) on many diverse national security topics. Most of these directives are undisclosed. Texts of the directives or descriptive fact sheets have been obtained for about a third of them (19). Titles alone have been ascertained for 8 more. Suspected or reported topic areas have been pro-posed for another 19. No data at all are available for at least ten others.[18]

Unlike the case of some other categories of "secret law," this does not represent a significant departure from recent past practice. The Clinton Administration, for example, issued a total of 75 Presidential Decision Directives, with a roughly comparable proportion of classified, unclassified, and unidentified directives.

Nevertheless, such national security directives are a vexing instrument of executive authority since they often combine significant national policy initia-tives with unwavering secrecy. They "commit the Nation and its resources as if they were the law of the land" and yet in most cases "they are not shared with Congress" or the public.[19]

Presidential directives, many of which carry the force of law, can take a be-wildering number of different forms, including memoranda, orders, proclama-tions, and more.[20] Because the President is not subject to the Freedom of Infor-mation Act, the public is dependent on the good graces of the Administration for access to many of these records.

Transportation Security Directives

The Transportation Security Administration [TSA] has imposed a control category known as "Sensitive Security Information" on many of its security policies with the result that some unclassified security regulations affecting ordinary airline passengers have been withheld from disclosure.

In the post-September 11, 2001 statute that created the TSA, Congress directed the agency to devise regulations to prohibit disclosure of "information obtained or developed in carrying out security [if disclosure would] be detrimental to the security of transportation."[21]

But in its implementing rule, TSA interpreted this mandate broadly to permit or require the withholding of an entire class of "security directives."[22]

Consequently, in an apparent departure from congressional intent, a whole series of binding regulations governing passenger inspection, personal identification and other practices were rendered inaccessible, to the frustration of some and the disgust of others. Some Americans understandably wondered why and how they could be required to comply with regulations that they could not see.[23]

Secret Law in Congress

It may be noted that the problem of secret law is not exclusively attributable to the executive branch. Congress has participated in the propagation of secret law through the adoption of classified annexes to intelligence authorization bills, for example. Such annexes may establish national policy, or require or prohibit the expenditure of public funds, all without public notice or a semblance of accountability. In a broader sense, Congress has acquiesced in the secret law practices identified above by failing to effectively challenge them.

On the other hand, Congress enacted legislation for the first time last year to require public disclosure of the amount of the National Intelligence Program budget, a step away from the inherited Cold War practice of secret law.

Conclusion

It should be possible to identify a consensual middle ground that preserves the security of genuinely sensitive national security information while reversing the growth of secret laws, regulations and directives.

The distinction advanced by the ACLU in its pursuit of FIS Court rulings between legal analysis which should be released and operational intelligence information which should be protected was appropriate and correct, in my opinion.

The fact that the FIS Court was unwilling (and believed itself unable) to adopt and apply this distinction in practice suggests that legislative action may be needed to reestablish the norm that secret laws are anathema. [...]

The rule of law, after all, is one of the fundamental principles that unites us all, and one of the things we are committed to protect. Secret law is inconsistent with that commitment.

STATEMENT FOR THE RECORD OF HEIDI KITROSSER
Introduction and Summary

Thank you for inviting me to testify on secret law and the threat that it poses to democratic and accountable government. My testimony will consider the light that constitutional law sheds on the topic. I teach constitutional law at the University of Minnesota Law School and I have written extensively on the constitutional separation of powers, government secrecy, and free speech.

I wish to make two main points today. First, the text, structure, and history of the Constitution reflect a brilliant design that reconciles the dangers of government secrecy with the occasional need for secrecy. Under the Constitution, policy decisions presumptively are transparent in nature, but the executive branch retains some limited leeway to implement those transparent policies in secret. Furthermore, the Constitution gives us structural mechanisms—such as Congress' oversight capacity—to check even secret implementation of transparent policies to ensure that it does not cloak circumvention of the law. Second, over the past several years, we have seen a disturbing trend whereby the executive branch has taken its structural capacities to secretly *implement* law and abused them to secretly *make* new law and to *circumvent* established law. The damage of this trend is exacerbated by the fact that the executive branch has circumvented not only substantive law but also procedural law, such as statutory mandates to share information with Congress.

On the first point, of constitutional design, we see a careful balance between secrecy's virtues and its risks in the Constitution's text and structure. Specifically, we see a negative correlation in the Constitution between the relative openness of each political branch and the relative control that each branch has over the other. Congress is relatively transparent and dialogue-driven. The executive branch, in contrast, is structurally capable of much secrecy, but it also is largely beholden to legislative directives. Thus, the executive branch can be given much leeway to operate in secret, but remains subject to being overseen or otherwise restrained in its secrecy by the legislature. Looking to history, we see an understanding by the founders that such a balance would indeed be struck. Among the President's claimed virtues was a structural capacity for secrecy. Yet it was equally crucial to the founders that the President would be constrained through legislation, oversight, and other means. As Alexander Hamilton put it, one person "will be more narrowly watched and most readily suspected." In short, then, the Constitution reconciles competing needs for openness and secrecy by giving us an executive branch that has the structural capacity to keep secrets, but that must operate within policy parameters that are themselves transparent and subject to revision.

On the second point, as to recent events, we increasingly see a dangerous breakdown in this constitutional structure. For example, we now know that for years the administration relied on a series of secret executive orders and secret legal opinions—many of which to this day remain classified—in order to run secret surveillance and interrogation programs. These programs not only operated under a regime of secret law, but they secretly circumvented statutory mandates. Their existence was made possible in part by the additional circumvention of statutory disclosure mandates. For example, as is now well known, the administration did not comply with its statutory obligation to inform the full congressional intelligence committees of its secret surveillance program.

These events turn the constitutional structure upside down, seizing for the executive branch the power not only to legislate, but to create secret, alternate legislative regimes. The only thing that could make matters worse would be for such events to become normalized in the eyes of Americans. Given the length of time in which these events have been unfolding and given the administration's continuing lack of cooperation with congressional and public information requests, I fear that we have already started down this road. I urge Congress to use its substantial constitutional powers of legislation and oversight to make clear to the executive branch and to all Americans that secret law has no place in our constitutional system.

I. The Constitutional Design: Policy Transparency and Limited Leeway for Secret Implementation[24]

A. Overview of the Constitutional Design

The Constitution's founders recognized their crucial task to "combin[e] the requisite stability and energy in government with the inviolable attention due to liberty and to the republican form."[25] One of the most important ways in which they met this challenge was by granting policy-making powers to the relatively open, transparent, and dialogue-driven legislature while leaving policy implementation predominantly to an executive branch with substantial capacities for secret, energetic, and efficient operation. The founders thus designed a Constitution under which laws and law-making presumptively are transparent and subject to political checking and revision. The laws themselves, however, can provide some room for secret implementation.

Of course, the line between law-making and law-implementation often is a fine one. As the Supreme Court observed in *Mistretta v. U.S.*,[26] "Congress simply cannot do its job absent an ability to delegate power under broad general directives."[27] Law implementation thus can entail the crafting of sub-policies, or "quasi-legislating."[28] But important protections remain to ensure that executive branch policy-making does not give way to a regime of secret law. First, the executive branch remains subject to statutes and thus cannot craft policies which circumvent (let alone secretly circumvent) those statutes. In this sense, the executive branch is obliged to act under a transparent statutory framework, however broad that framework might be. Second, Congress—both through legislation and through its constitutional power to create its internal rules[29]—may craft policies for conducting oversight to ensure that the executive branch does not secretly circumvent statutory law or otherwise abuse its implementation powers. Third, Congress can craft legislation requiring openness in executive branch policy-making. Congress did just this, for example, in creating the Administrative Procedure Act ("APA"). It created the APA partly to ensure that the administrative state not become a parallel, secret law-making regime.[30] Fourth, the judiciary retains the power to reign in executive branch activity that crosses the line from statutory implementation to unconstrained law-making. It famously did just this in the seminal case of *Youngstown Sheet & Tube Co. v. Sawyer*.[31] It also did this when it invalidated two delegations of power to the administrative state before the latter was constrained statutorily through the APA.[32]

B. Constitutional Text, Structure, and History

That the Constitution creates a structure in which policy-making presumptively must be open and subject to political checks is exemplified by several aspects of constitutional text, structure, and history.

First, there is a negative correlation between the relative openness of each political branch and the relative control that each branch has over the other. Congress is a relatively transparent and dialogue-driven branch,[33] and its core tasks are to pass laws that the executive branch executes and to oversee such execution.[34] The executive branch, in contrast, is capable of much secrecy,[35] but also is largely beholden to legislative directives in order to act.[36] This creates a rather brilliant structure in which the executive branch can be given leeway to operate in secret, but remains subject to being overseen or otherwise restrained in its secrecy by the legislature.

Second, historical references to secrecy as an advantage of a single President (as opposed to an executive council)—particularly two widely cited Federalist papers[37]—also cite accountability and the ability of other branches and the people to uncover wrongdoing as a major advantage of a single President. For instance, Alexander Hamilton famously stated that a single President is desirable because "[d]ecision, activity, secrecy, and dispatch will generally characterize the proceedings of one man in a much more eminent degree than the proceedings of any greater number."[38] Yet Hamilton, in the same Federalist Paper in which he made this statement, followed the statement with an approving explanation of the responsibility and potential transparency of a single President. Hamilton argued that "multiplication of the executive adds to the difficulty of detection," including the "opportunity of discovering [misconduct] with facility and clearness." One person "will be more narrowly watched and most readily suspected."[39] Similar observations were made at the Philadelphia convention in which the Constitution was written[40] and throughout the constitutional ratification period.[41] For example, William Davie explained in the North Carolina ratification debate:

> With respect to the unity of the Executive, the superior energy and secrecy
> wherewith one person can act, was one of the principles on which the
> Convention went. But a more predominant principle was, the more obvious
> responsibility of one person. It was observed that, if there were a plurality
> of persons, and a crime should be committed, when their conduct was to be
> examined, it would be impossible to fix the fact on any one of them, but that
> the public were never at a loss when there was but one man.[42]

The historical evidence thus reflects a balanced constitutional design whereby executive secrecy is expected but remains tethered to political accountability.

Third, the only explicit textual reference to secrecy occurs in Article I, § 5, of the Constitution, which requires Congress to keep journals of its proceedings, but allows each chamber to exempt "such Parts as may in their Judgment require Secrecy."[43] That fact by itself does not tell us very much, as one could argue that a secret-keeping prerogative is intrinsic in the President's executive and commander-in-chief duties. What it does reflect, however, is a constitutional structure that permits secrecy only under conditions that will ensure some political awareness of and ability to check such secrecy. The very framing of the congressional secrecy provision as an exception to an openness mandate, combined with a logical and historical expectation that a large and deliberative legislative body generally will operate in sunlight suggest a framework wherein final decisions as to political secrecy are trusted only to bodies likely to face internal and external pressures against such secrecy.

Finally, an executive branch that can keep secrets but that can be reigned [sic] in by Congress reflects the most logical reconciliation of competing constitutional values. On the one hand, the Constitution clearly values transparency as an operative norm. This is evidenced by myriad factors, including the necessities of self-government, the First Amendment, and Article I's detailed requirements for a relatively open and dialogic legislative process. On the other hand, the Constitution reflects an understanding that secrecy sometimes is a necessary evil, evidenced both by the congressional secrecy allowance and by the President's structural secrecy capabilities. Permitting executive branch secrecy, but requiring it to operate within policy parameters themselves open and subject to revision, largely reconcile these two values.

C. Justice Jackson's Three Zones of Presidential Power

The above analysis complements Justice Jackson's influential analysis from his concurrence in *Youngstown Sheet & Tube Co. v. Sawyer*.[44] In *Youngstown*, Justice Jackson described three basic zones of presidential power.[45] Presidential power is "at its maximum" in zone one.[46] In this first zone, "the President acts pursuant to an express or implied authorization of Congress."[47] In zone two, presidential power is at an uncertain, intermediate level.[48] In this second zone, "the President acts in absence of either a congressional grant or denial of authority."[49] Here, the President:

can only rely upon his own independent powers, but there is a zone of twilight in which he and Congress may have concurrent authority, or in which its distribution is uncertain. Therefore, congressional inertia, indifference or quiescence may sometimes, at least as a practical matter, enable, if not invite, measures on independent presidential responsibility. In this area, any actual test of power is likely to depend on the imperatives of events and contemporary imponderables rather than on abstract theories of law.[50]

In zone three the President's "power is at its lowest ebb."[51] In this third zone, he "takes measures incompatible with the express or implied will of Congress."[52] He thus "can rely only upon his own constitutional powers minus any constitutional powers of Congress over the matter."[53]

The first zone is the simplest from the perspective of the constitutional presumption of transparent law and policy. The President's authority is at his highest in this zone because his actions are legitimized by statutory authority, which itself is legitimized partly by the relative transparency of the legislative process. Hence, even where secrecy characterizes aspects of the President's implementation, the policy framework under which he operates itself is transparent. The second zone raises the possibility of inherent presidential powers or presidential powers pursuant to very broad, ambiguous statutory authority, while the third zone raises the barely more than theoretical possibility of a situation in which the president alone, and not Congress, is empowered to act. Actions in the respective zones indeed have progressively less presumptive legitimacy. The absence of a relatively clear policy-making process means the absence of legislative transparency. And in the third zone, not only is such process absent but in its place is a known, established policy whose presence gives false assurance to the public and to other branches.

II. Swallowing the Transparency Rule: The Arrival of Secret Law[54]

Secret law poses a very real and present threat to our constitutional system. Some striking, non-exhaustive, examples include the [legal interpretations authorizing the National Security Agency's secret warrantless electronic surveillance program and the claimed authority to override public executive orders in secret discussed by Steven Aftergood as well as the legal justifications for the CIA's secret interrogation program].

[...]

D. Some Key Conflicts between These Events and Constitutional Design

Some of the examples discussed above reflect direct violations of the constitutional separation of powers. At minimum, they all reflect a clash with the principles and purposes underlying the same. What follows are some key aspects of these conflicts.

1. Youngstown Zone Three Action as Troubling New Norm

Among the striking aspects of the warrantless surveillance and torture programs are the weakness in each case of the administration's claim that it complies with existing statutes and thus its implicit (and to some degree explicit) reliance on the notion that the administration may secretly circumvent existing statutes. In short, the administration in both cases is in Justice Jackson's *Youngstown* zone three, whereby the President "can rely only upon his own constitutional powers minus any constitutional powers of Congress over the matter." As discussed earlier, *Youngstown* zone three actions carry a deep presumption of illegality for very good reason. Such actions bypass the transparent and dialogic protections of the legislative process. And because they conflict with existing statutes, they mislead the public, particularly when the circumventing actions occur in secret.

Despite its exceedingly weak statutory arguments, the administration in each case provided no basis to conclude that Congress constitutionally was disabled from acting and that the Administration thus had exclusive constitutional right to craft and follow its own laws and to do so in secret. Instead, the administration offered bald assertions about the danger of making public the very existence of our laws. As explained earlier, those assertions barely pass the "laugh test."[55]

2. The Intra-Executive-Branch Analogue of the Zone Three Problem

While it may not share the legal ramifications of the secret override of statutes, secret revision by the executive branch of its own publicly announced policies—such as its executive orders—violates core purposes of separated powers. As with *Youngstown* zone three actions, such secret policy changes implicitly assure the public that certain policies are in place when in fact they have been altered or withdrawn. The President thus retains the power of law-making while avoiding political accountability.

Congress can and should take legislative and/or oversight action to prevent such abuses by the executive branch. As detailed throughout this statement and at greater length elsewhere,[56] Congress has ample constitutional prerogative to set legislative parameters by which the President may act in secret and by which he must disclose information to Congress or to the public.

3. Disregard for Statutory Oversight Mandates and for Congressional Oversight Generally

Effective congressional oversight must take place if limits on secret law-making are to be more than theoretical. Such oversight is a means, for example, to determine if legislatively sanctioned secrecy has been harnessed to cloak unauthorized policy-making or policy-circumvention. Yet as the experience with the surveillance and torture programs demonstrate, the oversight system too often cracks under the weight of executive branch disregard and legislative acquiescence in the same. Such disregard and acquiescence is facilitated in part by the same arguments used to justify the circumvention of substantive statutory directives. That is, the executive branch often simply asserts that statutorily required disclosures or requested disclosures would prove too dangerous, and these assertions too often are met with acquiescence.

This breakdown in oversight, in which the executive branch effectively calls the shots, gets things exactly backwards from a constitutional perspective. As discussed throughout this statement and in the sources cited throughout, the executive branch constitutionally is constrained by Congress' policy directives regarding information-sharing. It is for Congress, through statutory terms and through its constitutional power to make rules for its proceedings, to set the policy framework under which information disclosure, including negotiations about the same, can take place. Current statutory and chamber rules indeed strike myriad balances and provide flexibility to accommodate secrecy and other needs as they arise in hearings.[57] Openness can, of course, pose dangers. But so can secrecy, as recent events attest. The Constitution's founders struck a balance by leaving it to Congress to openly debate and establish policies, including rules on information disclosure. The executive is left to implement the rules, sometimes in secret, and sometimes through give-and-take with Congress as the rules provide.

4. The Troubling Ease With Which Secrecy "Needs" Are Invoked Generally

In the *Youngstown* zone three contexts described above and more generally, the administration has repeatedly invoked claims of "national security necessity" to justify secret policy-making. Yet as already noted, these claims often are made cavalierly, rarely rising beyond mere assertion. Congress ought not to accede to such empty claims.

CONCLUSION

Congress should use its substantial legislative and oversight powers to make clear to the administration and to the American people that secret law has no place in the United States of America.

Thank you for soliciting my views on this important topic. Please do not hesitate to let me know if I can be of further assistance.

NOTES FOR STATEMENT FOR THE RECORD BY STEVEN AFTERGOOD

Notes have been renumbered for this edition.

1. *Torres v. I.N.S.*, 144 F.3d 472, 474 (7th Cir. 1998).

2. 1 Stat. 68. Cited by Harold C. Relyea, "The Coming of Secret Law," *Government Information Quarterly*, Vol. 5, No. 2, 1988, pp. 97–116.

3. Relyea, "The Coming of Secret Law," p. 104, citing *Panama Refining Company v. Ryan*, 293 U.S. 388 (1935).

4. *Providence Journal Co. v. Department of the Army*, 981 F.2d 552, 556 (1st Cir. 1992).

5. Motion of the American Civil Liberties Union for Release of Court Records, August 8, 2007. Copy available at: http://www.fas.org/irp/agency/doj/fisa/aclu080807.pdf. The same records were independently sought by the Electronic Frontier Foundation under the Freedom of Information Act, without success.

6. Reply of the American Civil Liberties Union in Support of Motion for Release of Court Records, September 14, 2007, at pp. 1, 2, 10. Copy available at: http://www.fas.org/irp/agency/doj/fisa/aclu-reply091407.pdf.

7. Ibid., pp. 8, 12–13.

8. Motion of the American Civil Liberties Union for Release of Court Records, August 8, 2007, at p. 12.

9. Opposition to the American Civil Liberties Union's Motion for Release of Court Records, August 31, 2007, at p. 14. Copy available at: http://www.fas.org/irp/agency/doj/fisa/aclu-doj-resp083107.pdf.

10. Ibid., p. 14, footnote 9.

11. Memorandum Opinion by Judge John D. Bates, Foreign Intelligence Surveillance Court, Docket No. MISC. 07-01, December 11, 2007, at p. 16. Copy available at: http://www.fas.org/irp/agency/doj/fisa/fisc121107.pdf.

12. Ibid., at page 15.

13. http://www.usdoj.gov/olc/opinionspage.htm. Some opinions were not published until years after they were issued. Accordingly, publication of additional recent opinions might still be expected in years to come. Nevertheless, even allowing for such delays, there appears to be a real decline in the current pace of publication.

14. Principles to Guide the Office of Legal Counsel, a White Paper published by the American Constitution Society, December 2004, available at: http://www.acslaw.org/node/5561.

15. Statement of Sen. Whitehouse, December 7, 2007, Congressional Record, pp. S15011–S15012, available at: http://www.fas.org/irp/congress/2007_cr/fisa120707.html.

16. "United States Intelligence Activities," Executive Order 12333, 4 December 1981, preamble: ". . . by virtue of the authority vested in me by the Constitution and statutes of the United States of America, including the National Security Act of 1947, as amended . . ." Copy available at: http://www.fas.org/irp/offdocs/eo12333.htm.

17. Letter to me from Paul P. Colborn, Special Counsel, Office of Legal Counsel, February 5, 2008, denying a FOIA request dated December 18, 2007.

18. A collection of unclassified NSPDs, fact sheets and related material is available here: http://www.fas.org/irp/offdocs/nspd/index.html.

19. Relyea, "The Coming of Secret Law," op. cit., p. 108. See also U.S. General Accounting Office, "National Security: The Use of Presidential Directives to Make and Implement U.S. Policy," January 1992, report no. GAO/NSIAD-92-72.

20. See Harold C. Relyea, "Presidential Directives: Background and Overview," Congressional Research Service, updated August 9, 2007. Copy available at: http://www.fas.org/sgp/crs/misc/98-611.pdf.

21. The Aviation and Transportation Security Act, 49 U.S. Code 114(s)(1).

22. Protection of Sensitive Security Information, Interim Final Rule, Federal Register, May 18, 2004, pp. 28066–28086, section 15.5 (b)(2), copy available at: http://www.fas.org/sgp/news/2004/05/fr051804.html.

23. See my article "The Secrets of Flight," Slate, November 18, 2004, available at: http://www.slate.com/id/2109922/.

ENDNOTES FOR STATEMENT FOR THE RECORD BY HEIDI KITROSSER

24. Much of this discussion is drawn, and in some cases quoted directly (including internal citations), from three articles: Heidi Kitrosser, *Congressional Oversight of National Security Activities: Improving Information Funnels*, 29 CARDOZO L. REV. 1049 (2008); Heidi Kitrosser, *Macro-Transparency as Structural Directive: A Look at the NSA Surveillance Controversy*, 91 MINN. L. REV. 1163 (2007); Heidi Kitrosser, *Secrecy and Separated Powers: Executive Privilege Revisited*, 92 IOWA L. REV. 489 (2007)

25. The Federalist No. 37, at 194 (James Madison) (Clinton Rossiter ed., 1961).

26. 488 U.S. 361 (1989).

27. *Id.* at 372.

28. "Quasi-legislation" is a term often used in administrative law to describe agency crafting of rules under broad statutory directives. It is perhaps in administrative law, particularly in discussions of the non-delegation doctrine, that the line between policy-making and policy-implementation has been most thoroughly considered.

29. U.S. Const., art. I, §5, cl. 2.

30. *See, e.g.*, Erik Luna, *Transparent Policing*, 85 IOWA L. REV. 1107, 1165 (2000); William Mock, *On the Centrality of Information Law: A Rational Choice Discussion of Information Law and Transparency*, 17 JOHN MARSHALL J. OF INFO. & COMPUTER L., 1069, 1098 (1999).

31. 343 U.S. 579 (1952).

32. Panama Ref. Co. v. Ryan, 293 U.S. 388 (1935); A.L.A. Schecter Poultry Corp. v. United States, 295 U.S. 495 (1935). *See also, e.g.*, Cass Sunstein, *Constitutionalism After the New Deal*, 101 HARV. L. REV. 421, 446–48 (1987).

33. *See, e.g.*, U.S. Const., art. I, §5, cl. 2 (requiring Congress to keep and to publish journals of its proceedings); U.S. Const., Art. I, § 7 (laying out relatively open and dialogic process of legislating, including requirements that legislation be approved by both branches, that any presidential objections be communicated to Congress and considered by them, and that "the Names of the Persons voting for and against the Bill shall be entered on the Journal of each House respectively").

34. *Compare, e.g.*, U.S. Const., art. I, § 8 to U.S. Const., art. II, § 2.

35. *See, e.g.*, The Federalist No. 70, at 424 (Alexander Hamilton) (Clinton Rossiter ed., 1961)); The Federalist No. 64, at 392–93 (John Jay) (Clinton Rossiter ed., 1961)).

36. *See, e.g.*, Saikrishna Prakash, *A Critical Comment on the Constitutionality of Executive Privilege*, 83 MINN. L. REV. 1143, 1154–69 (1999).

37. *See supra* n. 12.

38. *See* Hamilton, *supra* n. 12, at 424.

39. *Id.* at 427–30.

40. 1 The Records of the Federal Convention of 1787, at 74, 254 (Max Farrand, ed., Yale Univ. Press 1966).

41. *See, e.g.*, Daniel N. Hoffman, Governmental Secrecy and the Founding Fathers 29–32 (1981).

42. *Id.* at 30 (quoting 3 The Records of the Federal Convention, supra note 17, at 347).

43. U.S. Const., art. I, § 5, cl. 3.

44. 343 U.S. 579, 634 (1952) (Jackson, J., concurring).

45. *Id.* at 635–38.

46. *Id.* at 635.

47. *Id.*

48. *Id.* at 637.

49. *Id.*

50. *Id.*

51. *Id.*

52. *Id.*

53. *Id.*

54. Some discussion in sections A & D, including some direct quotations (which incorporate their internal citations) is drawn from two articles: Heidi Kitrosser, *Congressional Oversight of National Security Activities: Improving Information Funnels*, 29 CARDOZO L. REV. 1049 (2008); Heidi Kitrosser, *Macro-Transparency as Structural Directive: A Look at the NSA Surveillance Controversy*, 91 MINN. L. REV. 1163 (2007).

55. Indeed, the testimonial explanation of then Attorney General Gonzales as to the need to keep the warrantless surveillance program secret literally did not pass the laugh test. The transcript reflects audience laughter following his stated justification. Gonzales Testimony, *supra* note 39, at 107.

56. *See* sources cited, *supra* note 1.

57. *See, e.g.*, Kitrosser, *Congressional Oversight*, *supra* note 31, at 1073–75, 1080–83, 1084–86 (detailing such rules).

*From 1993 to 2011 **Russell Feingold** represented the state of Wisconsin in the Senate, where he served on the Judiciary, Foreign Relations, Budget, and Intelligence Committees. After leaving the Senate, he founded Progressives United, a nonprofit organization that focuses on opposing corporate dominance in American politics.

Steven Aftergood directs the Project on Government Secrecy, which works to reduce the scope of official secrecy and to promote public access to government information.

Heidi Kitrosser is a professor of law at the University of Minnesota. Professor Kitrosser writes primarily about constitutional law, particularly free speech, separation of powers, and government secrecy.

Opening statement of Senator Russell Feingold and statements for the record of Steven Aftergood and Heidi Kitrosser before the Senate Subcommittee on the Constitution of the Committee on the Judiciary, April 30, 2008. "Secret Law and the Threat to Democratic and Accountable Government." 110th Cong.

Part 2: Striking the Proper Balance between Secrecy and Access to Information

Instinct might suggest that the more information that is kept out of the public domain, the more secure we will be. After all, if disclosure of some information is dangerous, why not err on the side of secrecy? As this section demonstrates, however, too much secrecy can also reduce security. Efforts to maximize the benefits to society of both access to information and secrecy face a difficult balancing act. The government has not had much success in reaching the proper balance, according to Elizabeth Goitein, who argues in "Overclassification: Its Causes and Consequences" that overclassification within the executive branch is a long-standing and intractable problem with significant adverse consequences. A former director of the federal government's Information Security Oversight Office, J. William Leonard, goes one step further, asserting that unnecessarily shielding information from public view is not the only cost of overclassification. Policy decisions, he argues, also suffer from excessive secrecy, harming our national security by leading to the adoption of ill-conceived policies that might not have survived public scrutiny.

And it is not just government actors who struggle to determine the appropriate level of information disclosure. The scientific community also faces particular challenges in this regard. The free flow of information is a long-established touchstone of the scientific community, in which researchers learn from one another and build upon one another's discoveries and insights. But as Elisa D. Harris and John D. Steinbruner explain, such openness can pose national security threats when the information relates to potentially dangerous scientific advances. Consider the discovery of a gene sequence for a highly contagious deadly virus or the blueprints to a new weapons delivery system. Harris and Steinbruner therefore argue that the scientific community needs to establish a system to weigh "the potential scientific, medical, or other benefits" of certain research areas against "the potential security risks."

As you read the selections, consider the following questions:
• What are the benefits of limiting access to information? What are the costs? Are there ways to reap the national security benefits of secrecy

without incurring those costs? If not, how will we know when the costs outweigh the benefits?

• How can we determine when disclosure of certain information will be more dangerous than nondisclosure? Who should be charged with making that assessment? Should it be government officials involved in policymaking in the relevant area—who may therefore be tempted to shield their decision making from public scrutiny? Or should it be disinterested decision-makers with no stake in policy decisions? If disinterested decision-makers are better, how can we ensure that such decision-makers are sufficiently knowledgeable about the potential impact of the information to make a wise decision?

• When it is difficult or impossible to determine whether certain information is better kept secret or shared, what should the default position be?

• Should scientists restrict access to their research when it has potential security implications? Should the government? Harris and Steinbruner suggest that the scientific community make decisions regarding what information to publish through a peer-reviewed balancing test, with the potential value of the information playing a role in determining whether it is made public. Is there any information that should never be published, no matter its scientific value?

Overclassification: Its Causes and Consequences

by Elizabeth Goitein*

Executive officials may classify information if its disclosure would threaten national security. This authority, judiciously exercised, can save lives. Any time important government information is withheld from the public, however, the mechanism of self-government is weakened. The trade-off is clear, and there is ample evidence that the government is failing to strike the correct balance in its current classification practices.

The unnecessary classification of information—"overclassification"—is rampant, and nearly everyone who works with classified information recognizes the problem. In 1993, Senator John Kerry, who reviewed classified documents while chairing the Senate Select Committee on POW/MIA Affairs, commented, "I do not think more than a hundred, or a couple of hundred, pages of the thousands of [classified] documents we looked at had any current classification importance."[1] The next year, Donald Rumsfeld acknowledged, "I have long believed that too much material is classified across the federal government as a general rule."[2]

The problem of overclassification demands attention in part because it jeopardizes national security. Excessive secrecy impedes the sharing of information within government, making it more difficult to draw connections and anticipate threats. Furthermore, it erodes respect for the classification system and necessitates the granting of security clearances to millions of people—two phenomena that increase the risk of leaks.

Overclassification also corrodes democratic government. Secret programs stifled public debate on our government's actions after the September 11, 2001, attacks. Should the military and CIA have used torture to extract information from detainees? Should the National Security Agency have eavesdropped on Americans' communications without warrants? Classification forced the nation to rely on leaked information to debate the legality and desirability of these measures, and to do so well after they were in place.

A notable aspect of the classification system is the persistent gap between written regulation and actual practice. Presidents since Franklin Delano Roosevelt have issued executive orders governing classification. These orders have long purported to impose commonsense limits, such as a ban on using classification to conceal wrongdoing. The current order—Executive Order 13,526, issued by President Obama—prohibits classification if significant doubt exists about the need for secrecy. In practice, however, such limits often fall by the wayside.

A 2011 report by the Brennan Center for Justice, which this essay's author co-wrote, concluded that the primary source of the "implementation gap" is a skewed incentive structure. Numerous incentives push powerfully in the direction of classification, ranging from the desire to conceal government misconduct to the simple press of business. By contrast, there are essentially no incentives to refrain from or challenge improper classification. Most notably, those who classify documents improperly are rarely if ever held accountable.[3]

In order to succeed, any effort to reduce overclassification must address these skewed incentives. Unfortunately, there are few efforts under way that would meaningfully tackle this problem.

THE SCOPE OF THE PROBLEM

Overclassification is as old as classification itself. A 1940 executive order by President Franklin Delano Roosevelt marked the beginning of the modern classification regime,[4] and each of the multiple government studies to address the issue since then—including the Coolidge Committee in 1956,[5] the Wright Commission in 1957,[6] the Moss Subcommittee in 1958,[7] the Seitz Task Force in 1970,[8] the Stilwell Commission in 1985,[9] the Joint Security Commission in 1994,[10] the Moynihan Commission in 1997,[11] and the 9/11 Commission in 2004[12]—has reported widespread overclassification.

Current and former government officials have given startling estimates of the problem's scope. Rodney B. McDaniel, who served as National Security Council executive secretary under President Ronald Reagan, estimated that only 10 percent of classification was for "legitimate protection of secrets."[13] A Department of Defense official in the George W. Bush administration estimated that overclassification stood at 50 percent.[14] Government statistics bear out these assessments. When a member of the public asks an agency to declassify a particular record (through a process called "mandatory declassification review"), the agency determines about 90 percent of the time that at least some of the information need not remain classified.[15]

Stark examples of overclassification have occurred throughout the history of the classification regime. Some border on the absurd, while others represent violations of the public trust:

- In 1947, an Atomic Energy Commission official issued a memo on nuclear radiation experiments that the government conducted on human beings. The memo instructed, "No document [shall] be released which refers to experiments with humans and might have [an] adverse effect on public opinion or result in legal suits. Documents covering such work . . . should be classified 'secret.'"[16]
- In the 1960s, the FBI wiretapped Dr. Martin Luther King Jr.'s telephone. Information about this activity was classified "top secret," meaning that its disclosure could cause "exceptionally grave damage to the national security,"[17] even though its sole purpose, in the FBI's own words, was to gain information about King's personal life that could be used to "completely discredit [him] as a leader of the Negro people."[18]
- In *New York Times Co. v. United States*,[19] the Nixon administration asked the Supreme Court to enjoin publication of the "Pentagon Papers"—government documents regarding relations between the United States and Vietnam. Before oral argument, Solicitor General Erwin Griswold reviewed the items that the government wanted to keep secret and "quickly came to the conclusion that most of them presented no serious threat to national security."[20]
- In responding to a Freedom of Information Act request, the Defense Intelligence Agency in 2004 blacked out portions of a biographical sketch of General Augusto Pinochet, even though the Clinton administration had already declassified the document. Redacted portions revealed that Pinochet "[d]rinks scotch and pisco sours; smokes cigarettes; likes parties. Sports interests are fencing, boxing and horseback riding."[21]
- A 2006 cable from a U.S. diplomat discussed a wedding he attended in Russia's Republic of Dagestan. The paragraph describing a typical Dagestani wedding, including the following observations, was classified:

> Dagestani weddings . . . take place in discrete parts over three days. On the first day the groom's family and the bride's family simultaneously hold separate receptions. . . . The next day, the groom's parents hold another reception, this time for the bride's family and friends. . . . On the third day, the bride's family holds a reception for the groom's parents and family.[22]

THE COSTS OF OVERCLASSIFICATION

If information that merits classification is released, the costs can be extraordinarily high—a fact that is well understood. The costs of overclassification are less evident, but they can be equally grave.

A. Risks to National Security

Excessive secrecy undermines intelligence efforts by inhibiting information sharing. There are legitimate reasons why information is not shared in some cases, including both security and privacy considerations. But needless restrictions can jeopardize national security.

The 9/11 Commission found that "the failure to share information was the single most important reason why the U.S. Government failed to detect and disrupt the September 11 plot."[23] It cataloged federal agencies' failures in this regard and concluded:

> What all of these stories have in common is a system that requires a demonstrated "need to know" before sharing. . . . Such a system implicitly assumes that the risk of inadvertent disclosure outweighs the benefits of wider sharing. Those Cold War assumptions are no longer appropriate.[24]

Despite efforts to encourage broader information sharing after 9/11, the problem persists. In 2008, the Homeland Security Advisory Council, responding to a request from then-secretary Michael Chertoff, issued a report titled *The Top Ten Challenges Facing the Next Secretary of Homeland Security*. The report noted that the classification system "is broken and is a barrier (and often an excuse) for not sharing pertinent information with homeland security partners."[25]

The problem is particularly acute with respect to information sharing between federal and local officials. Local law enforcement agencies increasingly are at the forefront of domestic counterterrorism efforts. Yet these officials are frequently unable to obtain key information in a timely manner (or at all) because it is classified. As the chief of police for the District of Columbia testified before Congress: "Information collected by the federal government is sometimes overly classified, causing valuable information that should be shared to remain concealed."[26]

Unnecessary secrecy also undermines respect for the classification system, thereby promoting leaks. As early as 1956, the Coolidge Committee found a "casual attitude toward classified information" within the Defense Department, and concluded: "When much is classified that should not be classified at all . . . respect for the system is diminished and the extra effort required to adhere faithfully to the security procedures seems unreasonable."[27] As Supreme Court justice Potter Stewart would later put it, "When everything is classified, then nothing is classified."[28]

Finally, when so much information is needlessly classified, even government employees and contractors who perform relatively nonsensitive jobs may require access to classified information. As of October 2012, nearly 5 million people held a security clearance.[29] As this pool grows, the chance that it will include some people who handle classified information irresponsibly increases. Granting clearances to roughly one in every 50 American adults is simply not an effective strategy for keeping secrets.

B. Harm to Democratic Decision Making

Information is the critical ingredient to responsible self-governance. James Madison famously wrote that "a popular Government, without popular information, or the means of acquiring it, is but a Prologue to a Farce or a Tragedy; or perhaps both."[30] The people require knowledge of their government's actions to debate the issues of the day, to hold their elected representatives accountable at the ballot box for choices that do not reflect their wishes, and to seek redress in the courts for violations of the law.

By limiting oversight, overclassification increases the likelihood of unwise or illegal activity. Consider the legal defenses of torture prepared by Department of Justice lawyers within the Office of Legal Counsel after 9/11. Not only were the actual interrogation techniques classified; so, too, was the legal analysis claiming that the statutes prohibiting torture do not apply to the president acting as commander in chief, and that the infliction of pain constitutes torture only if it approximates the sensation of "death, organ failure, or serious impairment of body functions."[31] This legal analysis was binding on the executive branch. It therefore constituted a type of "secret law," the classification of which was wholly inappropriate, according to the former head of the office that oversees the classification system (the Information Security Oversight Office, or ISOO).[32]

The torture memos are a prime example of how secrecy can promote unsound reasoning by policymakers and undermine democratic decision making. The improper classification and close holding of these opinions prevented other government lawyers from testing their legal soundness. Had this occurred, the memos might never have been issued; instead, they remained in place for several months until a new head of the Office of Legal Counsel concluded that they were poorly reasoned and withdrew them.[33]

More fundamentally, secrecy prevented the public and Congress from debating, before the fact, the use of torture to acquire intelligence from detainees. Whether one supports or opposes the use of torture, the decision to use it redefined our national identity and—through its effect on how others perceive us—may change the course of our history. The hallmark of a democracy is that the people have both a right and an obligation to participate in such consequential decisions.

C. Financial Costs

According to ISOO, the government spent $9.77 billion on classification in fiscal year 2012. This estimate does not include the classification budgets of some of the largest intelligence agencies—including the CIA, the NSA, and the Office of the Director of National Intelligence—because the amount they spend on classification is *itself* classified.[34]

Experts have repeatedly noted that the government would save money by reducing overclassification. In 1994, the Joint Security Commission reported that "overhauling the classification system will have cost-beneficial impacts on virtually every aspect of security. . . . If we classify less . . . we will have to clear fewer people, buy fewer safes, and mount fewer guard posts."[35] Similarly, the Moynihan Commission reported: "Classification means that resources will be spent throughout the information's life cycle . . . that would be unnecessary if the information were not classified."[36]

Although there are no studies on this point, the amount that the government would save by reducing overclassification is certain to be significant. To give just one example: Paper printouts of classified information must be stored in safes or special filing cabinets. A 1993 General Accounting Office study found that the average cost to the government of a regular five-drawer filing cabinet was $174.17, while the average cost of the equivalent container for classified information was $2,160[37]—a difference of an order of magnitude.

Why Overclassification Occurs

The prevalence of overclassification derives from an imbalance in incentives. Several forces unrelated to national security considerations push strongly in the direction of classifying documents. There are few if any countervailing forces, virtually ensuring that overclassification will occur.

A. Incentives to Overclassify

1. A Culture of Secrecy

In the words of Senator Moynihan, "a culture of secrecy took hold within American Government" during the Cold War.[38] This culture was premised on the notion that we knew who the adversary was; we knew that the adversary's spies were attempting to learn military secrets; and we knew exactly who, among trusted federal officials, needed to know the information that we were trying to keep out of enemy hands.[39]

As many commentators have observed, these Cold War assumptions no longer hold.[40] Deciding who has a "need to know" is a difficult and error-prone undertaking when the enemy is loosely defined and the means and targets of attack are unpredictable. Moreover, given terrorism's transnational nature and focus on civilian targets, information routinely must be shared among federal, state, local, and foreign governments, as well as private-sector partners and even members of the public.[41] Nonetheless, as one member of the 9/11 Commission stated, the "unconscionable culture of secrecy [that] has grown up in our Nation since the cold war" remains.[42]

While the modern culture of secrecy may have its proximate genesis in the Cold War, its roots go much deeper—to the very nature of bureaucracies and human interaction. Francis Bacon observed in 1597 that "knowledge itself is power."[43] Government officials use classification to confer importance on the information they are conveying—and, by extension, on themselves. As stated by one journalist in recounting a conversation with a retired intelligence official:

> [The official] . . . noticed that classification was used not to highlight the underlying sensitivity of a document, but to ensure that it did not get lost in the blizzard of paperwork that routinely competes for the eyes of government officials. If a document was not marked "classified," it would be moved to the bottom of the stack. . . . He observed that a security classification, by extension, also conferred importance upon the author of the document.[44]

Information control also can be a key weapon in turf wars between agencies. A former national security official under President Reagan estimated that "protection of bureaucratic turf" accounted for fully 90 percent of classification.[45] Former intelligence officers told *Washington Post* reporters that "the CIA reclassified some of its most sensitive information at a higher level so that National Counterterrorism Center staff . . . would not be allowed to see it."[46]

Organizational cultures affect everyone within the group, and they tend to be self-reinforcing. Accordingly, individual classifiers need not possess a Cold War mind-set, a desire to enhance their own status, or a sense of competition with other agencies to be influenced by this phenomenon. In an agency characterized by a culture of secrecy, classification simply becomes "how we do things"—a manifestation of the culture that in turn perpetuates it.

2. Concealment of Governmental Misconduct or Incompetence

Executive officials involved in instances of governmental misconduct or incompetence have an obvious motive to withhold the evidence. The executive order bans classification intended to "conceal violations of law, inefficiency, or administrative error," or to "prevent embarrassment to a person, organization, or agency."[47] There is no mechanism, however, for enforcing compliance with this provision. Moreover, the prohibition focuses on the classifier's intent. As long as he can posit some national security implication to disclosure—however tenuous or secondary—the classifier can maintain that hiding wrongdoing was not his motive.[48]

Since its inception, the classification system has been used for the improper purpose of concealing government misconduct. In the 1950s, the government, after receiving funds from Congress for heavy-duty military cargo planes, classified pictures showing that the aircraft "were converted to plush passenger planes." When a member of Congress sent a letter asking about the conversion, he "found that even his letter of inquiry was stamped 'Secret.'"[49]

A more recent example is the classification of the NSA's post-9/11 warrantless wiretapping program. At the time, the Foreign Intelligence Surveillance Act required the government to obtain a court order to wiretap communications involving a U.S. citizen or legal permanent resident. The program ignored this mandate. While Justice Department lawyers advanced creative arguments to justify its legality,[50] it is difficult to escape the conclusion that the program was classified because of its shaky legal footing. The alternative explanation—that the program would have lost its effectiveness if disclosed—appears to be off the mark, given that the administration persuaded Congress to amend the Foreign Intelligence Surveillance Act (publicly, of course) to allow the program to continue even after it was revealed.[51]

Some insiders have opined that mitigating political damage is classifiers' primary goal. Former solicitor general Erwin Griswold published an op-ed in which he wrote, "It quickly becomes apparent to any person who has considerable experience with classified material" that "the principal concern of the classifiers is not with national security, but rather with governmental embarrassment of one sort or another."[52] In describing the classified documents he reviewed on the Select Committee on POW/MIA Affairs, Senator Kerry stated that "more often than not" documents were classified "to hide negative political information, not secrets."[53]

3. Facilitation of Policy Implementation

From the early days of the Republic, it has been well understood that secrecy enables executive officials to act quickly and easily, unencumbered by the slow workings and uncertain outcomes of the democratic process. Even within the executive branch, initiatives may be implemented more smoothly when fewer people are involved. Alexander Hamilton had this fact in mind when he argued that there should be a single president to lead the executive branch: "Decision, activity, secrecy, and dispatch will generally characterise the proceedings of one man, in a much more eminent degree, than the proceedings of any greater number."[54]

Highly compartmented classification can be an attractive option for officials who know that their desired course of action may raise eyebrows among colleagues. In the words of one former CIA official: "One of the tried-and-true tactical moves is if you are running an operation and all of a sudden someone is a critic and tries to put roadblocks . . . you classify it and put it in a channel that that person doesn't have access to."[55] When the FBI wiretapped Dr. King's telephone, it sought to hide its activities even from the attorney general, lest his involvement scuttle the initiative.[56]

Classification also can be used to ease policy implementation by limiting congressional involvement. In the late 1980s, President Reagan sought congressional support for military aid to the government of El Salvador, which was fighting left-wing rebels. Some members, however, were concerned about the Salvadoran government's potential connections with right-wing paramilitary groups known as "death squads." In response to a Freedom of Information Act request, the administration released portions of a CIA report stating that Salvadoran military officers had pledged to punish human rights offenders—but classified the report's conclusion that the Salvadoran government was "incapable of undertaking a real crackdown on the death squads."[57] Through this selective classification, the administration was able to strengthen its case before Congress.

Finally, classification can be a tool to shape public opinion about controversial policies. After 9/11, the detention without charge of alleged "enemy combatants" at Guantánamo Bay, Cuba, became the subject of fierce public debate. Administration officials characterized the prisoners as "the worst of the worst" and claimed that their detention was critical to national security.[58] The government classified its individual assessments of the risks posed by detainees, however—many of which revealed only that there was "no reason recorded" for the detainee's transfer to Guantánamo.[59] Disclosing these documents would not have exposed intelligence sources or methods—there were none to expose—but it would have weakened the administration's public case for indefinite detention.

In short, it is simply easier to get things done—particularly controversial things—when fewer people have the information necessary to object. It is thus tempting for executive officials to withhold (or selectively release) information, regardless of whether the policy they seek to advance skirts the edges of the law or is squarely within the permissible bounds of government action.

4. Fear of Repercussions for Failing to Protect Sensitive Information

Classifiers who fail to protect sensitive national security information face serious repercussions. The Moss Committee noted the potential for "stern punishment,"[60] while the 9/11 Commission pointed to the possibility of "criminal, civil, and internal administrative sanctions."[61] A former intelligence official put it this way: "Revealing 'too much' generally has been considered career-threatening."[62] The specter of such consequences provides a strong incentive to classify.

Official sanctions aside, there is a natural tendency among government officials to be risk-averse when it comes to classification decisions.[63] After all, in matters of national security, the perceived stakes are generally high, and perceived failures on the part of institutions or individuals entrusted with protecting national security are not looked upon kindly by the public—as evidenced by the widespread criticism of the government's failure to anticipate and prevent the 2009 Fort Hood shootings or the 2013 Boston Marathon bombings.[64]

No government official wants to be responsible for releasing information that leads to the next terrorist attack, regardless of how remote that possibility might be. The harms caused by overclassification, while grave and certain, are more attenuated and unlikely to be traced to any one government official. It is not surprising, under these circumstances, that government officials feel pressure to err—and to err liberally—on the side of classification.

5. The Press of Business

Deciding whether information meets the criteria for classification can be difficult and time-consuming (although the actual process of classifying documents is relatively easy, as discussed below). Original classifiers—those who are authorized to determine, in the first instance, whether information should be classified—must assess whether disclosure "could reasonably be expected" to harm national security.[65] This may require them to consider a range of hypothetical scenarios and to assess the likelihood of each unfolding. Derivative classifiers, who are authorized to classify documents based on guidance provided by original classifiers, may be required to undertake a similarly subjective and complex analysis if the guidance provided to them is vague.

Although this analysis is essential to the integrity of the classification system, busy government officials who deal with large volumes of national security information may feel that they do not have the luxury of engaging in it. They are likely to default to classification, given the potential consequences of failing to classify sensitive information. This phenomenon was noted by the Project on National Security Reform, an independent organization that contracted with the Department of Defense to study the national security interagency system:

> To decide not to classify a document entails a time-consuming review to evaluate if that document contains sensitive information. Former officials within the Office of the Secretary of Defense, for example, who often work under enormous pressure and tight time constraints, admit to erring on the side of caution by classifying virtually all of their pre-decisional products.[66]

The practice of classification by default interacts with, and reinforces, the culture of secrecy in some agencies. Classifiers feel safe to follow this practice because they work in an environment in which secrecy is expected, not challenged. Newcomers quickly learn that classification is an acceptable time-saving option, and the cycle is perpetuated.

B. Lack of Incentives to Refrain from or Challenge Overclassification

1. Ease of Classifying Documents

Several features of the current system allow government officials to classify documents without careful consideration. First, the executive order governing classification requires an original classifier to be "*able to* identify and describe the damage" to national security that could result from unauthorized disclosure.[67] Under current ISOO guidelines, however, the classifier need not actually do so.[68]

Second, the executive order states that only specified categories of information, such as "intelligence sources or methods," are subject to classification.[69] Classifiers, however, need only "[cite] the applicable classification categor[y]";[70] they need not demonstrate its applicability. The Moynihan Commission concluded that merely citing a category "does little to lessen the tendency to classify by rote and does not adequately reflect the long-term consequences of an original classification decision."[71]

Classification based on instructions in a classification guide requires even less explanation. ISOO's guidelines allow a derivative classifier to cite an entire guide, which may be dozens or hundreds of pages, rather than the specific provision that justifies classifying the information in question.[72]

Advances in technology have exacerbated the problem by automating much of the classification process. When creating a document or email on a classified computer system, officials are presented with drop-down prompts that can include default settings for the classification level or other required information. Classification thus can be accomplished with a few quick (and unthinking) clicks of a mouse.[73]

In the absence of any system to enforce compliance, even the few basic steps that classifiers must take are often dispensed with. For example, every classified document should contain a line that states "Classified By" or "Derived From," to identify the source of classification authority.[74] In a typical year in which ISOO conducted document reviews at select agencies, 18 percent of reviewed documents contained no "Classified By" or "Derived From" line. In its fiscal year 2009 report, describing the results of its document review at 15 agencies, ISOO observed that "three-fourths of the agencies had discrepancies in more than 50 percent of their documents; several agencies had error rates higher than 90 percent."[75]

In short, despite the consequential nature of the decision to withhold government information from the public, classifying documents in accordance with current rules is a fairly easy exercise—and classifying documents without regard to the rules is an even easier one.

2. Lack of Accountability for Improper Classification

Government officials have little to lose when they classify documents unnecessarily. The 9/11 Commission observed, "No one has to pay the long-term costs of over-classifying information, though these costs—even in literal financial terms—are substantial. There are no punishments for *not* sharing information."[76] A former FBI official put it bluntly: "It is a truism that no one ever got in trouble for over-classifying."[77]

The executive order governing classification allows agencies to penalize officials who classify information improperly.[78] Even if agencies wanted to impose sanctions, however, there is no systematic mechanism in place to identify offenders. In 1994, the Joint Security Commission proposed that each agency appoint an overclassification ombudsman who would "routinely review a representative sample of the agency's classified material" to enable "real-time identification of the individuals responsible for classification errors," with an eye toward "attach[ing] penalties to what too often can be characterized as classification by rote."[79] This recommendation was not implemented.

The executive order does obligate each agency with classification authority to maintain a self-inspection program, including a review and assessment of the agency's classified product.[80] But there is no requirement that the agency use this process to identify employees who classify excessively, let alone hold them accountable. Moreover, many agencies simply fail to maintain the required program.[81]

Even strongly worded threats of punishment may be ineffective in the absence of a mechanism to measure compliance and a commitment to enforcing the rules. Remarkably, despite widespread acknowledgment within government that overclassification is a systemic problem, it does not appear that a classifier has ever been stripped of classification authority for improperly classifying information.[82]

3. Inadequate Training

Many of the factors that encourage overclassification could be countered by a strong training program that instilled a proper understanding of, and respect for, the limitations of classification authority. ISOO has long required training for all executive branch employees who create, process, or handle classified information. Nonetheless, agencies routinely have failed to adhere to their training obligations. For example, ISOO has found that many agencies failed to provide any refresher training whatsoever, despite ISOO's directive that such training be provided annually.[83]

When training is provided, its content is often limited. Government officials report that their training has emphasized the need to protect classified information, with little or no focus on the limits of their classification authority.[84] The results are predictable. According to the former head of ISOO, many derivative classifiers seem unaware that they lack authority to classify information that has not been deemed classified by an original classifier—a basic tenet of the classification system.[85]

President Obama's 2009 executive order for the first time requires that classifiers receive periodic training on avoiding overclassification.[86] If faithfully implemented, this requirement could begin to chip away at the culture of secrecy that pervades so many of the relevant agencies. Such an outcome, however, depends on agencies' conforming their training programs to applicable requirements—an area in which they consistently have fallen short in the past.

4. No Rewards for Challenges to Improper Classification Decisions

The executive order on classification recognizes that employees with access to classified documents are uniquely positioned to identify instances of overclassification. It provides that "authorized holders of information who, in good faith, believe that its classification status is improper are encouraged and expected to challenge the classification status of the information." It directs agencies to establish procedures for bringing such challenges and prohibits retaliation against participating employees.[87]

Yet classification challenges by federal employees are rare. While there were more than 95 million decisions to classify information in fiscal year 2012, officials brought only 402 formal challenges.[88] The reasons for the rarity of these challenges are evident.

First, agencies do not comply with their obligation to encourage classification challenges. A recent ISOO report noted that "many authorized holders of classified information are not aware of this provision, and therefore, do not challenge classification decisions as much as should be expected in a robust system." In some cases, ISOO found that agencies had put no procedures in place for employees to bring such challenges.[89]

Second, there are no incentives to challenge improper classification decisions—and strong incentives not to challenge them. ISOO's implementing directive states that employees "shall present [classification] challenges to an original classification authority [OCA] with jurisdiction over the information."[90] In some instances, this may be the very person who made the decision that the employee wishes to challenge. Even if an impartial OCA could be found, in an agency characterized by a culture of secrecy, there would be tremendous pressure—from one's peers, if not one's supervisors—not to challenge colleagues' classification decisions.

REFORM EFFORTS

Although the executive and legislative branches have been convening committees for decades to analyze the problem of overclassification, there have been surprisingly few efforts to reform classification practices, and fewer still that have met with success. One noteworthy exception is the Fundamental Classification Policy Review (FCPR) undertaken by the Department of Energy in 1995.[91]

The goal of the FCPR was to review the agency's classification guidance and practice against a presumption of disclosure. Fifty technical experts, divided into seven topical working groups, examined hundreds of classification guides, soliciting public input along the way. Ultimately, the Department of Energy declassified millions of documents, including the complete list of U.S. nuclear explosive tests.[92]

In 2009, President Obama attempted to re-create the success of the FCPR, ordering all relevant agencies to conduct a "Fundamental Classification Guidance Review" (FCGR). It is too soon to say whether this review, completed in 2012, was successful. There is some reason for optimism: of 3,103 classification guides reviewed, 869 were canceled or consolidated. For fiscal year 2012, ISOO reported a decline in the number of original classification decisions, which it attributed to the FCGR.[93]

Unfortunately, there is room for skepticism as well. The decline in original classification decisions was more than offset by the increase in derivative classification decisions.[94] If the FCGR merely results in original classifiers labeling more of their decisions as "derivative," its benefits will be limited.

More fundamentally, what propelled the success of the 1997 FCPR was leadership at the agency level. Energy Secretary Hazel O'Leary, reportedly motivated by personal horror at classified radiation experiments performed on human subjects during the Cold War, initiated and supported the review. By contrast, many of the reports agencies provided to ISOO during the recent FCGR suggest grudging compliance rather than active engagement.[95] Indeed, many agencies failed to provide the basic information ISOO requested.[96]

Congress has stepped into the mix, as well, passing the Reducing Over-Classification Act in 2010. The act allows agencies to consider an employee's "consistent and proper classification of information" in determining whether to make certain cash incentive awards. It also requires agencies' inspectors general to conduct two evaluations assessing employees' compliance with classification rules and identifying policies or practices that may be contributing to persistent misclassification. And it codifies certain enhanced training requirements contained in President Obama's executive order.[97]

Finally, at President Obama's request, the Public Interest Declassification Board—an independent advisory committee created by Congress—issued recommendations in November 2012 for a "transformation" of the classification system. A year later, the administration announced that it would create an interagency "Classification Reform Committee" to consider the recommendations and implement those that are accepted.[98] Some of the board's proposals could make a dent in the culture of secrecy, such as creating a "safe harbor" for classifiers who make good-faith decisions not to classify, requiring separate training units on avoiding overclassification, developing training models based on agencies' best practices, and providing incentives for employees to challenge improper classification decisions.[99]

Such changes would make it easier for classifiers to act responsibly. However, neither Congress nor the Public Interest Declassification Board put forward any proposals for holding officials accountable when they overclassify. They thus provided the carrot, but not the stick. Given that some incentives to overclassify are deeply ingrained in human nature, it is unlikely that any reforms will succeed if there are no consequences for misusing the system. Until accountability is introduced, the balance between security and openness will continue to be struck in a manner that serves neither end.

NOTES

1. *Mark-up of Fiscal Year 1994 Foreign Relations Authorization Act: Hearing before the Subcomm. on Terrorism, Narcotics and Int'l Operations of the S. Comm. on Foreign Relations*, 103rd Cong. 32 (1993) (statement of Sen. John Kerry) [hereinafter 1993 FRAA hearing].

2. Donald Rumsfeld, op-ed, *War of the Words*, WALL St. J., July 18, 2005, at A12.

3. *See generally* ELIZABETH GOITEIN AND DAVID M. SHAPIRO, REDUCING OVERCLASSIFICATION THROUGH ACCOUNTABILITY (Brennan Center 2012).

4. KEVIN R. KOSAR, CONG. RESEARCH SERV., 97-771, SECURITY CLASSIFICATION POLICY AND PROCEDURE: E.O. 12958, AS AMENDED 3 (2009).

5. DEF. DEP'T COMM. ON CLASSIFIED INFO., REPORT TO THE SECRETARY OF DEFENSE 6 (1956) [hereinafter COOLIDGE COMMITTEE REPORT].

6. COMM'N ON GOV'T SEC., 84TH CONG., REPORT OF THE COMMISSION ON GOVERNMENT SECURITY 174–75 (1957).

7. H.R. REP. No. 85-1884, at 4 (1958) [hereinafter MOSS SUBCOMMITTEE REPORT].

8. DEF. SCI. BD. TASK FORCE ON SECRECY, REPORT OF THE DEFENSE SCIENCE BOARD TASK FORCE ON SECRECY 2 (1970).

9. COMM'N TO REVIEW DOD SEC. POLICIES AND PRACTICES, KEEPING THE NATION'S SECRETS: A REPORT TO THE SECRETARY OF DEFENSE app. E, at 31 (1985).

10. JOINT SEC. COMM'N, REDEFINING SECURITY: A REPORT TO THE SECRETARY OF DEFENSE AND THE DIRECTOR OF CENTRAL INTELLIGENCE 6 (1994) [hereinafter JOINT SECURITY COMMISSION REPORT].

11. COMM'N ON PROTECTING AND REDUCING GOV'T SECRECY, REPORT OF THE COMMISSION ON PROTECTING AND REDUCING GOVERNMENT SECRECY, S. DOC. No. 105-2, at xxi (1997) [hereinafter MOYNIHAN COMMISSION REPORT].

12. NAT'L COMM'N ON TERRORIST ATTACKS UPON THE U.S., THE 9/11 COMMISSION REPORT: FINAL REPORT OF THE NATIONAL COMMISSION ON TERRORIST ATTACKS UPON THE UNITED STATES 417 (2004) [hereinafter 9/11 COMMISSION REPORT].

13. *See* Moynihan Commission Report, *supra* note 11, at 36 (quoting McDaniel).

14. *Too Many Secrets: Overclassification as a Barrier to Critical Information Sharing: Hearing before the Subcomm. on Nat'l Sec., Emerging Threats, and Int'l Relations of the H. Comm. on Gov't Reform*, 108th Cong. 82 (2004) (testimony of Carol A. Haave, Deputy Under Secretary of Defense, Counterintelligence and Security).

15. Info. Sec. Oversight Office, 2010 Report to the President 20 (2011) [hereinafter ISOO 2010 Report].

16. Memorandum from O. G. Haywood Jr., Colonel, Corps of Engineers, to Dr. [Harold] Fidler, Atomic Energy Commission, Medical Experiments on Humans (Apr. 17, 1947), *available at* http://www.hss.energy.gov/ HealthSafety/ohre/roadmap/overview/074930/index.html.

17. Exec. Order No. 13,526 § 1.2(a)(1), 75 Fed. Reg. 707, 707 (Jan. 5, 2010).

18. Final Report of the Senate Select Comm. to Study Government Operations: Intelligence Activities and the Rights of Americans, Book III, S. Rep. No. 94-755, at 125 (1976) [hereinafter Church Committee Final Report Book III].

19. New York Times Co. v. United States, 403 U.S. 713 (1971).

20. Erwin N. Griswold, Op-Ed, *Secrets Not Worth Keeping: The Courts and Classified Information*, Wash. Post, Feb. 15, 1989, at A25.

21. http://www.gwu.edu/~nsarchiv/NSAEBB/NSAEBB90/index2.htm.

22. http://www.nytimes.com/interactive/2010/11/28/world/20101128-cables-viewer.html#report/cables-06MOSCOW9533.

23. *Emerging Threats: Overclassification as a Barrier to Critical Information Sharing: Hearing before the Subcomm. on Nat'l Sec., Emerging Threats, and Int'l Relations of the H. Comm. On Gov't Reform*, 109th Cong. 115 (2005) (statement of Richard Ben-Veniste, Commissioner, National Commission on Terrorist Attacks upon the United States).

24. *See* 9/11 Commission Report, *supra* note 13, at 355–56, 417.

25. Homeland Sec. Advisory Council, Top Ten Challenges Facing the Next Secretary of Homeland Security 8 (2008).

26. *The Over-Classification and Pseudo-Classification: Part I, II, and III: Hearing before the Subcomm. on Intelligence, Info. Sharing, and Terrorism Risk Assessment of the House Comm. on Homeland Sec.*, 110th Cong. 27 (2007) (statement of Chief Cathy L. Lanier, Metropolitan Police Department, Washington, D.C.) (emphasis omitted).

27. Coolidge Committee Report, *supra* note 5, at 6, 9.

28. New York Times Co. v. United States, 403 U.S. 713, 730 (1971) (Stewart, J., concurring).

29. Office of the Dir. of Nat'l Intelligence, 2012 Report on Security Clearance Determinations 3 (2013).

30. Letter from James Madison to W. T. Barry (Aug. 4, 1822), *reprinted in* The Complete Madison 337 (Saul K. Padower ed., 1953).

31. Memorandum from John C. Yoo, Deputy Assistant Attorney Gen., to William J. Haynes II, Gen. Counsel of the Dep't of Defense 11-14, 39 (Mar. 14, 2003).

32. *See Secret Law and the Threat to Democratic and Accountable Government: Hearing before the Subcomm. on the Constitution of the S. Comm. on the Judiciary*, 110th Cong. 11 (2008) (statement of J. William Leonard, Former Director, Information Security Oversight Office).

33. Jack Goldsmith, The Terror Presidency 144–51, 167 (2007).

34. Info. Sec. Oversight Office, 2012 Annual Report to the President (2013) [hereinafter ISOO 2012 Report] at 24, 25.

35. Joint Security Commission Report, *supra* note 10, at 94.

36. Moynihan Commission Report, *supra* note 11, at 35.

37. U.S. Gen. Accounting Office, GAO/NSIAD-94-55, Classified Information: Costs of Protection Are Integrated With Other Security Costs 15 (1993).

38. Moynihan Commission Report, *supra* note 11, at xliv.

39. James B. Steinberg, et al., Building Intelligence to Fight Terrorism, Brookings Institution Policy Brief, No. 125 1–2 (2003).

40. *See, e.g.*, J. William Leonard, *The Corrupting Influence of Secrecy on National Policy Decisions*, in 19 Research in Social Problems and Public Policy, Government Secrecy 421, 423 (Susan Maret, ed., 2011).

41. Steinberg et al., *supra* note 40, at 2.

42. *2005 Overclassification Hearing*, *supra* note 24, at 89 (statement of Richard Ben-Veniste, former Commissioner, National Commission on Terrorist Attacks upon the United States).

43. Francis Bacon, Religious Meditations, Of Heresies (1597), *reprinted in* The Works of Francis Bacon: Literary and Religious Works pt. III, 179 (New York, Hurd & Houghton 1873).

44. Ted Gup, Nation of Secrets: The Threat to Democracy and the American Way of Life 44 (2007).

45. C3I: Issues of Command and Control 68 (Thomas P. Croakley ed., 1991) (*quoting* Rodney McDaniel, former Exec. Secretary of the Nat'l Sec. Council).

46. Dana Priest and William M. Arkin, *Top Secret America: A Hidden World, Growing beyond Control*, Wash. Post, July 19, 2010, at A1.

47. Exec. Order No. 13,526 § 1.7(a)(1)–(2), 75 Fed. Reg. at 710.

48. *See* ACLU v. Dep't of Defense, 628 F.3d 612 (D.C. Cir. 2011).

49. Moss Subcommittee Report, *supra* note 7 at 4 (1958).

50. http://www.justice.gov/opa/whitepaperonnsalegalauthorities.pdf.

51. *See* Joby Warrick & Walter Pincus, *How the Fight for Vast New Spying Powers Was Won*, Wash. Post, Aug. 12, 2007, at A1.

52. Griswold, *supra* note 20, at A25.

53. *1993 FRAA Hearing*, *supra* note 1 (statement of Sen. John Kerry).

54. The Federalist No. 70, at 424 (Alexander Hamilton) (Clinton Rossiter, ed., 1961).

55. Gup, *supra* note 44, at 28–29 (quoting former covert CIA operative Melissa Mahle).

56. Church Committee Final Report Book III, *supra* note 18, at 125.

57. *See* Jeffrey Richelson et al., eds., *Dubious Secrets*, 90 Nat'l Sec. Archive Electronic Briefing Room (May 21, 2003), http://www.gwu.edu/~nsarchiv/NSAEBB/NSAEBB90/index.htm.

58. *See, e.g.*, Katharine Q. Seelye, *Threats and Responses: The Detainees*, N.Y. Times, Oct. 23, 2002, at A14.

59. BBC, *WikiLeaks: Many at Guantanamo 'Not Dangerous,'* BBC News (Apr. 25, 2011), http://www.bbc.co.uk/news/world-us-canada-13184845.

60. Moss Subcommittee Report, *supra* note 7, at 158.

61. 9/11 Commission Report, *supra* note 12, at 417.

62. M. E. Bowman, *Dysfunctional Information Restrictions*, Fall/Winter 2006–2007 Intelligencer: Journal of U.S. Intelligence Studies 29, 34 (2007).

63. *See* J. William Leonard, Dir., Info. Sec. Oversight Office, at the National Classification Management Society Annual Training Seminar (June 12, 2003) ("There is no underestimating the bureaucratic impulse to 'play it safe' and withhold information").

64. *See, e.g.*, Jonah Goldberg, op-ed, *Fort Hood Killings: FBI Asleep on the Job*, Sun Sentinel (Fort Lauderdale), Nov. 17, 2009, at A21; David M. Herszenhorn, *Lawmakers Fault Pre-Marathon Bombing Efforts*, Boston Globe, June 3, 2013.

65. Exec. Order No. 13,526 § 1.4, 75 Fed. Reg. at 709.

66. Project on National Security Reform, Forging a New Shield 304 (2008).

67. Exec. Order No. 13,526 § 1.1(a)(4), 75 Fed. Reg. at 707 (emphasis added).

68. 32 C.F.R. § 2001.10(c) (2011).

69. Exec. Order No. 13,526 § 1.4(c), 75 Fed. Reg. at 709.

70. Exec. Order No. 12,958 § 1.7(a)(5), 60 Fed. Reg. 19,823, 19,828 (Apr. 20, 1995).

71. Moynihan Commission Report, *supra* note 11, at 30.

72. 32 C.F.R. § 2001.22(c)(1).

73. Little public information is available regarding the automated systems used by agencies engaged in classification activity. The description here is based on multiple interviews with current and former government employees who work or worked with classified computer systems.

74. 32 C.F.R. §§ 2001.21(a)(1), 2001.22(b)&(c).

75. INFO. SEC. OVERSIGHT OFFICE, 2009 REPORT TO THE PRESIDENT 18 (2010) [hereinafter ISOO 2009 REPORT].

76. 9/11 COMMISSION REPORT, *supra* note 12, at 417.

77. Bowman, *supra* note 62, at 34.

78. Exec. Order No. 13,526 § 5.5(c), 75 Fed. Reg. at 726.

79. JOINT SECURITY COMMISSION REPORT, *supra* note 10, at 25.

80. Exec. Order No. 13,526 § 5.4(d)(4), 75 Fed. Reg. at 725–26.

81. In fiscal year 2005, for example, ISOO visited 18 agencies and found that 7 of them had no self-inspection programs whatsoever, while 7 others had programs that did not include any review of classified documents. INFO. SEC. OVERSIGHT OFFICE, 2005 REPORT TO THE PRESIDENT 26 (2006) [hereinafter ISOO 2005 REPORT].

82. Leading classification experts were unaware of such an instance. Email from J. William Leonard, former Dir., Info. Sec. Oversight Office, to Elizabeth Goitein, Co-Dir., Liberty & Nat'l Sec. Program, Brennan Center for Justice (July 1, 2011, 3:39 p.m. EST) (on file with Brennan Center); email from Steven Aftergood, Dir., Project on Gov't Secrecy, Fed'n of Am. Scientists, to David M. Shapiro, Counsel, Brennan Center for Justice (June 22, 2010, 1:03 p.m. EST) (on file with Brennan Center).

83. *See, e.g.*, INFO.SEC. OVERSIGHT OFFICE, 2008 REPORT TO THE PRESIDENT 23 (2009); INFO. SEC. OVERSIGHT OFFICE, 2006 REPORT TO THE PRESIDENT 23 (2007); ISOO 2005 REPORT, *supra* note 81, at 26.

84. Information about the nature of classification trainings was provided/confirmed by current and former government employees who participated in such trainings and who asked not to be identified.

85. Telephone Interview with J. William Leonard, former Dir., Info. Sec. Oversight Office (Apr. 15, 2011).

86. Exec. Order No. 13,526 §§ 1.3(d) & 2.1(d), 75 Fed. Reg. at 708 & 712.

87. Exec. Order No. 13,526 § 1.8, 75 Fed. Reg. at 711.

88. ISOO 2012 REPORT, *supra* note 34, at 8.

89. ISOO 2010 REPORT, *supra* note 15, at 13; ISOO 2009 REPORT, *supra* note 76, at 9.

90. 32 C.F.R. § 2001.14(a).

91. U.S. DEP'T OF ENERGY, REPORT OF THE FUNDAMENTAL CLASSIFICATION POLICY REVIEW GROUP (1997).

92. *See* Steven Aftergood, *Reducing Government Secrecy: Finding What Works*, 27 YALE L. & POL'Y REV. 399, 409–11 (2009).

93. ISOO 2012 REPORT, *supra* note 34, at 18.

94. *See id.* at 8.

95. *See* http://www.archives.gov/isoo/fcgr/index.html.

96. *See* Memorandum from John P. Fitzpatrick, Dir., Info. Sec. Oversight Office, to Selected Senior Agency Officials (Jan. 23, 2012), *available at* http://www.fas.org/sgp/isoo/fcgr-012312.pdf.

97. 50 U.S.C.A. § 435 note (West 2009) (Promotion of Accurate Classification of Information).

98. EXEC. OFFICE OF THE PRESIDENT, THE OPEN GOVERNMENT PARTNERSHIP: SECOND OPEN GOVERNMENT NATIONAL ACTION PLAN FOR THE UNITED STATES OF AMERICA 4 (2013), *available at* http://www.whitehouse.gov/sites/default/files/docs/us_national_action_plan_6p.pdf.

99. PUB. INT. DECLASSIFICATION BD., TRANSFORMING THE SECURITY CLASSIFICATION SYSTEM 14–15 (2012).

*Elizabeth Goitein is the codirector of the Liberty & National Security Program at the Brennan Center for Justice at the New York University School of Law.

This chapter consists of edited and updated excerpts from the Brennan Center's 2011 report, *Reducing Overclassification through Accountability*, coauthored by Elizabeth Goitein and David M. Shapiro.

Used by permission.

The Corrupting Influence of Secrecy on National Policy Decisions

*by J. William Leonard**

Secrets can be the lifeblood of nations. Both treasure and blood of a nation's citizenry are readily spent to steal another nation's secrets and to safeguard its own. Yet, individuals also die—adversaries and citizens alike—simply because governments have secrets.

When employed by national governments, secrecy is a two-edged sword. Denying information to the enemy on the battlefield also increases the risk of a lack of awareness on the part of friendly forces, contributing to the potential for fratricide or other military failures. Strict compartmentalization in recruiting spies increases a nation's vulnerability to deception as a consequence of using sources that ultimately prove to be unreliable. Making purely bureaucratic policy decisions in secret such as which organizations to include within a larger agency devoted to countering terrorism can result in mission failure for an organization primarily devoted to responding to natural disasters. Simply put, official secrecy comes at a price—sometimes a deadly price—oftentimes through its impact on the decision-making process employed by national leaders.

Whether seeking advances in science and technology, formulating government policy, developing war plans or assessing intelligence, the end product can always be enhanced as a consequence of a far-reaching give and take during which underlying premises are challenged and alternative approaches are considered. As such, official secrecy just about guarantees the absence of an optimal decision by our government leaders. The challenge is ensuring that this tradeoff—that is, accepting a less than optimal decision in exchange for denying information to a potential national security adversary—is taken into account when making a decision to cloak certain information in secrecy. The consequences of not doing so is evidenced by many of the momentous decisions made by Federal government officials over the past decade that turned out to be exceptionally flawed due, in large part, to the fact that the process for making these decisions was shrouded in excessive and often needless official secrecy.

What I learned as the top classification overseer in the executive branch as Director of the Information Security Oversight Office, commonly known as ISOO, is secrecy can act like a toxin in the body politic. Much like chemotherapy in the human body, it can have beneficial results when used in an extremely controlled and limited manner. However, neither should be employed lightly as they can easily produce outcomes worse than the illness they are attempting to cure. In government, as in other institutions, excessive secrecy ultimately makes for flawed decisions. It undermines our constitutional form of government, weakens the rule of law, and facilitates actions inconsistent with our nation's core values and beliefs. It can contribute to the squandering of American blood and treasure and aid our adversaries in the recruitment of future extremists. Official government secrecy is in many regards a relic of the Cold War that has long outlived its usefulness.

As such, what is the proper role of secrecy within government today? What do we gain and what do we lose when our government conducts so much of its business in secret, especially when it comes to formulating national security policy? Our Declaration of Independence states, in part, that "Governments are instituted among Men, deriving their just powers from the consent of the governed." This strongly implies that for our nation's citizens to provide the consent upon which our government is based, it must be an informed consent, an increasingly difficult end to achieve when the government restricts the dissemination of information while making the most profound decisions possible, such as unleashing the brutality of war and sending our nation's youth to sacrifice life and limb for "the larger good." Absent the free flow of information, absent the ability of the citizenry to provide an informed consent, the Declaration implies that the exercise of power by the government through its decision-making process will inevitably become flawed. Yet, when many of the same individuals who helped frame such a bold and revolutionary declaration met 11 years later to draft a more effective framework for a new government, they would themselves produce a product whose flaws, in many ways, can be directly attributable to the framers desire to shroud their deliberations in official secrecy.

By 1787, the nation had divided into two ideological frameworks not much different from those in existence today; those who believed in a strong national government and those who favored the preponderance of political power being vested in either the States or in individual citizens. Many favored the continuation of the status quo under the Articles of Confederation, principally because the weak central government did not have the ability to tax. Others favored a strong national government with the ability to raise revenues on its own, free of the singular power of any State to effectively veto an enhancement of centralized government. Both sides feared tyranny; either emanating from a strong national government or from state legislatures who showed a willingness to usurp the rights of minorities. On the basis of subsequent history, both sides had a valid reason to be concerned and thus neither side had a monopoly on the truth.

By the time the delegates to the Philadelphia Convention met in 1787, the nationalists were in ascendancy. All recognized that momentous decisions upon which the fate of the young nation rested had to be made. Some, such as James Madison, believed that the most propitious decisions could be made in secret. Thus, notwithstanding temperatures as high as 94 degrees in June, 96 degrees in July, and 95 degrees in August (Vile, 2005), the delegates decided their four months of meetings in Philadelphia during the summer of 1787 would take place behind closed doors and windows. They opted to endure the fetid air of an isolated room to conduct their debates in official secrecy. No reporters or visitors were permitted at any session, and not one word of its historic deliberation was permitted to be disclosed to anyone who was not a delegate.[1]

Years later, Madison stated that he believed "no Constitution would ever have been adopted by the convention if the debates had been public."[2] In a contemporaneous letter to his son, George Mason wrote,

> It is expected our doors will be shut, and communications upon the business of the Convention be forbidden during its sitting. This I think myself a proper precaution to prevent mistakes and misrepresentation until the business shall be completed, when the whole may have a very different complexion from that in which the several crude and indigested parts might in their first shape appear if submitted to the public eye.[3]

An example of how seriously official secrecy was taken at the Convention is provided by no less an authority figure than General George Washington, who presided over the Convention. When the convention first opened, the delegates were provided a copy of a number of propositions brought forward as guiding principles for a new government. As recounted by William Pierce, a delegate from Georgia, one morning, one of the delegates to the Convention dropped his copy of the propositions. It was picked up by General Mifflin, a delegate from Pennsylvania, who then gave it to Washington, who proceeded to put it in his pocket and continued with business as usual. A the end of the day, after a motion for adjournment was made, Washington rose from his seat and said,

> Gentlemen: I am sorry to find that some one member of this Body, has been so neglectful of the secrets of the Convention as to drop in the State House a copy of their proceedings, which by accident was picked up and delivered to me this Morning. I must entreat Gentlemen to be more careful, least our transactions get into the News Papers, and disturb

the public repose by premature speculations. I know not whose Paper it is, but there it is (throwing it down on the table), let him who owns it take it.[4]

With that, Washington bowed, picked up his hat, and left the room with, as recounted by Pierce, "a dignity so severe that every Person seemed alarmed." No one ever came forward to collect the paper.[5]

And what did all that official secrecy succeed in facilitating? Some readily point out that the world's oldest democracy, the United States of America, was, in essence, "born behind closed doors" (Berenson, 2008). But was it?

When they reflect on American democracy and the role fulfilled by the U.S. Constitution and what it all means to their everyday lives, most Americans today frequently think about the liberties that are guaranteed by the Constitution—freedom of religion, of speech, and of the press; the right to be secure against unreasonable search and seizure; the right to not be deprived of life, liberty or property, without due process; and so on. What is important to acknowledge, however, is that by conducting business in such secrecy, even individuals as brilliant as our Constitution's framers came up short and made what proved to be extraordinarily faulty decisions. For what emerged from the locked doors of the Convention hall proved to be an exceedingly flawed product—one which failed to contain the basic limits to government authority, which we take for granted today but which were not codified until passage of what we know as the Bill of Rights—the first 10 amendments to the Constitution designed to protect the "unalienable" rights our Declaration of Independence recognizes we all possess.

Once the shackles of secrecy surrounding the framing of our Constitution were removed, a true national debate ensued over the future of our country. Out of this public discourse arose the recognition that the Constitution required explicit safeguards against tyranny. If not for the public commitment made in reaction to this debate to introduce and support during the First Congress under the new Constitution amendments providing a bill of rights, our government, which has proved to be the world's oldest democracy, would most likely have not even come into being, as least not as we know it today.

The arguments used at the time to justify the omission of recognized civil liberties have proven hollow in view of our nation's history. For example, Alexander Hamilton (1788) in *Federalist No. 84* expressed the fear that protecting specific rights might imply that any unmentioned rights would not be protected:

I go further, and affirm that bills of rights, in the sense and in the extent in which they are contended for, are not only unnecessary in the proposed constitution, but would even be dangerous. They would contain various exceptions to powers which are not granted; and on this very account, would afford a colorable pretext to claim more than were granted. For why declare that things shall not be done which there is not power to do?

Yet, even with the explicit incorporation of a Bill of Rights into our Constitution, the recognition of the full extent of individuals' civil liberties and limits of Federal and State government authority has steadily evolved over the last two and a quarter centuries as evidence by the 2010 U.S. Supreme Court decision in *McDonald v. Chicago* (see SCOTUS wiki, 2010) applying the Second Amendment to the states.

What lessons do we take from the experiences of the Framers?

The United States has assembled the most massive capability to steal other countries' secrets the world has ever seen. Exactly what we spend upwards of $66.5 billion dollars a year is itself a secret (Globalsecurity.org, 2009). And it is the conventional wisdom in almost every corner, both to the right and to the left of the political spectrum, that the withholding "national security information" from public disclosure is essential to our nation's well-being. No less of an advocate for openness in government than Senator Russ Feingold (2008) (D-WI) stated,

> Through the classification system and the common law, we've carved out limited exceptions for highly sensitive factual information about military operations, intelligence sources and methods, nuclear programs, and the like. That is entirely appropriate and important to protecting our national security.

Somehow as a nation, we have developed an almost all reflexive posture whereby we consistently genuflect at the altar of "national security" and accept as given that the withholding of sensitive information, be it relating to intelligence, military, or foreign policy matters, will invariably serve to preclude or minimize damage to our nation's well-being. In fact, as with the founding of our form of government, within the recent past, some of the most exceptionally grave instances whereby our nation's well-being has been severely damaged can be directly attributable to our government's withholding from public disclosure information, to include "sensitive" national security information relating to intelligence, military, or foreign policy matters. Classification of national security information, unless applied in a deliberative, thoughtful and informed manner, can actually cause the damage to our nation's security it is intended to preclude.

Reflexive classification can actually advance, rather than retard, the objectives of our nation's adversaries.

The litany almost goes without saying. First and foremost, our nation chose to unleash the unimaginable brutality of war when we optioned to invade Iraq, over eight years ago on March 19, 2003. Much has been written and said about how faulty the original rationale was for that decision. However, it is useful to also review the role that secrecy played in that tragically flawed commitment of national might and prestige.

To better inform their deliberations before the October 2002 vote to authorize the use of military force against Iraq, some members of Congress requested that a National Intelligence Estimate (NIE) (see Bruno and Otterman, 2008) be prepared on Iraq's programs for weapons of mass destruction. The NIE and its key judgments, in addition to being wrong, were classified. The NIE was delivered to Congress the week before its vote and, because it was classified, to read it, members had to go to a special room and sign a log. It [has] been variously reported how many senators actually read the classified report before authorizing the President to take our nation to war, but the publication *The Hill* quoted one senior congressional intelligence staffer as saying that "You can say with 100 percent certainty it's less than 10" (Raju, Schor, & Wurman, 2007). How many more would have read it had it not been classified is impossible to say—but we can only hope that it would have been more than 10.

And what would they have learned if they had read the original NIE rather than rely on the unclassified white paper (see National Security Archive, 2008), which was released by the Director of Central Intelligence at the same time and which was intended as an unclassified version of the NIE? According to the senate report on prewar intelligence on Iraq (U.S. Senate Select Committee on Intelligence, 2006), they would have learned of the State Department's Bureau of Intelligence and Research alternative view on whether Iraq would have a nuclear weapon this decade and that the dismissed attempts by Iraq to obtain high-strength aluminum tubes as being part of Iraq's effort to reconstitute its nuclear program. They would also have learned that while the key judgments were almost identical in layout and substance in both papers, the key judgments of the unclassified paper were missing many of the caveats that were used in the classified NIE. As concluded by the report, removing caveats such as "we judge" or "we assess" changed many sentences in the unclassified paper to statements of fact rather than assessments—an egregious act because a cardinal rule of the declassification process is to ensure that it does not alter the substance of the information released (U.S. Senate Select Committee on Intelligence).

What is equally disturbing is the rationale offered by drafters of the classified NIE as to why the unclassified paper omitted the fact that the intelligence community's own nuclear experts at the Department of Energy did not agree with the NIE's conclusion regarding the aluminum tubes, even though the allegation was being used by some of our leaders to stir up images of mushroom clouds appearing somewhere over the United States. Again according to the Senate Select Committee on Intelligence (2006), officials at the National Intelligence Council indicated that they did not refer to disagreements between intelligence agencies in unclassified documents out of concern that the country being discussed would be "tipped off to a potential cover story." Such a concern can understandably justify classification in some instances. However, to use it as a rationale for a decision that ultimately led to the production of a paper that has been judged as being misleading to both the Congress and the American people, in as grave a matter as a decision to go to war, is a perfect example of how the failure to balance the damage that results from disclosure, with the damage that results from classifying, can have exceedingly tragic consequences for our nation (U.S. Senate Select Committee on Intelligence, 2006).

The lead up to the Iraq War provides another excellent example of how even our own intelligence community can be hampered by excessive and needless classification and compartmentalization. Again, it is well known now that when Secretary of State Colin Powell spoke to the U.N. Security Council in February 2003 just before the war,[6] the most impressive part of his presentation which talked about eyewitness accounts of mobile biological labs and an accident that killed a dozen people was a fraud, based on debriefings by German intelligence officials of a human source aptly codenamed "Curveball." What is truly noteworthy, however—according to Los Angeles Times reporter Bob Drogin who wrote a book on Curveball—is that at the time of the U.N. presentation, and even not until well after the war had begun, the CIA did not even know the name of the source whose fabrications served as the basis upon which our nation chose to go to war. And, according to Drogin, the reason why is that German intelligence refused to share his name. They did so simply because they could; it was "pride of service," a form of one-upmanship (Koppelman, 2007).

There are yet other examples of how excessive classification can harm our national security. For example, even during the administration of George W. Bush, our national security strategy recognized that we are engaged in an ideological struggle against many forms of extremism. In fact, the first pillar of that strategy as articulated by the prior administration was in promoting freedom, justice, and human dignity, which includes offering people throughout the world a positive vision rooted in America's beliefs, thereby isolating and marginalizing violent extremists (see *National Security Strategy of the United States of America,* 2002). This strategy reflected our success in ending the Cold War, not by defeating the Soviet Union militarily, but rather by promoting American ideals and values that ultimately led to the demise of the most formidable foe our nation has ever confronted.

So how have we done over the past decade—how successful have we been in isolating and marginalizing violent extremists and offering the world's populace a positive vision of our society? Even many of our government's leaders acknowledge that we are not doing very well, and this perspective is supported by empirical evidence. For example, toward the end of the Bush administration, in June 2007, the Pew Global Attitudes Project released the results of a worldwide public opinion survey that focused on global unease with major world powers. Among other results, this poll revealed that widespread anti-American sentiment had significantly deepened since 2002. Specifically, in virtually every area of the world—Western Europe, Eastern Europe, Latin America, and Asia—overwhelming majorities of people viewed the United States favorably before 2002. But in virtually every single country in each of those regions, the percentage that viewed the United States favorably significantly decreased in 2007. The notable drop in U.S. credibility was as pronounced among America's traditional allies as it is in less friendly regions. More significantly still, significant majorities in Europe and Latin America who supported the United States in its war on terrorism in the immediate aftermath of 9/11 had notably reversed their positions (Pew Global Attitudes Project, 2007).

I would suggest our continuing failure to isolate the extremists is due, in part, to the worldwide perception that we continue to violate our own values and ideals, especially as they relate to human dignity and the rule of law. This perception was fostered by some of our own government officials when they refused during the Bush years to plainly state that physically restraining an individual and forcing his lungs to slowly fill up with water constitutes torture. They did this, in part, by hiding behind the classification system—by stating that to acknowledge limits to interrogation techniques used by our intelligence services (but not our military) would somehow disclose classified information—and thus harm our national security.

While a case may be made that the *unauthorized* disclosure of specific interrogation techniques can reasonably be expected to result in damage to the national security (a basic standard for classification), a far more compelling case can be made that greater harm to national security results by not unequivocally acknowledging whether specific techniques are consistent with American values and our commitment to preserving human dignity and the rule of law. Such evasion, rather than isolating and marginalizing violent extremists, instead provides them with fodder for their web sites and other mass media to further inflame passions and recruit new members to their cause.

In fact, the argument for classification of specific interrogation techniques has already been rejected by our military's combatant commanders. When releasing the Army's revised interrogation techniques in September 2006, Lt. Gen. John Kimmons, then Army Deputy Chief of Staff for Intelligence, acknowledged the Army considered classifying some of the techniques to keep them out of the hands of the enemy. Instead, they opted for transparency, in part to be, as General Kimmons stated, "as clear as we can be in the training of these techniques to our own soldiers, sailors, airmen, and Marines" (DoD News Briefing with Deputy Assistant Secretary Stimson and Lt. Gen. Kimmons from the Pentagon, 2006).

In that vein, the young men and women that we send into combat every day understand that if in the heat of battle they make a split-second decision that involves the indiscriminate use of force, it can result not only in the loss of innocent life but can also undercut our national security by feeding a negative vision of our nation to the rest of the world. As such, like the dozens of service members criminally charged to date for unlawful killings, they know that they can and will be held accountable. Indiscriminate government secrecy can have an equally deleterious impact on our national security strategy. Yet, we are a long way from instilling the same sense of discipline and accountability for all government officials who wield the critical national security tool of classification.

A prime example of indiscriminate secrecy was revealed a few years ago by Jack Goldsmith, the former head of the Office of Legal Counsel (OLC) in the Department of Justice during the Bush administration. Goldsmith wrote that senior officials within the government

> blew through [the Federal (sic) Intelligence Surveillance Act] in secret based on flimsy legal opinions that they guarded closely so no one could question the legal basis for the operations. (Rosen, 2007)

Goldsmith further recounted one of his first experiences with such extraordinary concealment, in late 2003 when, as he recalls, David Addington of the Office of the Vice President angrily denied a request by the National Security Agency's (NSA) Inspector General to see a copy of OLC's legal analysis supporting the oft-discussed secret NSA terrorist surveillance program. Goldsmith reported that "before I arrived in OLC, not even NSA lawyers were allowed to see the Justice Department's legal analysis of what NSA was doing" (Rosen, 2007).

I cannot recall a more blatant example of using classification not for its intended purpose of denying information to our nation's adversaries but rather to use it as a bureaucratic weapon to blunt potential opposition. The NSA lawyers had the highest of clearance levels and already knew the substance of the NSA's surveillance program, the very information most of value to our nation's adversaries. Yet, when it came to being afforded access to pure legal analysis, they were treated as if they were legal counsel for Al-Qaeda rather than for the Director of NSA who was responsible to ensure the legality of his agency's actions. Such antics give yet more fodder to our nation's adversaries to represent the United States as having nothing but contempt for the rule of law. Much like the 18-year-old soldier who indiscriminately fires his weapon, such conduct severely undermines our national security strategy of providing the world populace with a positive vision of the United States and thereby isolating and marginalizing violent extremists. The only difference is the 18-year-old soldier, who literally risks his life for his nation, would be held accountable.

The damage to the national interest as a consequence of excessive secrecy is not relegated solely to the national security arena; for example, the administration's decision to create the Department of Homeland Security in the wake of the attacks of September 11, 2001, the most massive reorganization of the Federal government since 1947, was cloaked in secrecy for purely bureaucratic reasons. One Homeland Security official was quoted at the time as stating that "the bureaucracy would have smothered this in its infancy if the White House had let it out" (Michael, 2002). Once again, however, excessive secrecy came at a price and there were consequences to be paid.

Harold Relyea formerly of the Congressional Research Service wrote of the consequences of the Bush administration developing somewhat hastily and in complete secrecy its proposal for a Department of Homeland Security. Specifically, Relyea (2003, p. 617) writes that "available reorganization expertise was not utilized and support from agencies and professional constituencies directly affected was not sought." Relyea (2003, p. 617) went on to point out that the president's proposal failed to address a definition of the organizing concept—that is, "a Department of Homeland Security was proposed but what was homeland security?" Absent such a common understanding, Relyea highlights that there was no standard for determining which existing agencies, programs, and functions merited transfer to the new department and, even more importantly, what should be done with the non-homeland security programs and functions of an agency being transferred (p. 617).

At the time, many were concerned that non-homeland security functions transferred to the new department, that is, those programs not directly related to countering terrorism, would become the victims of benign neglect; that programs not focused on the terrorist threat would be regarded as having a lower priority and would be allocated insufficient resources for their full and effective execution. For example, the House Committee on the Judiciary recommended transferring only the Office of National Preparedness of the Federal Emergency Management Agency (FEMA) to the new department, not the entire agency (Relyea, 2003, p. 618). Nonetheless, these and other voices of concern were drowned out and in the end the administration pretty much got what it wanted. Unfortunately, a little over two years later, the citizens of New Orleans and coastal Louisiana and Mississippi would discover the hard way that such concerns were well-founded. Had such a massive bureaucratic undertaking as the creation of the Department of Homeland Security not been undertaken in such secrecy, the lives of tens of thousands of Americans may not have been upended to the extent they were and continue to be as our government still struggles to meet its most basic commitment to provide for the common welfare of its most needy citizens.

Notwithstanding the above examples, one thing needs to be perfectly clear. Government secrecy is an essential national security tool that must be preserved. I make this observation having spent my 34-year federal career immersed in the arcane world of official government secrecy. The government's system of secrecy has had more than a theoretical application for my family. In service to their country, my two sons placed themselves in harm's way—one through overseas travel in support of our nation's intelligence efforts and the other as a combat infantry platoon leader in Iraq. Thus, their well-being was dependent, in part, on effective government secrecy. I know the value of government secrecy in an uncertain world.

The ability to surprise and deceive the enemy can spell the difference between life and death on the battlefield. Certain intelligence methods can work only if the adversary is unaware of their existence. Similarly, it is nearly impossible for our intelligence services to recruit human sources who often risk their lives aiding our country or to obtain assistance from other countries' intelligence services, unless such sources can be assured complete and total confidentiality. The successful discourse between nations often depends on constructive ambiguity and plausible deniability as the only way to balance competing and divergent national interests.

However, much the same way our nation's military leaders—in developing and implementing a new counterinsurgency strategy—have come to the conclusion that the more force you use, the less effective it can be, our nation's bureaucracies must similarly use government secrecy more selectively and recognize that in today's environment, less secrecy and increased transparency can, at times, be more effective in denying adversaries the ability to harm our nation.

NOTES

1. As recorded in Madison's notes of the Federal Convention, the following additional rules were recorded for Tuesday, May 29, 1787: "That no copy be taken of any entry on the journal during the sitting of the House without leave of the House. That members only be permitted to inspect the journal. That nothing spoken in the House be printed, or otherwise published or communicated without leave."

2. Farrand, M. (Ed.), *The records of the federal convention of 1787* (Vol. III, Yale University Press, New Haven, CT., 1911, p. 479)—"Jared Sparks: Journal, Notes of a visit to James Madison," also available at http://memory.loc.gov/ammem/amlaw/lwfr.html. Accessed on 7 July 2010.

3. *Ibid.*, p. 28—George Mason to George Mason, Jr., Philadelphia, May 27, 1787.

4. *Ibid.*, p. 86—William Pierce: Anecdote.

5. *Ibid.*, p. 86.

6. Full text of Powell's speech, see *The Guardian*, available at www.guardian.co.uk/world/2003/feb/05/iraq.usa. Accessed on 8 July 2010.

REFERENCES

Berenson, B.A. (2008). Secret law and the threat to democratic and accountable government. Testimony before the United States Senate Committee on the Judiciary, Subcommittee on the Constitution, S. Hrg. 110-604, 110th congress, 2nd session, April 30. Available at www.fas.org/sgp/congress/200g/law.html. Retrieved on 7 July 2010.

Bruno, G., & Otterman, S. (2008). The council on foreign relations. *National Intelligence Estimates Backgrounder*, May 15. Available at www.cfr.org/publication/7758/national_intelligence_estimates.html. Retrieved on 8 July 2010.

Feingold, R. (2008). Secret law and the threat to democratic and accountable government. Opening Statement, United States Senate Committee on the Judiciary, Subcommittee on the Constitution, 110 Congress, 2nd session, 110-604, April 30. Available at www.fas.org/sgp/congress/2008/law.html. Retrieved on 7 July 2010.

Globalsecurity.org (2009). 2009 intelligence budget. Available at www.globalsecurity.org/intell/library/budget/index.html. Retrieved on 8 July 2010.

Hamilton, A. (1788). The federalist papers no. 84, Avalon project. Available at http://avalon.law.yale.edu/18th_century/fed84.asp. Retrieved on 7 July 2010.

Koppelman, A. (2007). The man who sold the war. Salon.com, October 16. Available at www.salon.com/books/int/2007/10/16/curveball. Retrieved on 5 July 2010.

Michael, W. (2002). Security blanket: Here are details of the proposed Department of Homeland Security and the inside story of how it was planned in utmost secrecy. Will Congress agree to this major reorganization and will it be good for the United States? *Insight on the News*, July 22. Available at www.highbeam.com/doc/lGl-90041157.html. Retrieved on 11 July 2010.

National Security Archive. (2008). PR push for Iraq war preceded intelligence findings. August 22. Available at http://www.gwu.edu/~nsarchiv/NSAEBB/NSAEBB254/. Retrieved on 8 July 2010.

Pew Global Attitudes Project. (2007). Global unease with major world powers. Available at http://pewglobal.org/2007/06/27/global-unease-with-major-world-powers/. Retrieved on November 27, 2010.

Raju, M., Schor, E., & Wurman, I. (2007). Few senators read Iraq NIE report. *The Hill*, June 17. Available at http://thehill.com/homenews/news/12304-few-senators-readiraq-niereport. Retrieved on 8 July 2010.

Relyea, H. C. (2003). Organizing for homeland security. *Presidential Studies Quarterly, 33*(3), 602–624.

Rosen, J. (2007). Conscience of a conservative. *New York Times Magazine*, September 9. Available at http://nytimes.come/2007/09/09/magazine/09rosen.html?_r=1. Retrieved on 7 July 2010.

SCOTUS wiki. (2010). Available at http://www.scotuswiki.com/index.php?title=McDonald_v._City_of_Chicago. Retrieved on 8 July 2010.

The President of the United States. (2002). The National Security Strategy of the United States of America, September. Available at www.globalsecurity.org/military/library/policy/national/nss-020920.pdf. Retrieved on 5 July 2010.

U.S. Department of Defense (DOD). (2006). DoD News Briefing with Deputy Assistant Secretary Stimson and Lt. Gen. Kimmons from the Pentagon. September 6. Available at http://www.defense.gov/Transcripts/Transcript.aspx?TranscriptID=3712. Retrieved on 5 July 2010.

U.S. Senate Select Committee on Intelligence. (2006). Report of the select committee on intelligence postwar findings about Iraq's WMD programs and links to terrorism and how they compare with prewar assessments together with additional views. S. Report. 109-331, 109th congress, 2nd session, September 8. Available at http://intelligence.senate.gov/phaseiiaccuracy.pdf. Retrieved on November 27, 2010.

Vile, J. R. (2005). *The constitutional convention of 1787: A Comprehensive Encyclopedia of America's Founding* (Vol. 2). ABC-CLIO: Santa Barbara.

*J. William Leonard retired in 2008 after 34 years of federal service. In his most recent government position as the director of the Information Security Oversight Office, he was responsible to the president for policy oversight of the executive branch–wide national security information classification system. He is currently the chief operating officer of a private, nonprofit foundation in Washington, D.C., dedicated to the growth and strengthening of democratic institutions around the world.

Leonard, J. William. "The Corrupting Influence of Secrecy." In *Government Secrecy*, edited by Susan Maret, 421–434. Research in Social Problems and Public Policy 19. Greenwich, CT: JAI Press, 2011.

Scientific Openness and National Security after 9-11

by Elisa D. Harris and John D. Steinbruner*

Fear of bioterrorism has emerged as a priority concern of American security policy as a result of the anthrax letters of 2001. That event resonating with the September 11 terrorist attacks crystallized a much more urgent sense of threat than had previously been perceived. It is now commonly assumed that malicious organizations will attempt to exploit the destructive potential of biotechnology, and it is also implicitly conceded that a dedicated effort is likely to succeed.[1]

In response to this surge of fear, the American political system has sharply increased investment in biodefence research intended to provide protection against deliberate biological attack. Nowhere is this more true than at the National Institutes of Health (NIH), which has seen its funding for biodefence grow by over 3,200%, from $53 million in fiscal year 2001 to a record $1.8 billion (requested) in fiscal year 2006.[2] These funds have resulted in a 1,500% increase in the number of grants for research on anthrax, plague and other top biological warfare agents, from 33 between 1996–2000, to almost 500 between 2001 and January 2005.[3] This research is dedicated to determining the character and magnitude of potential threat in order to develop better methods of protection. But at least some of this effort will assuredly identify more advanced methods of attack as well.

That unavoidable fact poses a sharp dilemma and a fundamental problem of policy. By its very nature, biodefence research generates information that the global medical community has strong reason and arguably an inherent right to know. Unrestricted dissemination of that information, however, might inform those dedicated to destruction. Moreover, as in other areas of technology, it is likely that offensive applications of biotechnology will prove to be substantially easier than defensive ones and could therefore emerge more rapidly in open competition.

In principle, the dilemma might be substantially mitigated by a new oversight system under which sensitive information vital to public health protection is restricted to those professionally qualified and explicitly authorized to have it and those individuals are in turn monitored to document responsible use. Such an arrangement does not exist within any country or internationally, however, and is not as yet even being officially discussed. But for such an arrangement to be effective at any level, there is a need to devise principles to guide decisions on whether to restrict or classify information. Fortunately, there are useful precedents in that regard.

EVOLVING PRACTICE

In the past, all NIH-funded research has been unclassified. But in October 2001, President Bush signed an Executive Order extending classification authority to the Department of Health and Human Services, which includes NIH. Anthony Fauci, who heads the NIH institute responsible for biodefence research, later said that although most NIH-funded research would remain unclassified, some limitations on access could not be ruled out. "As we move into more research on counter-bioterrorism," Fauci said, "we should examine this issue on a case-by-case basis."[4]

By the spring of 2002, it was clear that the Bush Administration was seriously considering the possibility of restrictions on the dissemination of scientific findings that could have national security implications—what has been called "sensitive but unclassified" information. In a memorandum to federal agencies in March, White House Chief of Staff Andrew Card raised the need to protect sensitive but unclassified information.[5] At the same time, the US Department of Defense (DOD) circulated a draft directive containing proposals for new categories of controlled information and for prepublication review of certain DOD-funded research, even if it was unclassified.[6] Because of strong criticism from the scientific community, the Pentagon draft was withdrawn. However reports continued to emerge about White House plans to develop rules for the dissemination of information that could have national security implications.

US scientific organizations moved quickly to minimize the possibility of government-mandated restrictions on fundamental research, offering governance by scientists themselves as an alternative. In August 2002, the American Society for Microbiology (ASM), which publishes eleven leading US peer-reviewed scientific journals, adopted guidelines for handling manuscripts dealing with sensitive microbiological issues. As part of the traditional peer-review process, all reviewers were now required to inform the Editor of any manuscript that contained information on methods or materials "that might be misused or might pose a threat to public health safety." Any manuscript thus identified would be held until a decision concerning its disposition had been rendered by the Editor-in-Chief in consultation with the ASM Publication Board.[7] As Board Chairman Samuel Kaplan later described it, the goal was to establish a practice for trying to prevent the publication of information that could be a "clear and imminent danger to the public."[8] A few months later, the *Proceedings of the National Academy of Sciences* (PNAS) quietly adopted a similar review process for biological agents that had been identified by the Centers for Disease Control and Prevention as posing the highest security risk.[9]

By October 2002, the Presidents of the National Academies of Science were weighing in, declaring in a formal statement that a balance was needed between the restrictions necessary to safeguard "strategic secrets" and the openness required to accelerate the progress of technical knowledge. The NAS Presidents called upon scientists and policymakers to work together to develop clear criteria for determining what information needed to be restricted or classified and how best to accomplish that task.[10]

In January 2003, in response to a request from ASM, the National Academy of Sciences hosted a day-long meeting of scientists and security experts to begin to explore how to balance openness and national security. Scientific journal editors were generally dismissive of the idea that any research should be publicly withheld. But others cautioned that unless scientists took the lead in defining what was sensitive and proposing how it could be protected, the government would act. If scientists do not take these security concerns seriously, former Deputy Secretary of Defense John Hamre warned, politicians with little understanding of science will step in with "blanket restrictions" that would have "devastating effects on the conduct of science."[11]

The following day, thirty journal editors and scientists agreed in a signed statement to support the development of new processes for considering the security implications of proposed manuscripts and, where necessary, to modify or refrain from publishing papers whose potential harm outweighed their potential benefits. In an editorial accompanying release of the statement, the PNAS elaborated upon the thinking behind the effort. No one would publish a "cookbook recipe" for a weapon, which would in any event not pass scientific muster. But it is nearly impossible, the editorial said, to determine in advance exactly what type of manuscript should not be published, as any work of value to terrorists would also be of value in countering terrorism. For this reason, the journal editors had focused on developing a common set of publication policies.[12] But as Stanford Professor Stanley Falkow later pointed out, the journal editors had failed to provide guidance not only on who exactly would make these publication decisions but also what information constituted a potential threat.[13]

Precedents and Possible Guidelines

The need to balance scientific openness and national security is not a new issue. As former ASM president Ron Atlas has noted, since the beginning of modern science in the 1600s, scientists have confronted questions of secrecy and science. In an essay in 1626, Sir Francis Bacon observed: "And this we do also; we have consultations, which of the inventions and experiences which we have discovered shall be published, and which not; and take all an oath of secrecy for the concealing of those which we think fit to keep secret . . ."[14]

During the Cold War, concerns that the Soviet Union had benefited militarily from access to US scientific and technical information, especially in computer science and other areas of the physical sciences, prompted discussions not unlike today's about possible restrictions on scientific communication, including prepublication review by the Pentagon of research in certain areas relevant to national security. In response, the National Academy of Sciences convened an expert panel under the chairmanship of former Cornell University President Dale Corson to examine how to balance scientific communication and national security. The Corson Report, which was published in 1982, concluded that the national welfare, including national security, is best served by allowing the free flow of all scientific and technical information "not directly and significantly connected with technology critical to national security." Accordingly, the report recommended that most fundamental research at universities should be unclassified; that a limited amount might require classification; and that a small grey area could require limited restrictions short of classification.[15]

The Reagan Administration accepted the Corson Report recommendations, embodying them in National Security Decision Directive 189, which stated: "to the maximum extent possible, the products of fundamental research [shall] remain unrestricted. . . . No restrictions may be placed upon the conduct or reporting of federally-funded fundamental research that has not received national security classification, except as provided in applicable US Statutes." NSDD 189 defined fundamental research as "basic and applied research in science and engineering, the results of which ordinarily are published and shared broadly within the scientific community . . ."[16]

Following the controversy over the Card memo, the President's Science Advisor, John Marburger, publicly reaffirmed the Bush Administration's commitment to NSDD 189,[17] referring to an earlier letter from National Security Advisor Condoleezza Rice. "The key to maintaining US technological preeminence is to encourage open and collaborative basic research," Rice wrote in November 2001. "[T]he policy on the transfer of scientific, technical, and engineering information set forth in National Security Decision Directive 189 shall remain in effect, and we will ensure that this policy is followed."[18]

In addition to upholding the principle of scientific openness, the Corson Report also outlined criteria for making classification decisions in fundamental research, criteria that could serve as a model for classification decisions in the life sciences, including biodefence research, today. Admittedly, the context is very different: the Soviet Union as compared to a much more diffuse set of national and possibly subnational actors; the physical sciences as compared to the life sciences. But no US adversary, much less terrorist group, that exists today is better capable than the Soviet Union was of adapting fundamental research results for military purposes. If these criteria were deemed by the NAS as appropriate to deal with the Soviet military threat, they should be at least as effective against the much less sophisticated adversaries we currently face.

Drawing on the Corson Report, one could establish the principle that no basic or applied research, including biodefence research, at university, industry or government labs should be restricted or classified unless the following criteria are met:

1. the technology is developing rapidly and time from basic science to application is short;

2. the technology has identifiable direct military applications; or it is dual-use and involves process or production related technologies;

3. the transfer of technology would give a BW proliferator (e.g. a nation-state or subnational group) a significant near-term military benefit;

4. the US is the only source of information about the technology, or other nations that could also be the source have control systems as secure as those in the US; and,

5. the duration and nature of the proposed restrictions would not seriously compromise existing public health practice.

There are two main differences between these criteria and those outlined in the Corson Report: the term "Soviet Union" has been replaced by "BW proliferator;" and a fifth criterion has been added to take account of the public health implications of any proposed restrictions.

Whether it is possible to identify a more specific list of fundamental research for which restrictions or classification is warranted is unclear. One proposal, in 2003, included the following examples: alterations in virulence that defeat vaccine; alterations that greatly accelerate disease course or delay diagnosis; engineering drug resistance; and, delivery systems.[19] But this and other proposals like it are far too broad, and would capture a wide swath of fundamental research critical to future medical, agricultural and other peaceful applications.

Interestingly, a much more limited approach to the classification of biodefence information has been promulgated by the US Army. In Army regulation 380-86, dated 1 February 2005, only one area of research is proposed for classification: the results of medical research revealing operational deficiencies or vulnerabilities in biological defence. By comparison, the identity of microorganisms and toxins being studied, their characteristics, and the consequences of their administration to appropriate hosts is considered unclassified information, as is general medical research and procedures for protecting personnel against biological agents.[20]

There are sound scientific reasons for avoiding dissemination restrictions or classification in the life sciences, including in the area of biodefence research. As the NAS has noted, none of the research that has been the focus of recent attention has pointed the way toward the production of biological weapons in any specific way. Many additional experimental steps are required in order to translate basic research results into a useable biological warfare agent, much less an actual weapon.[21] In addition, as the rapid response to SARS showed, scientific progress depends upon open communication and the ability to replicate research and validate results. Restrictions on the flow of scientific information will undermine not only efforts to develop defences against biological weapons but also to protect the public against the threat from naturally occurring disease. New restrictions could also have a chilling effect on the willingness of scientists to work in areas in which there are limits on their ability to communicate with other scientists and to publish their research results.[22]

There are also compelling security reasons for avoiding restrictions or classification, especially in the area of biodefence research. As Mark Wheelis has pointed out, secrecy about the nature and scope of US biodefence efforts makes it more difficult for Congress to exercise its oversight responsibilities and limits opportunities for expert or public input into the policymaking process. The result could be policies that fail to address the real threats facing the United States. Limits on the dissemination of information about US biodefence research activities could also raise suspicions about US intentions to comply with the Biological Weapons Convention (BWC), thus leading others to pursue the very illicit activities the US programme is designed to counter. Lack of openness on the part of the US could also serve as a justification for others to be more secretive about their own purported biodefence activities, thereby complicating

US efforts to detect genuine violations of the BWC. Finally, limits on the dissemination of biodefence information denies the US the deterrent value that comes from an adversary being aware of the robust nature of US biodefence preparations.[23]

Many of these arguments are similar to those made in the 1980s by US officials concerned about secrecy at Soviet biological institutes, including the possibility that Moscow was using recombinant DNA technology for offensive BW purposes. At a 1988 roundtable, ACDA official Robert Mikulak stated that there was "no justification" for secret biological research labs or classified research. He also argued that openness could help reduce suspicions of noncompliance with the Biological Weapons Convention. At the same meeting, DOD official Thomas Dashiell argued that by making DOD biodefence efforts "visible," the programme could act as a deterrent to potential adversaries.[24]

Both Mikulak and Dashiell also disavowed the need for classified research involving recombinant DNA technology. "There is no justification for classified military research on recombinant DNA . . . anywhere," Mikulak declared. Dashiell agreed, noting that classification was unnecessary because the relevant work involved "basic science areas" and the possible application was a number of years away.[25]

CLASSIFICATION AND OVERSIGHT MECHANISMS

If certain types of fundamental research in the life sciences are to be reviewed for possible dissemination restrictions or classification, however limited in scope, how might this best be pursued?

One possibility would be to rely upon scientific journals to review manuscripts, as proposed in the February 2003 statement by journal editors and scientists. This is also the approach recommended in October 2003 by an expert panel convened by the National Research Council under the chairmanship of MIT professor Gerald Fink. In their report, *Biotechnology Research in an Age of Terrorism*, the Fink Committee argued that "imposing mandatory information controls on research in the life sciences, if attempted, [would] be difficult and expensive with little likely gain in genuine security." As a consequence, the Committee recommended self-governance by scientists and scientific journals to review publications for their potential security risks.[26]

The Fink Committee recognized, however, that scientists have available to them many other opportunities for sharing the results of their research efforts short of publication. This includes presentations at scientific meetings, Internet postings, and normal e-mail and other exchanges between scientists working in similar areas. For this and other reasons, the Committee called for a concerted effort to educate scientists about the dual-use nature of biotechnology research. They also recommended adding seven so-called "experiments of concern" to the NIH Guidelines, the oversight process which is to be followed by all academic and other institutions that receive funding from NIH for recombinant DNA research. In the view of the Committee, this layered system of self-governance, involving individual scientists, the local and national committees responsible for implementing the NIH Guidelines (known respectively as Institutional Biosafety Committees and the Recombinant DNA Advisory Committee), and journal publishers, would provide an effective oversight arrangement. In March 2004, the Bush Administration announced plans to create a National Science Advisory Board for Biosecurity to develop guidelines for implementing these recommendations. But the Board, which has yet to be named or to hold its first meeting, is strictly advisory and both industry and classified research are formally outside its jurisdiction.[27]

Another possibility would be to rely upon a more formalized process for considering potential dissemination restrictions or classification requirements before funding has been approved and the research begun. This is the approach enshrined in NSDD 189, which states: "Each federal government agency is responsible for . . . determining whether classification is appropriate prior to the award of a research grant, contract, or cooperative agreement."[28] It is also reflected in the broader oversight proposal we have been developing at the Center for International and Security Studies at Maryland aimed at preventing advanced research in the life sciences from being applied, either inadvertently or deliberately, for destructive purposes.[29]

Under our proposed oversight system, all proposals in certain clearly defined research areas would go through a peer review process in which the potential scientific, medical, or other benefits are weighed against the potential security risks. Consideration would be given not only to whether and under what conditions the proposed research should proceed but also the possible need for restrictions on the dissemination of the research results, including through classification. This peer review process would be applied comprehensively to all relevant institutions, whether government, industry or academic. This is in contrast to the Fink Committee approach, which formally would apply only to academic or other institutions that are subject to the NIH Guidelines. Thus, neither industry nor government biodefence programs, which the Fink Committee singled out as raising particular dual-use concerns, would be required to adhere to its proposed rules.

To encourage compliance with our oversight system and adequate funding for its implementation, the obligations would be mandatory, unlike the Fink Committee approach, which relies on the voluntary compliance of scientists with the NIH Guidelines. And consistent with the globally distributed nature of the research itself, our system would seek to establish uniform procedures and rules among all participating countries. The Fink Committee recommendations, by comparison, apply only to the United States, although the Committee acknowledged in its report that only internationally harmonized standards would minimize the risk of misuse of dual-use research.

Like the NIH Guidelines, our oversight system would be tiered, with the level of risk of the proposed research determining the nature and extent of the oversight requirements. At the foundation would be a local review body, responsible for overseeing and approving what we call potentially dangerous research activities, particularly those that increase the potential for otherwise benign pathogens to be used for destructive purposes. This local oversight body would be similar to the existing Institutional Biosafety Committees, though better resourced, both financially and in terms of dedicated personnel.[30] The vast majority of research would fall into this category or not be affected at all.

At the next level there would be a national review body, which would be responsible for overseeing and approving what we call moderately dangerous research activities, particularly those that would enhance the weaponization potential of pathogens or toxins that already have been identified as posing a security threat. This national oversight body would be similar to the Recombinant DNA Advisory Committee.

At the top would be a global implementing body, which would be responsible for overseeing and approving the most dangerous research activities, especially research that involves or could result in the creation of pathogens significantly more dangerous than those that currently exist. The closest precedent for this would be the WHO Advisory Committee on Variola Virus Research, which oversees and approves all smallpox virus research conducted in the USA and Russia, the only countries authorized to retain the virus following its successful eradication in nature.

If the relevant peer review body determined that the results of a particular research project needed to be restricted, every effort would be made to share the restricted information with other scientists with a legitimate need-to-know. One model for this is the process that was used by the NAS to allow limited access to certain portions of its 2002 study on agricultural bioterrorism. In response to security concerns from the Department of Agriculture, which funded the study, NAS officials developed guidelines for the types of individuals who could be given access to the controlled information. Anyone interested had to submit a written request and be interviewed by NAS staff before being provided a copy of the controlled information.[31] It might also be possible to use a secure, password-controlled website to make controlled information available to those who have been vetted and found to have a legitimate need for access to the information.[32]

Clearly, the success of an oversight system like that described above depends very heavily on the willingness of the scientific community to help develop and implement the procedures and rules that are at the heart of the system. But security experts will also be critical to the peer review process, especially at the national level, where most biodefence research proposals likely would be vetted. Security clearances may be necessary for some or all of the individuals that serve on the national oversight body. Nondisclosure agreements, with appropriate penalties for violations, could also be used to help prevent unauthorized disclosures of sensitive information. And at every level, independent scientists and security experts, without a vested interest in the outcome of the review process, would be required to help ensure the integrity of the overall system.

NOTES

1. Prepared Testimony of Porter J Goss, Director of Central Intelligence, "Global Intelligence Challenges 2005: Meeting Long-Term Challenges with a Long-Term Strategy," Senate Select Committee on Intelligence, 16 February 2005, available at http://www.cia.gov/cia/public_affairs/speeches/2004/Goss_testimony_02162005.html.

2. In addition to basic research, these figures also cover construction of new biosafety laboratories and development of medical countermeasures. Prepared Testimony of Anthony Fauci, Director, National Institute of Allergies and Infectious Diseases, Senate Committee on Health, Education, Labor & Pensions, 8 February 2005, available at http://help.senate.gov/testimony/t184_tes.html.

3. "An Open Letter to Elias Zerhouni," Science, 4 March 2005, available at http://www.sciencemag.org/feature/misc/microbio/307_5714_1409c.pdf.

4. Erika Check, "Biologists apprehensive over US moves to censor information flow," Nature, 21 February 2002.

5. US Department of Justice, Office of Information and Privacy, FOIA Post, "Guidance on Homeland Security Issued," released 19 March 2002, available at http://www.usdoj.gov/oip/foiapost/2002foiapost10.htm.

6. US Department of Defense, "Mandatory Procedures for Research and Technology Protection with the DOD," Draft, March 2002, available at http://www.fas.org/sgp/news/2002/04/dod5200_39r_dr.html.

7. Prepared Testimony of Ronald Atlas, "Conducting Research During the War on Terrorism: Balancing Openness and National Security," House Committee on Science, 10 October 2002, available at http://www.asm.org/Policy/index.asp?bid=5703.

8. Samuel Kaplan, PhD, "Current Policies and Proposals," at Scientific Openness and National Security Workshop, National Academy of Sciences, Washington, DC, 9 January 2004.

9. Nicholas R Cozzarelli, "PNAS policy on publication of sensitive material in the life sciences," Proceedings of the National Academy of Sciences, 18 February 2003, available at http://www.pnas.org/cgi/content/full/100/4/1463?etoc.

10. Bruce Alberts, Wm. A. Wulf, and Harvey Fineberg, "Statement on Science and Security in an Age of Terrorism," 18 October 2002, available at http://www4.nationalacademies.org/news.nsf/isbn/s10182002b?OpenDocument.

11. Diana Jean Schemo, "Scientists Discuss Balance of Research and Security," *New York Times*, January 10, 2003.

12. Cozzarelli, "PNAS policy on publication of sensitive material in the life sciences," 18 February 2003.

13. Stanley Falkow, "Statement on scientific publication and security fails to provide necessary guidelines," *Proceedings of the National Academy of Sciences*, 13 May 2003, available at http://www.pnas.org/cgi/content/full/100/10/5575.

14. Essay, "The New Atlantis," quoted in Ronald Atlas, "Preserving Scientific Integrity and Safeguarding Our Citizens: Challenges for Scientific Publishers in the Age of Terrorism," at Scientific Openness and National Security Workshop, National Academy of Sciences, Washington, DC, 9 January 2003.

15. US National Academies of Science, "Scientific Communication and National Security," Washington, DC: National Academy Press, 1982, available at http://www.nap.edu/books/0309033322/html/.

16. "National Policy on the Transfer of Scientific, Technical and Engineering Information," (NSDD 189), 21 September 1985, available at http://www.fas.org/irp/offdocs/nsdd/nsdd-189.htm.

17. Remarks by John Marburger at Scientific Openness and National Security Workshop, National Academy of Sciences, Washington, DC, 9 January 2004.

18. Condoleezza Rice Letter to Dr Harold Brown, co-Chairman, Center for Strategic and International Studies, 1 November 2001, available at http://www.aau.edu/research/Rice11.1.01.html.

19. Stephen S Morse, "Bioterror R&D: Assessing the Threat," powerpoint presentation at Scientific Openness and National Security Workshop, National Academy of Sciences, Washington, DC, 9 January 2004.

20. US Department of the Army, "Classification of Former Chemical Warfare, Chemical and Biological Defense, and Nuclear, Biological, and Chemical Contamination Survivability Information" (Army Regulation 380-86), 1 February 2005, available at http://www.fas.org/irp/doddir/army/ar380-86.pdf.

21. Cozzarelli, "PNAS policy on publication of sensitive material in the life sciences," 18 February 2003; and US National Academies of Science, "Background Paper on Science and Security in an Age of Terrorism," 18 October 2002, available at http://www4.nationalacademies.org/news.nsf/isbn/s10182002?OpenDocument.

22. At least one of the Principal Investigators for the most contentious experiments—mousepox, smallpox protein, and poliovirus—has left the field because of the controversy surrounding publication of the work. Private communication, 3 March 2005.

23. Mark Wheelis, "Transparency and Biodefense," unpublished powerpoint presentation, 5 December 2003. See also, Jeanne Guillemin, "National Security and Biodefense: Is There a Case for Full Transparency?" 21st Workshop of the Pugwash Study Group on the Implementation of the Chemical and Biological Weapons Conventions, Geneva, 4–5 December 2004.

24. "Biological Warfare Issues Weighed," *ASM News*, vol 54 no 7, 1988.

25. Jonathan B. Tucker, "Gene Wars," *Foreign Policy*, no 57 (Winter 1984–85), p. 70.

26. National Research Council, *Biotechnology Research in an Age of Terrorism*, (Washington, DC: National Academies Press), Oct. 2003, available at http://www.nap.edu/books/0309089778/html/.

27. Information on the NSABB, including its charter, is available at http://www.biosecurityboard.gov/index.htm.

28. "National Policy on the Transfer of Scientific, Technical and Engineering Information," (NSDD 189), 21 September 1985.

29. John Steinbruner and Stacy Okutani, "The Protective Oversight of Biotechnology," *Biosecurity and Bioterrorism: Biodefense Strategy, Practice, and Science*, vol 2 no 2, 2004, available at http://www.liebertonline.com/doi/pdf/10.1089/bsp.2004.2.273; and John D Steinbruner and Elisa D Harris, "Controlling Dangerous Pathogens," *Issues in Science and Technology*, vol 19 no 3 (Spring 2003), available at http://www.issues.org/19.3/steinbruner.htm.

30. The limitations of the current Institutional Biosafety Committees has been documented in Sunshine Project, "Mandate for Failure: The State of Institutional Biosafety Committees in an Age of Biological Weapons Research," 4 October 2004, available at http://www.sunshine-project.org/.

31. Martin Ensirenk, "Entering the Twilight Zone of What Material to Censor," *Science*, 22 November 2002.

32. Raymond A Zilinskas and Jonathan B Tucker, "Limiting the Contribution of the Open Scientific Literature to the Biological Weapons Threat," *Journal of Homeland Security*, December 2002.

*Elisa D. Harris is a senior research scholar at the Center for International and Security Studies at Maryland (CISSM) and former director for nonproliferation and export controls at the National Security Council.

John D. Steinbruner is a professor in the School of Public Policy and director of CISSM.

Harris, Elisa D., and John D. Steinbruner. "Scientific Openness and National Security after 9-11." *CBW Conventions Bulletin* 67 (March 2005): 1–5.

Used by permission.

Part 3: Legislative Access to Information

The Constitution assigns to Congress a significant role in formulating national security policy. The powers to "declare war," "define and punish piracies and felonies committed on the high seas, and offenses against the law of nations," "make rules concerning captures on land and water," "raise and support armies," "provide and maintain a navy," and "make rules for the government and regulation of the land and naval forces" are all included in the list of Congress's enumerated powers.

For Congress to legislate responsibly pursuant to any of these powers, it requires access to some information held by the executive branch. Only with information generated by and in possession of executive branch officials—military officers, the intelligence community, the diplomatic corps—can legislators effectively evaluate policy proposals, weigh the costs and benefits of military action, or legislate wisely to protect the homeland. Yet as sociologist Max Weber observed in the early 1900s, bureaucracies tend to "figh[t] every attempt of the parliament to gain knowledge. . . . Bureaucracy naturally welcomes a poorly informed and hence a powerless parliament."[1] The U.S. executive branch is no different; it often resists requests to provide classified or otherwise sensitive information to Congress.

This section looks at the question of the proper scope of information to which Congress should have access from two very different perspectives. In "Congressional Access to National Security Information," Louis Fisher takes a Congress-centric approach, arguing for a robust interpretation of Congress's duty and right to access national security information. In testimony before Congress on proposed legislation regarding what right members of the intelligence community have to disclose classified information to Congress as "whistle-blowers"—that is, to share information that might implicate government misconduct—former deputy assistant attorney general Randolph Moss presents the opposite argument. He asserts that the control of information is assigned by the Constitution exclusively to the president, leaving no role for Congress to assert independent authority over information access.

As you read the selections, consider the following questions:
- Under what circumstances does Congress need access to information?

Is there certain information that should never be disclosed to Congress?

• What are the potential costs of denying Congress access to information? What are the benefits? Is it possible to predict in advance (and thus to make rules about) what kinds of information will incur more costs than benefits if disclosed to Congress?

• How does granting Congress access to information differ from granting access to the American people more broadly? Should Congress have more or less information than the general public? Why or why not?

• If Randolph Moss is correct that the Constitution reserves to the president complete control over national security information, will fraud, waste, abuse, or violations of the law within the executive branch ever be uncovered? Will Congress—and in particular the committees on intelligence, armed services, and foreign affairs—be able to exercise oversight obligations effectively?

• Are Fisher's and Moss's positions entirely incompatible, or is there some middle ground? Do you think that Fisher would object to adopting the more limited disclosure provisions in S. 3829 rather than the broader ones in S. 1668?

• Moss argues for a case-by-case resolution of information disputes, rather than a general rule regarding when Congress is entitled to access information. What does he see as the benefit of that rule? Can you think of any drawbacks to that rule?

NOTE

1. Max Weber, "Bureaucracy," in *Essays in Sociology*, ed. and trans. H. H. Gerth and C. Wright Mills, 233–34 (New York: Oxford University Press, 1946).

Congressional Access to National Security Information

by Louis Fisher*

In debates over access to executive branch information, the President often receives a heightened privilege when documents involve national security information. Writing for the Court in the Watergate Tapes Case, Chief Justice Warren Burger rejected an "absolute, unqualified" presidential privilege to be independent of judicial process.[1] However, in careless and overbroad dicta, Justice Burger appeared to allow information to remain privileged if the President claimed a "need to protect military, diplomatic, or sensitive national security secrets."[2] A footnote drew attention to the fact that the case only addressed access to information by the Judiciary, and not by Congress: "We are not here concerned with . . . congressional demands for information."[3]

Despite the Court's dicta in *Nixon*, courts have long gained access to information regarding military issues, diplomacy, and national security. As the Court noted in 1962: "[i]t is error to suppose that every case or controversy which touches foreign relations lies beyond judicial cognizance."[4] In recent decades, as a result of congressional legislation, courts have had increasing access to national security documents through such statutes as the 1974 amendments to the Freedom of Information Act,[5] the Foreign Intelligence Surveillance Act of 1978,[6] and the Classified Information Procedures Act of 1980.[7] To the extent the judiciary decides to defer to executive branch arguments for secrecy in national security matters, such deference has no direct application to Congress, as Article I of the Constitution vests in Congress explicit powers and responsibilities concerning national security issues.[8]

The purpose of this Article is to identify the duties and needs of Congress to obtain national security information from the Executive Branch. The Article begins by examining claims by the Office of Legal Counsel in the Department of Justice that the President's roles as Commander in Chief, head of the Executive Branch, and "sole organ" of the United States in external relations, vest in the President a preeminent position in controlling national security information. It concentrates next on changes that place federal judges increasingly closer to secret and classified documents. The Article concludes by examining the state secrets privilege, which is invoked by the Executive Branch to keep documents from private litigants. Federal courts vary widely in interpreting their duties when the Executive Branch claims this privilege. Some courts insist that the trial judge should receive the disputed documents and examine them in camera.[9] Others adopt judicial standards ranging from "deference"[10] to "utmost deference"[11] to treating the privilege as an "absolute."[12]

The conflicts over access to information are primarily between the Executive Branch and the courts, but Congress has an interest in assuring that a judge maintains control over the courtroom and assures fairness to litigants who sue the Executive Branch. Congress should pass legislation that clarifies the state secrets privilege. It debated such legislation in the late 1960s and early 1970s, but decided against the bill language presented to it by an expert panel.[13] The frequency with which the Bush administration has invoked the state secrets privilege in recent years has triggered new interest in legislation to strengthen judicial independence and the adversary process by limiting the privilege. On May 31, 2007, the Constitution Project released a report recommending that Congress conduct hearings to investigate the scope of the privilege and "craft statutory language to clarify that judges, not the Executive Branch, have the final say about whether disputed evidence is subject to the state secrets privilege."[14] On August 13, 2007, the American Bar Association House of Delegates adopted a statement on state secrets recommending that Congress "enact legislation governing federal civil cases implicating the state secrets privilege (including cases in which the government is an original party or an intervenor)."[15]

I. CONTROL OVER NATIONAL SECURITY INFORMATION

The Executive Branch's views establishing a broad privilege to withhold national security information from the other branches result from a mischaracterization of the President's constitutional roles. In 1996, the Office of Legal Counsel (the "OLC") in the Department of Justice prepared a memo that set forth what it considered to be the principles governing access to national security information:

> [T]he President's roles as Commander in Chief, head of the Executive Branch, and sole organ of the Nation in its external relations require that he have ultimate and unimpeded authority over the collection, retention and dissemination of intelligence and other national security information in the Executive Branch. There is no exception to this principle for those disseminations that would be made to Congress or its Members. In that context, as in all others, the decision whether to grant access to the information must be made by someone who is acting in an

official capacity on behalf of the President and who is ultimately responsible, perhaps through intermediaries, to the President.[16]

This memo's analysis rests on faulty generalizations and misconceptions about the President's roles as Commander in Chief, head of the Executive Branch, and "sole organ" of the nation in its external relations. The next three sections will look at these respective roles and how they affect access to security information.

A. Commander in Chief

The Constitution empowers the President to be Commander in Chief, but the scope of that power must be understood in the context of military responsibilities that the Constitution grants to Congress. Article II reads as follows: "The President shall be Commander in Chief of the Army and Navy of the United States, and of the Militia of the several States, when called into the actual Service of the United States."[17] For the militia, Congress—not the President—does the calling. The Constitution vests in Congress the power "[t]o provide for calling forth the Militia to execute the Laws of the Union, suppress Insurrections and repel invasions."[18]

A key purpose of the Commander in Chief Clause is to preserve civilian supremacy. Attorney General Edward Bates explained in 1861 that the President is Commander in Chief "not because the President is supposed to be, or commonly is, in fact, a military man, a man skilled in the art of war and qualified to marshal a host in the field of battle. No, it is for quite a different reason."[19] A soldier knows that whatever military victories might occur, "he is subject to the orders of the *civil magistrate*, and he and his army are always 'subordinate to the civil power.'"[20]

The Constitution protects civilian supremacy by delegating war powers to both the President and the elected members of Congress. To associate civilian supremacy solely with the President would undermine democratic principles, constitutional limits, and the republican system of government. Article I empowers Congress to declare war, raise and support armies, and make rules for the land and naval forces. The debates at the Philadelphia Convention make clear that the Commander in Chief Clause does not grant the President unilateral, independent authority other than the power to "repel sudden attacks."[21] Roger Sherman, for example, said that the President should be able "to repel and not to commence war."[22] The consensus at the debate was that taking the country from a state of peace to a state of war was to be done through a deliberative process that included congressional debate and approval, either by a declaration or authorization of war.[23] George Mason told his colleagues that he was for "clogging rather than facilitating war."[24]

At one point in the debates, Pierce Butler wanted to give the President the power to make war, arguing that he "will have all the requisite qualities, and will not make war but when the Nation will support it."[25] No one joined Butler in those sentiments. Elbridge Gerry said that he "never expected to hear in a republic a motion to empower the Executive alone to declare war."[26] Mason was against giving the power of war to the Executive "because [he was] not <safely> to be trusted with it."[27] At the Pennsylvania ratifying convention, James Wilson assured his colleagues that the Constitution's system of checks and balances "will not hurry us into war; it is calculated to guard against it. It will not be in the power of a single man, or a single body of men, to involve us in such distress."[28]

The Framers entrusted Congress with the power to initiate war because they believed that Executives, in their search for fame and personal glory, had a natural bias to favor war at the cost of the interests of their country.[29] John Jay explicitly made this point in his essay in Federalist No. 4. He warned:

> [a]bsolute monarchs will often make war when their nations are to get nothing by it, but for purposes and objects merely personal, such as, a thirst for military glory, revenge for personal affronts, ambition, or private compacts to aggrandize or support their particular families, or partisans. These, and a variety of other motives, which affect only the mind of the sovereign, often lead him to engage in wars not sanctioned by justice, or the voice and interests of his people.[30]

One might read "absolute monarchs" to apply only to royal regimes, not to the democratic system of the United States, but the Framers based their judgment on human nature, not on any particular form of government.[31] James Madison called war:

> the true nurse of executive aggrandizement . . . . In war, the honours and emoluments of office are to be multiplied; and it is the executive patronage under which they are to be enjoyed. It is in war, finally, that laurels are to be gathered; and it is the executive brow they are to encircle.[32]

The costly and misconceived military operations in Korea, Vietnam, and Iraq pursued by Harry Truman, Lyndon B. Johnson, and George W. Bush underscore the miscalculations and partisan calculations that accompany presidential wars.[33] Unless Congress and the federal courts have access to executive branch information, the President and his advisers can initiate military activities on insufficient and erroneous grounds.

B. Head of the Executive Branch

The Framers placed the President at the head of the Executive Branch to provide unity, responsibility, and accountability. The Framers expressed the principle of unity in the Constitution by placing upon the President, and no one else, the duty to "take Care that the Laws be faithfully executed."[34] The delegates at the Philadelphia Convention rejected the proposal for a plural executive, deciding to vest the executive duties in one person. Said John Rutledge: "A single man would feel the greatest responsibility and administer the public affairs best."[35]

The Framers' placement of the President at the head of the Executive Branch does not support an inference that Congress should be denied access to information within the Executive Branch necessary to discharge its legislative and oversight duties. The Framers never intended to make the President personally responsible for executing all of the laws.[36] Instead, he was to take care that the laws be faithfully executed, including laws that limited his control over certain decisions within the Executive Branch.[37] To assure that the laws are faithfully executed, Congress has an independent duty to supervise federal agencies and departments.[38] To fulfill that duty it needs access to executive branch information, including information about national security affairs.

From an early date, Congress directed certain subordinate executive officials to carry out specified "ministerial" functions without interference from the President. In 1789, during debate on the creation of the Department of the Treasury, James Madison insisted that the Comptroller should not serve at the pleasure of the President. The role of the office was to determine the legality of public expenditures, and Madison argued that this function was "not purely of an Executive nature."[39] It seemed to Madison "that they partake of a Judiciary quality as well as Executive. . . ."[40] He questioned whether the President "can or ought to have any interference in the settling and adjusting the legal claims of individuals against the United States."[41] As a result of this debate and others, Congress created a number of officers operating independently from the President so long as they were faithfully executing the laws.[42]

Even the heads of executive departments do not serve solely as political agents of the President. They perform legal duties assigned to them by Congress. In 1803, Chief Justice John Marshall distinguished between two types of duties for a Cabinet head: ministerial and discretionary. Congress may direct a Secretary to carry out certain activities as ministerial duties. Discretionary duties are owed to the President alone. When a Secretary performs ministerial duties he is bound to obey the laws. "He acts . . . under the authority of law, and not by the instructions of the President. It is a ministerial act which the law enjoins on a particular officer for a particular purpose."[43]

The dispute over ministerial duties reappeared in 1838. In *Kendall v. United States*, the Court held that Congress could mandate that certain payments be made to authorized individuals and that neither the head of the department nor the President could deny or control these ministerial decisions.[44]

On many occasions Attorneys General have advised Presidents that they had no legal right to interfere with administrative decisions made by auditors and comptrollers in the Treasury Department, pension officers, and other officials.[45] The President is responsible for seeing that administrative officers faithfully perform their duties, "but the statutes regulate and prescribe these duties, and he has no more power to add to, or subtract from, the duties imposed upon subordinate executive and administrative officers by the law, than those officers have to add or subtract from his duties."[46]

Executive agencies, including those in the field of national security, have a direct responsibility to Congress, the body that created them. In 1854, Attorney General Caleb Cushing advised department heads that they had a threefold relation: to the President, to execute his will in cases in which the President possessed a constitutional or legal discretion; to the law, which directs them to perform certain acts; and to Congress, "in the conditions contemplated by the Constitution."[47] Agencies are created by law and "most of their duties are prescribed by law; Congress may at all times call on them for information or explanation in matters of official duty; and it may, if it see[s] fit, interpose by legislation concerning them, when required by the interests of the Government."[48]

These limitations on the President's authority to direct the activities of executive officials were recognized by Chief Justice William Howard Taft when he wrote broadly about the power of the President to remove executive officials. Looking to the congressional debates of 1789, Taft concluded that the executive officials served at the President's pleasure and could be removed, but he also acknowledged that two classes of executive officials required a measure of independence, the first class being ministerial and the second being quasi-judicial:

> Of course there may be duties so peculiarly and specifically committed to the discretion of a particular officer as to raise a question whether the President may overrule or revise the officer's interpretation of his statutory duty in a particular instance. Then there may be duties of a quasi-judicial character imposed on executive officers and members of executive tribunals whose decisions after hearing affect interests of individuals,

the discharge of which the President can not in a particular case properly influence or control.[49]

In recent years, federal courts have repeatedly directed the President to carry out laws to which he personally objected or with which he had failed to comply as enacted.[50] The President is head of the Executive Branch, but what the Executive Branch does depends on statutory direction from Congress, in matters of both domestic and national security policy.

C. "Sole Organ" in Foreign Affairs

During debate in the House of Representatives in 1800, John Marshall said that the President "is the sole organ of the nation in its external relations, and its sole representative with foreign nations."[51] Justice George Sutherland later included that sentence in dicta in his *Curtiss-Wright* opinion in 1936 to suggest that the President's authority in foreign affairs is exclusive, plenary, independent, inherent, and extra-constitutional.[52] However, Justice Sutherland took Marshall's statement out of context to imply a position Marshall never held.

At no time in Marshall's career, as Secretary of State, member of Congress, or Chief Justice of the Supreme Court, did he ever suggest that the President could act unilaterally to make foreign policy in the face of statutory limitations. As a Justice, in a war powers case concerning a proclamation issued by President John Adams to naval commanders during the Quasi-War with France, Marshall ruled that the proclamation was invalid because it conflicted with a statute governing the seizure of foreign vessels.[53] As a legislator, Marshall made his "sole organ" comment in the context of a particular situation. The floor debate concerned the decision by President Adams to turn over to England someone charged with murder. Because the case was already pending in an American court, some members of Congress objected that Adams had violated the doctrine of separation of powers and should be impeached or censured.[54] In his floor speech, Marshall denied that there were any grounds to find fault with the President.[55] He argued that by carrying out an extradition treaty with England, Adams had discharged his constitutional duty to see that the law was faithfully executed and was not attempting to make national policy single-handedly or to act unilaterally without law. He further argued that in this case, Adams was carrying out a policy made jointly by the President and the Senate through the treaty-making process.[56] He provided that in other cases the President carried out policy made through the statutory process and that only after national policy had been formulated by the collective effort of both branches did the President become the "sole organ" in implementing the policy.[57]

In reaction to Justice Sutherland's analysis of Marshall's "sole organ" statement, Justice Robert Jackson in 1952 stated that the most that can be drawn from Sutherland's opinion is the intimation that the President "might act in external affairs without congressional authority, but not that he might act contrary to an Act of Congress."[58] Jackson specifically downplayed Sutherland's opinion, noting that "much of the [Sutherland] opinion is *dictum*."[59] In 1981, the D.C. Circuit similarly cautioned against placing undue reliance on "certain dicta" in Sutherland's opinion: "To the extent that denominating the President as the 'sole organ' of the United States in international affairs constitutes a blanket endorsement of plenary Presidential power over any matter extending beyond the borders of this country, we reject that characterization."[60]

The OLC reference to the "sole organ" implies an exclusive and independent role for the President in foreign and national security affairs. In context, however, John Marshall clearly stated that President Adams was operating under treaty and statutory authority as shaped and enacted by the legislative branch. Adams was not attempting to create national policy on his own—he was carrying out the will of Congress. As such, lawmakers had every right to determine whether the President was faithfully carrying out congressional policy formulated in statutes and treaties, and thus they should have been able to obtain foreign and national security information from the executive branch to assure compliance.

II. CHANGING ROLE OF THE COURTS

In the period immediately after World War II, federal courts regularly deferred to presidential decisions in military and diplomatic affairs. In 1948, in *Chicago & Southern Air Lines, Inc. v. Waterman*, the Supreme Court said:

> It would be intolerable that courts, without the relevant information, should review and perhaps nullify actions of the Executive taken on information properly held secret. Nor can courts sit *in camera* in order to be taken into executive confidences. But even if courts could require full disclosure, the very nature of executive decisions as to foreign policy is political, not judicial.[61]

The Court's judicial deference was not afforded solely to the President. "Such decisions," said the Court, "are wholly confided by our Constitution to the political departments of the government, Executive and Legislative."[62]

The *Waterman* decision was overly deferential when issued, compared not only with contemporary standards but even with those established much earlier. Federal courts had often decided cases involving military and diplomatic affairs, as reflected in Chief Justice Marshall's ruling in *Little v. Barreme*.[63] From 1789 to World War II, federal courts would rarely avoid ruling on a case because it involved foreign affairs or national security.[64] In 1952, the Supreme Court struck down President Truman's decision to seize steel mills as part of his effort to prosecute the war in Korea.[65] Yet a year later, the Court avoided a clash with the Executive Branch over national security documents. A district court had ordered the United States, as defendant, to produce a military accident report to permit the court, in camera, to determine whether it contained matter relevant to a tort claims case.[66] The Supreme Court reversed, ruling that the judiciary "should not jeopardize the security which the [government's] privilege is meant to protect by insisting upon an examination of the evidence, even by the judge alone, in chambers."[67] As explained in Section III, the Court was misled about the contents of the accident report.

A. Statutory Authorizations

Judicial attitudes of the 1940s and early 1950s have been superseded by grants of congressional authority to the courts. In 1973, the Supreme Court decided that it lacked authority to examine certain documents in camera merely to sift out "nonsecret components" for release.[68] Congress responded by passing an amendment to the Freedom of Information Act ("FOIA"),[69] clearly authorizing courts to examine executive records in judges' chambers to determine if the records fit into one of the nine categories of FOIA exemptions.[70] The Foreign Intelligence Surveillance Act ("FISA") of 1978[71] requires a court order to engage in electronic surveillance within the United States for purposes of obtaining foreign intelligence information.[72] The statute created the FISA Court to review applications submitted by government attorneys.[73] Congress granted more authority to courts in 1980, when it passed the Classified Information Procedures Act ("CIPA").[74] The Act establishes procedures allowing a judge to screen classified information to determine whether it could be used during a criminal trial.[75]

In the late 1960s, efforts were made to define and narrow the state secrets privilege, which had been used by the Executive Branch to withhold documents and testimony from federal courts and private litigants. An advisory committee, appointed by Chief Justice Earl Warren, began working on a draft of proposed rules of evidence in 1965. Its initial report defined "secrets of state" in this manner: "A 'secret of state' is information not open or theretofore officially disclosed to the public concerning the national defense or the international relations of the United States."[76] The chief officer of the executive department administering the subject matter that the secret concerned would be required to make a showing to the judge, "in whole or in part in the form of a written statement," allowing the trial judge to hear the matter in chambers, "but all counsel [would be] entitled to inspect the claim and showing and to be heard thereon."[77] Under the proposed rule, the judge would be able to "take any protective measure which the interests of the government and the furtherance of justice may require."[78]

The Committee identified several options for when a judge sustains a claim of privilege for a state secret in a case involving the government as a party. When sustaining the claim deprived a private party of "material evidence," the judge could make "any further orders which the interests of justice require, including striking the testimony of a witness, declaring a mistrial, finding against the government upon an issue as to which the evidence is relevant, or dismissing the action."[79] The advisory committee prepared two more drafts, but in 1973 Congress blocked passage of all the rules of evidence, including the one on state secrets.[80]

B. The Significance of Egan

The 1996 OLC memo[81] relied in part on *Department of the Navy v. Egan*[82] to maximize presidential power over classified documents.[83] As explained below, *Egan* is fundamentally a case of statutory construction and should not be read to grant the President any type of exclusive control over classified documents. The dispute in *Egan* involved the Navy's denial of a security clearance to Thomas Egan, who worked on the Trident submarine. After the denial, Egan was discharged from the Navy and sought review of his discharge by the Merit Systems Protection Board ("MSPB"). The Supreme Court upheld the Navy's action by ruling that the denial of a security clearance is a sensitive call of discretionary judgment committed by law to the executive agency that had the necessary expertise for protecting classified information.[84] The conflict in this case was entirely within the Executive Branch (Navy versus MSPB). It was not between Congress and the Executive Branch or the judiciary and the Executive Branch.

The focus on questions of statutory interpretation appeared at each stage of the lawsuit. The Justice Department stated in its brief: "The issue in this case is one of statutory construction and 'at bottom . . . turns on congressional intent.'"[85] The Court directed the parties to respond to this question: "Whether, in the course of reviewing the removal of an employee for failure to maintain a required security clearance, the Merit Systems Protection Board is authorized by statute to review the substance of the underlying decision [by the Navy] to deny or revoke the security clearance."[86]

The specific statutory questions concerned 5 U.S.C. §§ 7512, 7513, and 7701. The Justice Department, after analyzing the relevant statutes and their legislative history, could find no basis to conclude that Congress intended the MSPB to review the merits of security clearance determinations.[87] The entire oral argument before the Court on December 2, 1987 focused on the meaning of statutes and what Congress intended by them.[88] At no time did the Justice Department suggest that classified information could be withheld from Congress. The Court examined the "narrow question" of whether the MSPB had statutory authority to review the substance of a decision to deny a security clearance.[89]

At different points in its opinion the Court referred to constitutional powers of the President, including those as Commander in Chief and head of the Executive Branch,[90] and made reference to the President's responsibility over foreign policy.[91] Nevertheless, the case was decided solely on statutory grounds. In stating that courts "traditionally have been reluctant to intrude upon the authority of the Executive in military and national security affairs," the Court identified this fundamental exception: *"unless Congress specifically has provided otherwise."*[92] The Court appears to have borrowed this thought, if not the language, from the Justice Department, which argued that: "Absent an unambiguous grant of jurisdiction by Congress, courts have traditionally been reluctant to intrude upon the authority of the executive in military and national security affairs."[93]

During oral argument before the Supreme Court, the Justice Department and Egan's attorney, William J. Nold, debated the statutory issues. After the Department of Justice completed its presentation, Nold told the Justices: "I think that we start out with the same premise. We start out with the premise that this is a case that involves statutory interpretation." Nold objected that the Department kept trying to slip in some constitutional dimensions:

> What they seem to do in my view is to start building a cloud around the statute. They start building this cloud and they call it national security, and as their argument progresses . . . the cloud gets darker and darker and darker, so that by the time we get to the end, we can't see the statute anymore. What we see is this cloud called national security.[94]

In describing the President's role as Commander in Chief, the Court stated that the President's authority to protect classified information "flows primarily from [a] constitutional investment of power in the President and exists quite apart from any explicit congressional grant."[95] Thus if Congress had never enacted legislation regarding classified information, the President would be at liberty to use his best judgment to protect classified information. That is the legal and political reality when Congress is silent. But if Congress acts by statute, it can narrow the President's range of action and the courts would then seek guidance from statutory policy.

III. THE STATE SECRETS PRIVILEGE

In 1953, in the case of *United States v. Reynolds*, the Supreme Court for the first time recognized the state secrets privilege.[96] The case involved questions about the authority of the Executive Branch to withhold certain documents from three widows who sued the government for the deaths of their husbands in a military plane crash over Waycross, Georgia.[97] As part of their suit under the Federal Tort Claims Act,[98] the widows asked the Air Force for the official accident report and statements taken from three surviving crew members.[99] Both the district court and the Third Circuit held that the government had to produce the documents.[100] The government refused to release the documents and lost at both levels. Without ever looking at the documents, the Supreme Court sustained the government's claim of privilege. The decision contains conflicting positions. According to the Court:

> Judicial control over the evidence in a case cannot be abdicated to the caprice of executive officers. Yet we will not go so far as to say that the court may automatically require a complete disclosure to the judge before the claim of privilege will be accepted in any case. It may be possible to satisfy the court, from all the circumstances of the case, that there is a reasonable danger that compulsion of the evidence will expose military matters which, in the interest of national security, should not be divulged. When this is the case, the occasion for the privilege is appropriate, and the court should not jeopardize the security which the privilege is meant to protect by insisting upon an examination of the evidence, even by the judge, alone, in chambers.[101]

No persuasive case can be made that a judge examining a document in chambers risks the exposure of military matters or in any way jeopardizes national security. Judges take an oath of office to defend the Constitution in the same manner as the President, members of Congress, and executive officers.[102] Moreover, in deciding not to review the accident report and the statements of the surviving crew members, the Court was in no position to know if there had been "executive caprice." In short, the judiciary did what it said it could not do: abdicate to the Executive Branch.

The Court advised the three widows to return to district court and depose the three surviving crew members, and from that stage to consider relitigating the case.[103] The widows' attorneys took depositions,[104] but after debating the emotional and financial costs of continuing the lawsuit, the women decided to settle for seventy-five percent of what they would have received under the original district court ruling.[105]

We now know that the accident report and the statements by the three surviving crew members contained no state secrets. After the Air Force declassified the documents in the 1990s, the daughter of one of the civilians who died in the crash gained access to the material by means of an Internet search in February 2000.[106] The report made mention of "secret equipment," but anyone reading newspaper stories the day after the crash was aware that a secret plane on a secret mission carried secret equipment.[107] The three families decided to return to court in 2003 on a petition of coram nobis, charging that the judiciary had been misled by the government and that there had been fraud against the court.[108] The families lost in district court and in the Third Circuit, and on May 1, 2006, the Supreme Court denied certiorari.[109]

The Third Circuit decided the second case on the basis of judicial finality.[110] Central to the appellate court's decision was avoiding having to revisit and redo an earlier decision, even if there was substantial evidence that the Executive Branch had misled the judiciary, particularly the Supreme Court. In support, the Third Circuit cited another ruling that "perjury by a witness is not enough to constitute fraud against the court."[111] Such a position is reasonable in cases involving private parties, because litigants are expected to expose false statements through the regular adversary process.[112] Perjury and misleading statements by the government, however, are far more ominous when the Department of Justice is the major litigant in court and has a unique capacity to abuse or misuse political power. The Japanese-American cases in the 1980s highlighted the corrupting influence of having officers of the court (government attorneys) present misleading documents and testimony.[113]

The courts should not permit litigants, especially the federal government, to mislead a court to the point where it issues a ruling it would not have issued had it received correct information. The interests at stake are not only those of a private party suing the government, but also the court's interest in the integrity and credibility of the courtroom. With such decisions, private citizens will begin to view the judiciary not as an independent branch, freely participating in the system of checks and balances, but as a trusted arm of the Executive. Congress needs to consider legislation that will restore trust in the capacity of the judiciary to assure litigants an opportunity to fairly and effectively challenge government actions that may be abusive, illegal, or unconstitutional.

IV. Conclusions

Much of our national security information, such as information on military plans and atomic secrets, is legitimately classified and withheld from the public.[114] Other information may be kept secret to hide blunders, corruption, and illegality. Unless someone looks behind the secrecy label, no one knows what is being hidden or why. Members of Congress need access to national security information to discharge their duties under Article I, give vigor to the system of checks and balances, and prevent the dangers of concentrated power. Congress must also assure that the judiciary functions with the full independence needed to protect the rights of private litigants in court and to avoid the appearance of judicial subservience to executive interests.

In 1971, the D.C. Circuit ordered the government to produce documents for in camera review to assess a claim of executive privilege. The court argued that "[a]n essential ingredient of our rule of law is the authority of the courts to determine whether an executive official or agency has complied with the Constitution and with the mandates of Congress which define and limit the authority of the executive."[115] Mere claims and assertions of executive power or presidential prerogatives "cannot override the duty of the court to assure that an official has not exceeded his charter or flouted the legislative will."[116] The court issued an admonition that applies equally to Congress and the judiciary:

> [N]o executive official or agency can be given absolute authority to determine what documents in his possession may be considered by the court in its task. Otherwise the head of an executive department would have the power on his own say to cover up all evidence of fraud and corruption when a federal court or grand jury was investigating malfeasance in office, and this is not the law.[117]

The independent duty of Congress and the courts to exercise their coequal powers exists partly to protect their institutions. It also serves to apply effective checks on the capacity of the Executive Branch to violate individual rights and liberties. Therefore, it is not only permissible, but desirable that Congress pass legislation that gives courts access to national security documents.

Notes

1. United States v. Nixon, 418 U.S. 683, 706 (1974).
2. Id.
3. Id. at 712 n.19
4. Baker v. Carr, 369 U.S. 186, 211 (1962).

5. Pub. L. No. 93–502, 88 Stat. 1561 (codified as amended at 5 U.S.C. § 552 (2006)).

6. Pub. L. No. 95–511, 92 Stat. 1783 (codified in scattered sections of 50 U.S.C.).

7. Pub. L. No. 96–456, 94 Stat. 2025 (codified at 18 U.S.C.A. App.3 (2006)). For further discussion of these statutes, see *infra* Part II.A.

8. U.S. CONST. art. I, § 8 (vesting in Congress the power to "declare War," "raise and support Armies," "provide and maintain a Navy," and "define and punish Piracies").

9. Reynolds v. United States, 192 F.2d 987 (3d Cir. 1951).

10. Arar v. Ashcroft, 414 F. Supp. 2d 250, 283 (E.D.N.Y. 2006) (internal quotation marks omitted) (citing Jama v. Immigration and Customs Enforcement, 543 U.S. 335, 335 (2005)).

11. El-Masri v. United States, 479 F.3d 296, 305 (4th Cir. 2007), *cert denied*, 2007 WL1646914 (internal quotation marks omitted) (citing United States v. Nixon, 418 U.S. 683, 709 (1974)).

12. El-Masri v. Tenet, 437 F. Supp. 2d 530, 537 (E.D. Va. 2006).

13. *See* Pub. L. No. 93–12, 87 Stat. 9 (1973); *see also* LOUIS FISHER, IN THE NAME OF NATIONAL SECURITY: UNCHECKED PRESIDENTIAL POWER AND THE REYNOLDS CASE 140–45 (2006).

14. THE CONSTITUTION PROJECT, REFORMING THE STATE SECRETS PRIVILEGE, at ii (2007), http://www.constitutionproject.org/pdf/Reforming_the_State_Secrets_Privilege_Statement1.pdf.

15. Report to the House of Delegates, 2007 A.B.A. SEC. OF INDIVIDUAL RTS. AND RESPONSIBILITIES 116A, *available at* http://www.fas.org/sgp/jud/statesec/aba081307.pdf.

16. Memorandum from Christopher H. Schroeder, Acting Assistant Attorney Gen., Office of Legal Counsel, Dep't. of Justice, to Michael J. O'Neil, Gen. Counsel, Cent. Intelligence Agency 4 (November 26, 1996) [hereinafter OLC Memo] (quoting Brief for Appellees, Am. Foreign Serv. Ass'n. v. Garfinkel, 488 U.S. 923 (1988) (No. 87–2127)) (copy on file with author).

17. U.S. CONST. art. II, § 2.

18. *Id.* art. I, § 8, cl. 15.

19. 10 Op. Att'y Gen. 74, 79 (1861).

20. *Id.*

21. 2 THE RECORDS OF THE FEDERAL CONVENTION OF 1787, at 318–19 (Max Farrand ed., 1937).

22. *Id.* at 318.

23. LOUIS FISHER, PRESIDENTIAL WAR POWER 1–16 (2d ed. 2004).

24. 2 THE RECORDS OF THE FEDERAL CONVENTION OF 1787, at 319 (Max Farrand ed., 1937).

25. *Id.* at 318.

26. *Id.*

27. *Id.* at 319.

28. 2 THE DEBATES IN THE SEVERAL STATE CONVENTIONS ON THE ADOPTION OF THE FEDERAL CONSTITUTION 528 (Jonathan Elliot ed., 1896).

29. *See* William Michael Treanor, *Fame, the Founding, and the Power to Declare War*, 82 CORNELL L. REV. 695, 700 (1997).

30. THE FEDERALIST NO. 4 (John Jay).

31. FISHER, *supra* note 23, at 8–10.

32. James Madison, *Letters of Helvidius, No. IV*, *in* 6 THE WRITINGS OF JAMES MADISON, 1790–1802, at 171, 174 (Gaillard Hunt ed., 1906).

33. FISHER, *supra* note 23, at 97–104, 128–44, 211–35.

34. U.S. CONST. art. II, § 3.

35. 1 THE RECORDS OF THE FEDERAL CONVENTION OF 1787, *supra* note 15, at 65.

36. *See infra* notes 39–50 and accompanying text.

37. *See id.*

38. Louis Fisher, The Politics of Executive Privilege 3–25 (2004).

39. 39 1 Annals of Cong. 636 (Joseph Gales ed., 1789).

40. Id.

41. Id. at 638.

42. Louis Fisher, The Politics of Shared Power 111–12, 127–32 (4th ed. 1998).

43. Marbury v. Madison, 5 U.S. (1 Cranch) 137, 158 (1803).

44. Kendall v. United States, 37 U.S. (1 Pet.) 524 (1838). See also United States v. Louisville, 169 U.S. 249 (1898); United States v. Price, 116 U.S. 43 (1885); United States v. Schurz, 102 U.S. 378 (1880); Clackamus County, Or. v. McKay, 219 F.2d 479, 496 (D.C. Cir. 1954), vacated as moot, 349 U.S. 901, 909 (1955).

45. 1 Op. Att'y Gen. 624 (1823); 1 Op. Att'y Gen. 636 (1824); 1 Op. Att'y Gen. 678 (1824); 1 Op. Att'y Gen. 705 (1825); 1 Op. Att'y Gen. 706 (1825); 2 Op. Att'y Gen. 480 (1831); 2 Op. Att'y Gen. 507 (1832); 2 Op. Att'y Gen. 544 (1832); 4 Op. Att'y Gen. 515 (1846); 5 Op. Att'y Gen. 287 (1851); 11 Op. Att'y Gen. 14 (1864); 13 Op. Att'y Gen. 28 (1869).

46. 19 Op. Att'y Gen. 685, 686–87 (1890).

47. 6 Op. Att'y Gen. 326, 344 (1854).

48. Id.

49. Myers v. United States, 272 U.S. 52, 135 (1926).

50. E.g., Train v. City of New York, 420 U.S. 35 (1975); Lear Siegler, Inc., Energy Prods. Div. v. Lehman, 842 F.2d 1102, 1124 (9th Cir. 1988); Ameron, Inc. v. U.S. Army Corps of Eng'rs, 787 F.2d 875 (3d Cir. 1986), aff'd on reh'g, 809 F.2d 979 (3d Cir. 1986); Nat'l Treasury Employees Union v. Nixon, 492 F.2d 587 (D.C. Cir. 1974).

51. 10 Annals of Cong. 613 (1800).

52. See United States v. Curtiss-Wright Corp., 299 U.S. 304, 318–20 (1936).

53. See Little v. Barreme, 6 U.S. (2 Cranch) 170, 177–79 (1804).

54. 6 Annals of Cong. 552 (1800).

55. Id. at 605–06.

56. Id. at 597, 613–14.

57. Id. at 613–14.

58. Youngstown Sheet & Tube Co. v. Sawyer, 343 U.S. 579, 636 n.2 (1952) (Powell, J. concurring).

59. Id.

60. Am. Int'l Group, Inc. v. Islamic Republic of Iran, 657 F.2d 430, 438 n.6 (D.C. Cir. 1981). For an evaluation of the deficiencies of Justice Sutherland's dicta, see Louis Fisher, Presidential Inherent Power: The "Sole Organ" Doctrine, 37 Presidential Stud. Q. 139 (2007).

61. 333 U.S. 103, 111 (1948).

62. Id.

63. U.S. (2 Cranch) 169 (1804) (finding a commander of a warship of the United States actionable for damages because he acted pursuant to a presidential proclamation that exceeded the policy established by Congress in a statute).

64. Louis Fisher, Judicial Review of the War Power, 35 Presidential Stud. Q. 466 (2005).

65. Youngstown Sheet & Tube Co. v. Sawyer, 343 U.S. 579 (1952).

66. Brauner v. United States, 10 F.R.D. 468 (D. Pa. 1950), aff'd sub nom. Reynolds v. United States, 192 F.2d 987 (3d Cir. 1951).

67. United States v. Reynolds, 345 U.S. 1, 10 (1953).

68. EPA v. Mink, 410 U.S. 73, 81 (1973) (declining to examine documents regarding a planned underground nuclear test); see Fisher, supra note 13, at 130–36.

69. Freedom of Information Act, Pub. L. No. 93–502, 88 Stat. 1562 (codified at 5 U.S.C. § 552 (2006)).

70. *Id.; see* H.R. Rep. No. 93–1380, at 8–9, 11–12 (1974); Fisher, *supra* note 13, at 136–40.

71. Foreign Intelligence Surveillance Act of 1978, Pub. L. No. 95–5111, 92 Stat. 1783 (codified in scattered sections of 50 U.S.C.A.).

72. *Id.*

73. *Id.* at 1788, § 103; *see* Fisher, *supra* note 13, at 145–52.

74. Classified Information Procedures Act, Pub. L. No. 96–456, 94 Stat. 2025 (1980) (codified at 18 U.S.C.A. App. 3. § 3 (2006)).

75. *Id.; see* Fisher, *supra* note 13, at 152–53.

76. Preliminary Draft of Proposed Rules of Evidence for the U.S. District Courts and magistrates, 46 F.R.D. 161, 273 (1969).

77. *Id.*

78. *Id.*

79. *Id.* at 273–74.

80. Fisher, *supra* note 13, at 141–44.

81. *See id.*

82. 484 U.S. 518 (1988).

83. OLC Memo, *supra* note 16, at 6–7.

84. *Egan,* 484 U.S. at 529–30.

85. Brief for the Petitioner at 22, *Dept. of the Navy v. Egan,* 484 U.S. 518 (1988) (No. 86–1552) (citing Clarke v. Sec. Indus. Ass'n, 479 U.S. 388, 400 (1987)).

86. *Id.* at (I).

87. Petition for Writ of Certiorari at 4–5, 13, 15–16, 18, *Dept. of the Navy v. Egan,* 484 U.S. 518 (1988) (No. 86–1552).

88. Transcript of Oral Argument at 19, Dep't of the Navy v. Egan, 484 U.S. 518 (1988) (No. 86–1552).

89. *Egan,* 484 U.S. at 520.

90. *Id.* at 527.

91. *Id.* at 529.

92. *Id.* at 530 (emphasis added).

93. Brief for the Petitioner, *supra* note 83, at 21.

94. Transcript of Oral Argument at 19, Dep't of the Navy v. Egan, 484 U.S. 518 (1988) (No. 86–1552).

95. *Egan,* 484 U.S. at 527.

96. 345 U.S. 1, 6–7 (1953).

97. *Id.* at 2–4; *see also* Fisher, *supra* note 13.

98. 28 U.S.C. §§ 1346, 2674 (2006).

99. *Reynolds,* 345 U.S. at 3; *see also* Fisher, *supra* note 13, at 35–36.

100. Brauner v. United States, 10 F.R.D. 468 (D. Pa. 1950), *aff'd sub nom.* Reynolds v. United States, 192 F.2d 987 (3d Cir. 1951).

101. *Reynolds,* 345 U.S. at 9–10.

102. *See* 28 U.S.C.A. § 453 (2006).

103. Fisher, *supra* note 13, at 115–18.

104. *Id.* at 115–16.

105. *Id.* at 117.

106. *Id.* at 166–67.

107. *Id.* at 1–2.

108. Herring v. United States, 2004 WL 2040272, at *2 (E.D. Pa. Sept. 10, 2004).

109. Herring v. United States, 547 U.S. 1123 (2006).

110. Herring v. United States, 424 F.3d 384, 386 (3d Cir. 2005).

111. *Id.* at 390.

112. *Id.*

113. FISHER, *supra* note 13, at 171–74 (coram nobis cases vacating the convictions of Gordon Hirabayashi and Fred Korematsu because the government misled the Supreme Court).

114. *See, e.g.,* 42 U.S.C. §§ 2014(i)(y), 2274 (2000).

115. Comm. for Nuclear Responsibility, Inc. v. Seaborg, 463 F.2d 788, 793 (D.C. Cir. 1971).

116. *Id.*

117. *Id.* at 794.

*Louis Fisher is among the nation's foremost experts on constitutional law and public policy, with particular expertise in (among other areas) executive authority, separation of powers, and war powers.

Fisher, Louis. "Congressional Access to National Security Information." *Harvard Journal on Legislation* 45 (2008): 219–235.

Statement of Randolph Moss

Statement of Randolph Moss
Before the Permanent Select Committee on Intelligence,
U.S. House of Representatives
"Whistleblower Protections for Classified Disclosures"

May 20, 1998

[. . .]

My name is Randolph Moss. I am a Deputy Assistant Attorney General in the Office of Legal Counsel at the Department of Justice. I am pleased to be here to present the analysis of the Department of Justice concerning the constitutionality of S. 1668 and H.R. 3829, two bills that address disclosure to Congress of classified "whistleblower" information concerning the intelligence community.

As the Department has previously indicated, it is our conclusion that S. 1668, like the Senate passed version of section 306 of last year's Intelligence Authorization bill, is unconstitutional.[1] It is unconstitutional because it would deprive the President of the opportunity to determine how, when and under what circumstances certain classified information should be disclosed to Members of Congress—no matter how such a disclosure might affect his ability to perform his constitutionally assigned duties. In contrast, H.R. 3829 is constitutional because it contains provisions that allow for the exercise of that authority.

I begin by briefly summarizing the principal provisions of S. 1668 and H.R. 3829. I then review the relevant constitutional history and doctrine. I conclude by applying the relevant constitutional principles to the two bills. Because other witnesses at the hearing today can best address the practical concerns posed by legislation in this area, my remarks are limited to the relevant constitutional considerations.

I.

A.

S. 1668 would require the President to inform employees of covered federal agencies (and employees of federal contractors) that their disclosure to Con-

gress of classified information that the employee (or contractor) reasonably believes provides direct and specific evidence of misconduct "is not prohibited by
law, executive order, or regulation or otherwise contrary to public policy."[2] The
misconduct covered by the bill includes not only violations of law, but also violations of "any . . . rule[] or regulation," and it encompasses, among other things,
"gross mismanagement, a gross waste of funds, [or] a flagrant abuse of authority."[3]

S. 1668 would thus vest any covered federal employee having access to classified information with a unilateral right to circumvent the process by which the
executive and legislative branches accommodate each other's interests in sensitive information. Under S. 1668, any covered federal employee with access to
classified information that—in the employee's opinion—indicated misconduct
could determine how, when and under what circumstances that information
would be shared with Congress. Moreover, the bill would authorize this no matter what the effect on the President's ability to accomplish his constitutionally
assigned functions. As discussed below, such a rule would violate the separation
of powers.[4]

B.

H.R. 3829 would amend the Central Intelligence Agency Act and the Inspector General Act of 1978 to provide a means for covered executive branch
employees and contractors to report to the Intelligence Committees certain
serious abuses or violations of law or false statements to Congress that relate
to "the administration or operation of an intelligence activity," as well as any
reprisal or threat of reprisal relating to such a report. Under H.R. 3829, any employee or contractor who wishes to report such information to Congress would
first make a report to the inspector general for the Central Intelligence Agency
or their agency, as appropriate. If the complaint appears credible, the relevant
inspector general would be required to forward the complaint to the head of his
or her agency, and the head of the agency would generally be required to forward
the report to the Intelligence Committees. Moreover, if the inspector general
does not transmit the complaint to the head of the agency, the employee or contractor would generally be permitted to submit the complaint—under defined
conditions—to the Committees directly.

Significantly, unlike S. 1668, H.R. 3829 provides that the head of the agency
or the Director of Central Intelligence may determine "in the exceptional case
and in order to protect vital law enforcement, foreign affairs, or national security interests" not to transmit the inspector general's report to the Intelligence
Committees and not to permit the employee or contractor directly to contact

the Intelligence Committees.[5] Whenever this authority is exercised, the head of the agency or the Director of Central Intelligence must promptly provide the Intelligence Committees with his or her reasons for precluding the disclosure. In this manner, H.R. 3829 would provide a mechanism for congressional oversight while protecting the executive interest in maintaining the strict confidentiality of classified information when necessary to the discharge of the President's constitutional authority. As a result, unlike S. 1668, H.R. 3829 is consistent with the constitutional separation of powers.

II.

A host of precedents, beginning at the founding of the Republic, support the view that the President has unique constitutional responsibilities with respect to national defense and foreign affairs.[6] As was recognized in the *Federalist Papers* and by the first Congresses, secrecy is at times essential to the executive branch's discharge of its responsibilities in these core areas. Indeed, Presidents since George Washington have determined on occasion, albeit very rarely, that it was necessary to withhold from Congress, if only for a limited period of time, extremely sensitive information with respect to national defense or foreign affairs.[7]

Perhaps the most famous of the Founders' statements on the need for secrecy is John Jay's discussion in the *Federalist Papers*. Jay observed:

There are cases where the most useful intelligence may be obtained, if the persons possessing it can be relieved from apprehensions of discovery. Those apprehensions will operate on those persons whether they are actuated by mercenary or friendly motives; and there doubtless are many of both descriptions who would rely on the secrecy of the President, but who would not confide in that of the Senate, and still less in that of a large popular assembly. The convention have done well, therefore, in so disposing of the power of making treaties that although the President must, in forming them, act by the advice and consent of the Senate, yet he will be able to manage the business of intelligence in such manner as prudence may suggest.[8]

Our early history confirmed the right of the President to decide to withhold national security information from Congress under extraordinary circumstances. In the course of investigating the failure of General St. Clair's military expedition of 1791, the House of Representatives in 1792 requested relevant documents from the executive branch.[9] President Washington asked the Cabinet's advice as to his proper response "because [the request] was the first example, and he wished that so far as it should become a precedent, it should be rightly conducted."[10] Washington's own view was that "he could readily conceive there might be papers of so secret a nature, as that they ought not to be given up."[11]

A few days later a unanimous Cabinet—including Secretary of State Thomas Jefferson, Secretary of the Treasury Alexander Hamilton, and Attorney General Edmund Randolph—concurred. The Cabinet advised the President that, although the House "might call for papers generally," "the Executive ought to communicate such papers as the public good would permit, and ought to refuse those, the disclosure of which would injure the public."[12] The Executive "consequently w[as] to exercise a discretion" in responding to the House request.[13] The Cabinet subsequently advised the President that the documents in question could all be disclosed consistently with the public interest.[14]

Although President Washington ultimately decided to produce the requested documents, they were actually produced only after the House, on April 4, 1792, substituted a new request apparently recognizing the President's discretion by asking only for papers "of a public nature."[15]

Two years later, President Washington adhered to his conclusion regarding the respective authorities of the executive and legislative branches. Acting upon the advice of Attorney General William Bradford and other Cabinet officers, Washington responded to an unqualified request from the Senate for correspondence between the Republic of France and the United States minister for France by providing the relevant correspondence, except for "those particulars which, in [his] judgment, for public considerations, ought not to be communicated."[16]

In 1796, when a controversy arose regarding whether President Washington could be required to provide the House of Representatives with records relating to the negotiation of the Jay Treaty, James Madison—who was then a Member of the House—conceded that even where Congress had a legitimate purpose for requesting information the President had authority "to withhold information, when of a nature that did not permit a disclosure of it at the time."[17]

Congressional recognition of this power in the President extends well into recent times.[18] Moreover, since the Washington Administration, Presidents and their senior advisers have repeatedly concluded that our constitutional system grants the executive branch authority to control the disposition of secret information. Thus, then-Attorney General Robert Jackson declined, upon the direction of President Franklin Roosevelt, a request from the House Committee on Naval Affairs for sensitive FBI records on war-time labor unrest, citing (among other grounds) the national security.[19] Similarly, then-Assistant Attorney General William Rehnquist concluded almost thirty years ago that "the President has the power to withhold from [Congress] information in the field of foreign relations or national security if in his judgment disclosure would be incompatible with the public interest."[20]

The Supreme Court has similarly recognized the importance of the President's ability to control the disclosure of classified information. In considering the statutory question whether the Merit Systems Protection Board could review the revocation of an executive branch employee's security clearance, the Court in *Department of the Navy v. Egan* also addressed the President's constitutional authority to control the disclosure of classified information:

> The President . . . is the "Commander in Chief of the Army and Navy of the United States." U.S. Const., Art. II, § 2. His authority to classify and control access to information bearing on national security . . . flows primarily from this constitutional investment of power in the President and exists quite apart from any explicit congressional grant. . . . This Court has recognized the Government's "compelling interest" in withholding national security information from unauthorized persons in the course of executive business. . . . The authority to protect such information falls on the President as head of the Executive Branch and as Commander in Chief.[21]

Similarly, in discussing executive privilege in *United States v. Nixon*, a unanimous Supreme Court emphasized the heightened status of the President's privilege in the context of "military, diplomatic, or sensitive national security secrets."[22] Although declining in the context of that criminal case to sustain President Nixon's claim of privilege as to tape recordings and documents sought by subpoena, the Supreme Court specifically observed that the President had not "place[d] his claim of privilege on the ground that they are military or diplomatic secrets. As to these areas of Art. II duties the courts have traditionally shown the utmost deference to Presidential responsibilities."[23]

Other statements by individual Justices and the lower courts reflect a similar understanding of the President's power to protect national security by maintaining the confidentiality of classified information.[24] Justice Stewart, for example, discussed this authority in his concurring opinion in *New York Times v. United States* (the "Pentagon Papers" case):

> [I]t is elementary that the successful conduct of international diplomacy and the maintenance of an effective national defense require both confidentiality and secrecy. . . . In the area of basic national defense the frequent need for absolute secrecy is, of course, self-evident.

I think there can be but one answer to this dilemma, if dilemma it be. The responsibility must be where the power is. If the Constitution gives the Executive a large degree of unshared power in the conduct of foreign affairs and the maintenance of our national defense, then under the Constitution the Executive must have the largely unshared duty to determine and preserve the degree of internal security necessary to exercise that power successfully. . . . [I]t is clear to me that it is the constitutional duty of the Executive . . . to protect the confidentiality necessary to carry out its responsibilities in the fields of international relations and national defense.[25]

III.

In applying these constitutional principles to S. 1668 and H.R. 3829, we take as a given that Congress has important oversight responsibilities and a corollary interest in receiving information that enables it to carry out those responsibilities.[26] Those interests obviously include Congress's ability to consider evidence of misconduct and abuse by the executive's agents. H.R. 3829, however, demonstrates that it is possible to develop procedures for providing Congress information it needs to perform its oversight duties, while not interfering with the President's ability to control classified information when necessary to perform his constitutionally assigned duties.

A.

In analyzing S. 1668, there is no need to resolve the precise parameters of the President's authority to control access to classified diplomatic and national security information. Instead, we have focused on the specific problem presented by the bill, which, in defined circumstances, gives a unilateral right of disclosure to every executive branch employee with access to classified information.[27] The reach of S. 1668 is sweeping: it would authorize any covered federal employee to foreclose or circumvent a presidential determination that restricts congressional access to certain classified information in extraordinary circumstances.

S. 1668 is inconsistent with Congress's traditional approach to accommodating the executive branch's interests with respect to national security information. In the National Security Act, for example, Congress itself recognized the need for heightened secrecy in certain "extraordinary circumstances affecting vital interests of the United States," and authorized the President to sharply limit congressional access to information relating to covert actions in such cases.[28] An example of accommodation between the branches that is even more directly applicable to the present context is the National Security Act's recognition that the intelligence agencies on occasion need to redact sources and methods and other exceptionally sensitive intelligence information from materials they provide to the Intelligence Committees.[29]

In contrast, S. 1668 would deprive the President of his authority to decide, based on the national interest, how, when and under what circumstances particular classified information should be disclosed to Congress.[30] This is an impermissible encroachment on the President's ability to carry out core executive functions. In the congressional oversight context, as in all others, the decision whether and under what circumstances to disclose classified information must be made by someone who is acting on the official authority of the President and who is ultimately responsible to the President. The Constitution does not permit Congress to authorize subordinate executive branch employees to bypass these orderly procedures for review and clearance by vesting them with a unilateral right to disclose classified information—even to Members of Congress. Such a law would squarely conflict with the Framers' considered judgment, embodied in Article II of the Constitution, that, within the executive branch, all authority over matters of national defense and foreign affairs is vested in the President as Chief Executive and Commander in Chief.[31]

It has been suggested that S. 1668 (at least with modest revisions) would strike an acceptable balance between the competing executive and legislative interests relating to the control of classified information, and would thus survive review under ordinary separation of powers principles.[32] That balance under S. 1668, however, would be based on an abstract notion of what information Congress might need to know relating to some future inquiry and what information the President might need to protect in light of some future set of world events. Such an abstract resolution of the competing interests at stake is simply not consistent with the President's constitutional responsibilities respecting national security and foreign affairs. He must be free to determine, based on particular—and perhaps currently unforeseeable—circumstances, that the security or foreign affairs interests of the Nation dictate a particular treatment of classified information.

Furthermore, S. 1668 also undermines the traditional, case-by-case process of accommodating the competing needs of the two branches—a process that reflects the facts and circumstances of particular situations. As one appellate court has observed, there exists "an implicit constitutional mandate to seek optimal accommodation [between the branches] through a realistic evaluation of the needs of the conflicting branches *in the particular fact situation*."[33] Rather than enabling balances to be struck as the demands of specific situations require, S. 1668 would attempt to legislate a procedure that cannot possibly reflect what competing executive and legislative interests may emerge with respect to some future inquiry. It would displace the delicate process of arriving at appropriate accommodations between the branches with an overall legislated "solution" that paid no regard to unique—and potentially critical—national security and foreign affairs considerations that may arise. This approach contrasts with that of H.R. 3829, which would balance the competing legislative and executive interests at stake in a manner that would permit rational judgments to be made in response to real world events.

B.

H.R. 3829 does not present the constitutional infirmity posed by S. 1668. H.R. 3829 does not vest any executive branch employee who has access to classified information with a unilateral right to determine how, when and under what circumstances classified information will be disclosed to Members of Congress and without regard for how such a disclosure might affect the President's ability to perform his constitutionally assigned duties.

Instead, H.R. 3829 would establish procedures under which employees who wish to report to Congress must first submit their complaint to an inspector general, who would review it for credibility and then submit the complaint to the agency head before it is forwarded to Congress. This process would allow for the executive branch review and clearance process that S. 1668 would foreclose. H.R. 3829 would further authorize heads of agencies and the Director of Central Intelligence, upon the completion of that process, to decide not to transmit an employee's complaint to the Intelligence Committees, or allow the employee to contact the Committees directly, "in the exceptional case and in order to protect vital law enforcement, foreign affairs, or national security interests."[34] If such a decision were made, then the head of agency or Director of Central Intelligence would be required to provide the Committees with the reason for the determination.

Not only would H.R. 3829 thus avoid the constitutional infirmity of S. 1668 by allowing for review by the President or officials responsible to him, it would also allow for the operation of the accommodation process traditionally followed between the legislative and executive branches regarding disclosure of confidential information. Upon receipt of the explanation for a decision not to allow an employee complaint to go forward, the Intelligence Committees could contact the agency head or Director of Central Intelligence to begin the process of seeking to satisfy the Committees' oversight needs in ways that protect the executive branch's confidentiality interests. The bill's procedures are thus consistent with our constitutional system of separation of powers.

IV.

We recognize that Congress has significant interests in disclosure of evidence of wrongdoing or abuse. There is an inevitable tension, however, between preserving the secrecy necessary to permit the President to perform his constitutionally assigned duties and permitting the disclosures necessary to permit congressional oversight. Under relevant constitutional doctrine, Congress may not resolve this tension by vesting in individual federal employees the power to control disclosure of classified information. For this reason, we have concluded that S. 1668 is unconstitutional. H.R. 3829 does not contain this constitutional infirmity and is constitutional.

Notes

1. In addition, the Department of Justice took a similar position with respect to comparable legislation in a brief that it filed in the Supreme Court in 1989. *See* Brief for Appellees, *American Foreign Serv. Ass'n v. Garfinkel*, 488 U.S. 923 (1988) (No. 87-2127).

2. Section 1(a)(1)(A).

3. Section 1(a)(2)(A), (C).

4. The Supreme Court has employed three principles in resolving separation of powers disputes. First, where "[e]xplicit and unambiguous provisions of the Constitution prescribe and define . . . just how [governmental] powers are to be exercised," *INS v. Chadha*, 462 U.S. 919, 945 (1983), the constitutional procedures must be followed with precision. Second, where the effect of legislation is to vest Congress itself, its members, or its agents with "'either executive power or judicial power,'" the statute is unconstitutional. *Metropolitan Wash. Airports Auth. v. Citizens for Abatement of Aircraft Noise, Inc.*, 501 U.S. 252, 274 (1991) (citation omitted). Finally, legislation that affects the functioning of the executive may be unconstitutional if it either "'impermissibly undermine[s]' the powers of the Executive Branch" or "'disrupts the proper balance between the coordinate branches [by] prevent[ing] the Executive Branch from accomplishing its constitutionally assigned functions.'" *Morrison v. Olson*, 487 U.S. 654, 695 (1988) (citations omitted). Because we conclude that S. 1668 would violate separation of powers under even the most lenient of these tests, there is no need to resolve whether one of the more stringent standards applies.

5. *See id.* § 2(a), proposed new paragraph (5)(E) to be added to subsection (d) of section 17 of the Central Intelligence Agency Act of 1949, 50 U.S.C. § 403q (1994); *id.* § 2(b)(1), proposed new section 8H(e) to be added to the Inspector General Act of 1978, 5 U.S.C. app. 3 § 8 (1994 & Supp. II 1996).

6. The President's national security and foreign affairs powers flow, in large part, from his position as Chief Executive, U.S. Const. art. II, § 1, cl. 1, and as Commander in Chief, *id.* art. II, § 2, cl. 1. They also derive from the President's more specific powers to "make Treaties," *id.* art. II, § 2, cl. 2; to "appoint Ambassadors . . . and Consuls," *id.*; and to "receive Ambassadors and other public Ministers,"*id.* art. II, § 3. *See The Federalist* No. 64, at 392–94 (John Jay) (Clinton Rossiter ed., 1961). The Supreme Court has repeatedly recognized the President's authority with respect to foreign policy. *See, e.g., Department of the Navy v. Egan*, 484 U.S. 518, 529 (1988) (the Supreme Court has "recognized 'the generally accepted view that foreign policy was the province and responsibility of the Executive'") (quoting *Haig v. Agee*, 453 U.S. 280, 293–94 (1981)); *Alfred Dunhill of London, Inc. v. Republic of Cuba*, 425 U.S. 682, 705-06 n.18 (1976) ("'[T]he conduct of

[foreign policy] is committed primarily to the Executive Branch."); *United States v. Louisiana*, 363 U.S. 1, 35 (1960) (the President is "the constitutional representative of the United States in its dealings with foreign nations"); *New York Times Co. v. United States*, 403 U.S. 713, 741 (1971) (Marshall, J., concurring) ("it is beyond cavil that the President has broad powers by virtue of his primary responsibility for the conduct of our foreign affairs and his position as Commander in Chief"); *id.* at 761 (Blackmun, J., dissenting) ("Article II . . . vests in the Executive Branch primary power over the conduct of foreign affairs and places in that branch the responsibility for the Nation's safety."); *see also United States v. Kin-Hong*, 110 F.3d 103, 110 (1st Cir. 1997) ("[O]ur constitutional structure . . . places primary responsibility for foreign affairs in the executive branch. . . ."), *reh'g den.*, 110 F.3d 121 (1st Cir. 1997) (en banc); *Ward v. Skinner*, 943 F.2d 157, 160 (1st Cir. 1991) (Breyer, J.) ("[T]he Constitution makes the Executive Branch . . . primarily responsible" for the exercise of "the foreign affairs power."), *cert. denied*, 503 U.S. 959 (1992); *Sanchez- Espinoza v. Reagan*, 770 F.2d 202, 210 (D.C. Cir. 1985) (Scalia, J.) ("[B]road leeway" is "traditionally accorded the Executive in matters of foreign affairs.").

7. *See History of Refusals by Executive Branch Officials to Provide Information Demanded by Congress*, 6 Op. O.L.C. 751 (1982) (compiling historical examples of cases in which the President withheld from Congress information the release of which he determined could jeopardize national security).

8. *The Federalist* No. 64, at 392–93 (John Jay) (Clinton Rossiter ed., 1961).

9. For recent scholarly discussions of this episode and its significance for the development of separation of powers, *see* Gerhard Casper, *Separating Power* 28–31 (1997); David P. Currie, *The Constitution in Congress: The Federalist Period 1789–1801* 163–64 (1997).

   An earlier episode had occurred in 1790 when, in response to a request from the House of Representatives, Secretary of State Thomas Jefferson furnished that body with a report on Mediterranean trade. The report also touched on advice provided by a confidential European source on the possibility of buying peace with Algiers, which was endangering that trade. Jefferson relayed the source's advice to the House, but stated that his or her "name is not free to be mentioned here." Report of Secretary of State Jefferson, Submitted to the House of Representatives (Dec. 30, 1790) and Senate (Jan. 3, 1791), *in* 1 *American State Papers: Foreign Relations* 105 (1791). Jefferson also submitted the report with a request that the Speaker treat it as a secret document; and when the report was received, the House's galleries were cleared. *See* Casper at 47–50. The executive branch continues the practice of redacting identifying information on confidential sources when providing secret information to Congress.

10. 1 *Writings of Thomas Jefferson* 303 (Andrew Lipscomb ed. 1903) (The Anas).

11. *Id.*

12. *Id.* at 304.

13. *Id.*

14. *Id.* at 305.

15. 3 Annals of Cong. 536 (1792); *see also* Abraham D. Sofaer, *War, Foreign Affairs and Constitutional Power* 82–83 (1976); Casper at 29.

16. 4 Annals of Cong. 56 (1794); *see* Sofaer at 83-85. The Cabinet officers whom Washington consulted and who all agreed that he could withhold at least part of the material from the Senate were Hamilton, Randolph and Knox. *Id.* at 83. Randolph also informed Washington that he had met privately with Madison and with Justice James Wilson (another influential Framer), who provided similar advice. *Id.* at 83–4 n.*." [N]o further Senate action was taken to obtain the material withheld." *Id.* at 85.

17. 5 Annals of Cong. 773 (1796). As President Washington observed in declining the House's request:

    The nature of foreign negotiations requires caution, and their success must often depend on secrecy; and even when brought to a conclusion, a full disclosure of all the measures, demands, or eventual concessions which may have been proposed or contemplated would be extremely impolitic: for this might have a pernicious influence on future negotiations; or produce immediate inconveniences, perhaps danger and mischief, in relation to other Powers. *Id.* at 760. Washington had previously sought and received advice from Alexander Hamilton, then in private practice in New York. Hamilton provided Washington with a draft answer to the House, which had stated in part: "A discretion in the Executive Department how far and where to comply in such cases is essential to the due conduct of foreign negotiations." Letter from Alexander Hamilton to George Washington (Mar. 7, 1796), *in* 20 *The Papers of Alexander Hamilton*, at 68 (Harold C. Syrett ed., 1974).

    Although the Executive's concerns with the confidentiality of diplomatic materials certainly loomed large in the 1796 dispute, it would overstate the point to view the entire controversy as turning exclusively on the issue of "executive privilege." Washington rested his position partly on the alternative ground that the

Constitution gave the House no role in the treaty-making process. Moreover, it appears that the controversy "had a somewhat 'academic' character because the Senate had received all the papers, and the House members apparently could inspect them at the Senate." Casper at 65.

18. *See, e.g.*, S. Rep. No. 86-1761 at 22 (1960) (the Senate Committee on Foreign Relations, after failing to persuade President Kennedy to abandon his claim of executive privilege with respect to information relating to the U-2 incident in May, 1960, criticized the President for his refusal to make the information available but acknowledged his legal right to do so: "The committee recognizes that the administration has the legal right to refuse the information under the doctrine of executive privilege.").

19. *See Position of the Executive Department Regarding Investigative Reports*, 40 Op. Att'y Gen. 45, 46 (1941).

20. Memorandum from John R. Stevenson, Legal Adviser, Department of State, and William H. Rehnquist, Assistant Attorney General, Office of Legal Counsel, *Re: The President's Executive Privilege to Withhold Foreign Policy and National Security Information* at 7 (Dec. 8, 1969).

21. *Department of the Navy v. Egan*, 484 U.S. at 527 (citations omitted).

22. *United States v. Nixon*, 418 U.S. 683, 706 (1974); see also *id.* at 710, 712 n.19.

23. *Id.* at 710; *see also United States v. Reynolds*, 345 U.S. 1 (1953) (recognizing privilege in judicial proceedings for "state secrets" based on determination by senior Executive officials).

24. *See, e.g., Webster v. Doe*, 486 U.S. 592, 605–06 (1988) (O'Connor, J., concurring in part and dissenting in part) ("The functions performed by the Central Intelligence Agency and the Director of Central Intelligence lie at the core of 'the very delicate, plenary and exclusive power of the President as the sole organ of the federal government in the field of international relations.' . . . The authority of the Director of Central Intelligence to control access to sensitive national security information by discharging employees deemed to be untrustworthy flows primarily from this constitutional power of the President. . . .") (citation omitted); *New York Times Co. v. United States*, 403 U.S. at 741 (Marshall, J., concurring) (case presented no issue "regarding the President's power as Chief Executive and Commander in Chief to protect national security by disciplining employees who disclose information and by taking precautions to prevent leaks"); *Greene v. McElroy*, 360 U.S. 474, 513 (1959) (Clark, J., dissenting) (it is "basic" that "no person, save the President, has a constitutional right to access to governmental secrets"); *Guillot v. Garrett*, 970 F.2d 1320, 1324 (4th Cir. 1992) (President has "exclusive constitutional authority over access to national security information"); *Dorfmont v. Brown*, 913 F.2d 1399, 1405 (9th Cir. 1990) (Kozinski, J., concurring) ("Under the Constitution, the President has unreviewable discretion over security decisions made pursuant to his powers as chief executive and Commander-in-Chief."), *cert. denied*, 499 U.S. 905 (1991).

25. *New York Times Co. v. United States*, 403 U.S. at 728–30 (Stewart, J., concurring) (footnote omitted).

26. *See, e.g., McGrain v. Daugherty*, 273 U.S. 135 (1927).

27. We do not use the word "right" in the sense of a legally enforceable right. Rather, the term is intended to convey our understanding that the bill would purport to require the President to inform employees that they have standing authorization or permission to convey national security information directly to Congress without receiving specific authorization to convey the particular information in question. We have not analyzed the possible implications this legislation might have with respect to judicial enforcement of employee legal rights.

28. *See* 50 U.S.C. § 413b(c)(2) (1994) ("If the President determines that it is essential to limit access to the finding to meet extraordinary circumstances affecting vital interests of the United States, the finding may be reported to the chairmen and ranking members of the intelligence committees, the Speaker and minority leader of the House of Representatives, the majority and minority leaders of the Senate, and such other member or members of the congressional leadership as may be included by the President.") Even with this more protective standard, President Bush expressly reserved his constitutional authority to withhold disclosure for a period of time. *See* S. Rep. No. 102-85 at 40 (1991). *See also* 50 U.S.C. § 413b(c)(3) (1994) ("Whenever a finding is not reported pursuant to paragraph (1) or (2) of this section, the President shall fully inform the intelligence committees in a timely fashion and shall provide a statement of the reasons for not giving prior notice.").

29. *See* 50 U.S.C. § 413a (1994) ("To the extent consistent with due regard to the protection from unauthorized disclosure of classified information relating to sensitive intelligence sources and methods or other exceptionally sensitive matters, the Director of Central Intelligence and the heads of all departments, agencies, and other entities of the United States Government involved in intelligence activities shall . . . keep the intelligence committees fully and currently informed of all intelligence activities . . .").

30. *Cf. United States ex rel. Touhy v. Ragen*, 340 U.S. 462, 468 (1951) ("When one considers the variety of information contained in the files of any government department and the possibilities of harm from

unrestricted disclosure . . . , the usefulness, indeed the necessity, of centralizing determination as to whether subpoenas duces tecum will be willingly obeyed or challenged is obvious.").

31. This is not to suggest that Congress wholly lacks authority regarding the treatment of classified information, see New York Times Co. v. United States, 403 U.S. at 740 (White, J., concurring), but rather that Congress may not exercise that authority in a manner that undermines the President's ability to perform his constitutionally assigned duties.

32. See Whistleblower Protections for Classified Disclosures: Hearings Before the Senate Select Comm. on Intelligence, 105th Cong. 8 (1998) (statement of Prof. Peter Raven-Hansen).

33. United States v. American Tel. & Tel. Co., 567 F.2d 121, 127 (D.C. Cir. 1977) (emphasis added).

34. In light of S. 1668's focus on the intelligence community and classified information, the Department's analysis of the bill's constitutionality has focused on its interference with the President's authority to protect confidential national security and foreign affairs information. Of course, other constitutionally-based confidentiality interests can be implicated by employee disclosures to Congress. H.R. 3829 appropriately recognizes that such disclosures also should not compromise vital law enforcement interests.

*Randolph Moss served from 1998 to 2001 as assistant attorney general for the Office of Legal Counsel, where he issued opinions on a broad range of constitutional issues, questions of administrative law, and on the meaning of federal laws in areas involving privacy, copyright, ethics, immigration, appropriations, Native American sovereignty, electronic surveillance, national security, the environment, antitrust, immunity from civil suit, civil rights, international trade, and criminal proceedings. He is currently chair of Wilmer Hale's Regulatory and Government Affairs Department and a member of the Litigation/Controversy Department.

Statement for the record of Randolph Moss before the Permanent Select Committee on Intelligence, U.S. House of Representatives. May 20, 1998. "Whistleblower Protections for Classified Disclosures." 105th Cong.

Part 4: The State Secrets Privilege

One powerful tool through which the executive branch restricts access to national security information is the state secrets privilege. This privilege allows the executive branch to resist disclosure in court of information whose public dissemination would create a reasonable danger of harm to national security. Because the privilege allows the executive branch to withhold information that might represent evidence vital to one party's efforts to prove its case, the effect of an assertion of the privilege is sometimes to prevent a suit from going forward at all. The privilege has been invoked with this effect by the executive in several high-profile legal challenges to post-9/11 counterterrorism policies.

The Constitution Project's essay, "Reforming the State Secrets Privilege," provides a critique of the foundations of the state secrets privilege and suggests two types of reform. The first suggestion is that Congress pass legislation limiting the scope of the privilege; the second is that courts should be more skeptical of executive claims of privilege. Former attorney general Michael Mukasey, by contrast, presents a robust defense of the executive branch's use of the privilege and against legislative action in a statement of administrative position on proposed congressional legislation aimed at reforming the privilege. Mukasey's defense of the privilege is then subject to scrutiny in a response issued by the Brennan Center for Justice. Finally, we hear from several courts that, finding themselves faced with executive claims of privilege, have endorsed the government's position while simultaneously recognizing the troubling real-world consequences of those claims.

As you read the selections, consider the following questions:
• Should judges defer to executive-branch assessments of the harm certain disclosures would cause because they lack national security expertise? If so, is there any reason a judge could not enlist a national security expert disinterested in the outcome of the particular case to advise her on the possible dangers of disclosure?
• What is the proper scope of information over which the government may invoke the state secrets privilege? Should information that poses any reasonable danger of harm to national security be sufficient, or should it have to pass a higher bar? Should Congress have a role in determining the answer to that question?

- Currently, the state secrets privilege is absolute, meaning that so long as the government can show that the information poses a reasonable danger of causing harm to national security, the government is entitled to keep that information secret. Is that the appropriate result, or should the rule be more conditional? For example, should litigants be able to access the information by proving that the possible harm to national security is outweighed by the value of disclosure?
- If the proper invocation of the state secrets privilege prevents a plaintiff who was actually harmed by government action from being made whole, should other remedies be available? Who should provide them? Two of the courts who dismissed cases on state secrets grounds stressed the possibility of alternative remedies. Should the availability (or non-availability) of such remedies affect a judge's decision whether to dismiss a case on state secrets grounds? If so, how?

Reforming the State Secrets Privilege

*by The Constitution Project's Liberty and Security Committee & Coalition
to Defend Checks and Balances**

As interpreted by some courts, the state secrets doctrine places absolute power in the executive branch to withhold information to the detriment of constitutional liberties. We, the undersigned members of the Constitution Project's
Liberty and Security Committee and the Project's Coalition to Defend Checks
and Balances, urge that the "state secrets doctrine" be limited to balance the interests of private parties, constitutional liberties, and national security. Specifically, Congress should enact legislation to clarify the scope of this doctrine and
assure greater protection to private litigants. In addition, courts should carefully
review any assertions of this doctrine, and treat it as a qualified privilege, not
an absolute one.

Since the terrorist attacks of September 11, 2001, the government has repeatedly asserted the state secrets privilege in court, in a variety of lawsuits
alleging that its national security policies violate Americans' civil liberties. In
these cases, the government has informed federal judges that litigation would
necessitate disclosure of evidence that would risk damage to national security, and that consequently, the lawsuits must be dismissed. The government is
presently invoking the privilege in such cases as NSA eavesdropping and the
"extraordinary rendition" cases of Maher Arar and Khalid El-Masri. The fundamental issue: what constitutional values should guide a federal judge in evaluating the government's assertion?

The state secrets privilege was first recognized in the United States Supreme
Court decision *United States v. Reynolds*, 345 U.S. 1 (1953). Because of ambigui-
ties in this landmark case, federal judges have discharged their responsibilities
in widely different ways. Some have insisted on examining the document *in
camera* to decide whether the private party should receive the document un-
changed or in some redacted form. Other judges adopt the standard of (1) "deference," (2) "utmost deference," or (3) treat the privilege as an "absolute" when
appropriately invoked. The conduct of courts in these cases raises important
questions about the principle of judicial independence, the concept of a neutral
magistrate, fairness in the courtroom, the adversary model, and the constitutional system of checks and balances. The reforms we outline below would help
to safeguard these important principles.

The Problem with *Reynolds*. The Supreme Court's 1953 ruling in *Reynolds* involved the authority of the executive branch to withhold certain documents from three widows who sued the government for the deaths of their husbands in a B-29 crash. They asked for the Air Force accident report and statements from three surviving crew members. In bringing suit under the Federal Tort Claims Act, they won in district court as well as on appeal to the U.S. Court of Appeals for the Third Circuit. Both those courts told the government that if it failed to surrender the documents, at least to the district judge to be read in chambers, it would lose the case. Under the tort claims statute, the government is liable "in the same manner" as a private individual and is entitled to no special privileges.

However, without ever looking at the report, the Supreme Court sustained the government's claim of privilege. It stated: "Judicial control over the evidence in a case cannot be abdicated to the caprice of executive officers. Yet we will not go so far as to say that the court may automatically require a complete disclosure to the judge before the claim of privilege will be accepted in any case. It may be possible to satisfy the court, from all the circumstances of the case, that there is a reasonable danger that compulsion of the evidence will expose military matters which, in the interest of national security, should not be divulged. When this is the case, the occasion for the privilege is appropriate, and the court should not jeopardize the security which the privilege is meant to protect by insisting upon an examination of the evidence, even by the judge alone, in chambers." *Reynolds*, 345 U.S. at 9–10.

In deciding not to examine the report, the Court was in no position to know if there had been "executive caprice" or not. On its face, the Court's ruling marked an abdication by the judiciary to a governmental assertion. What principled objection could be raised to the executive branch showing challenged documents to a district judge in chambers? Unless an independent magistrate examined the accident report and the statements of surviving crew members, there was no way to determine whether disclosure posed a reasonable danger to national security, that the assertion of the privilege was justified, or that any jeopardy to national security existed.

Moreover, the Court's ruling left unclear the meaning of "disclosure." Why would a federal court "jeopardize the security which the privilege is meant to protect" by examining the document in private? On what ground can it be argued that federal judges lack authority, integrity, or competence to view the contents of disputed documents in their private chambers to determine the validity of the government's claim? No jeopardy to national security emerges with *in camera* inspection.

The Court advised the three widows to return to district court and depose the three surviving crew members. There is evidence that depositions were taken, but after weighing the emotional and financial costs of reviving the litigation, the women decided to settle for 75% of what they would have received under the original district court ruling. As noted below, it was revealed years later that there were no state secrets to protect and that the government was simply seeking to avoid releasing embarrassing information.

Application of Reynolds. The inconsistent signals delivered in *Reynolds* regarding judicial responsibility, reappear in contemporary cases. For example, on May 12, 2006, a district judge held that the state secrets privilege was validly asserted in a civil case seeking damages for "extraordinary rendition" and torture based on mistaken identity, and on March 2, 2007, this decision was upheld on appeal. Khalid El-Masri sued the government on the ground that he had been illegally detained as part of the CIA's "extraordinary rendition" program, tortured, and subjected to other inhumane treatment. His treatment resulted from U.S. government officials mistakenly believing that he was someone else.

The district court offered two conflicting frameworks. On the one hand, the court noted that it is the responsibility of a federal judge "to determine whether the information for which the privilege is claimed qualifies as a state secret. Importantly, courts must not blindly accept the Executive Branch's assertion to this effect, but must instead independently and carefully determine whether, in the circumstances, the claimed secrets deserve the protection of the privilege. . . . In those cases where the claimed state secrets are at the core of the suit and the operation of the privilege may defeat valid claims, courts must carefully scrutinize the assertion of the privilege lest it be used by the government to shield 'material not strictly necessary to prevent injury to national security.'" *El-Masri v. Tenet*, 437 F.Supp.2d 530, 536 (E.D. Va. 2006), quoting *Ellsberg v. Mitchell*, 709 F.2d 51, 58 (D.C. Cir. 1983).

Those passages suggest an independent role for the judiciary. However, the district court also offered reasons to accept executive claims. When undertaking an inquiry into state secret assertions, "courts must also bear in mind the Executive Branch's preeminent authority over military and diplomatic matters and its greater expertise relative to the judicial branch in predicting the effect of a particular disclosure on national security." *Id.* The state secrets privilege "is in fact a privilege of the highest dignity and significance." *Id.* The state secrets privilege "is an evidentiary constitutional authority over the conduct of this country's diplomatic and military affairs and therefore belongs exclusively to the Executive Branch." *Id.* at 535. The court stated that, "unlike other privileges, the state secrets privilege is absolute and therefore once a court is satisfied that the claim is validly asserted, the privilege is not subject to a judicial balancing of the various interests at stake." *Id.* at 537. Ultimately, the court upheld the government's claim of privilege and dismissed the case. On appeal, the Fourth Circuit affirmed the District Court's ruling, noting that "in certain circumstances a court may conclude that an explanation by the Executive of why a question cannot be answered would itself create an unacceptable danger of injurious disclosure." *El-Masri v. United States*, 479 F.3d 296, 305 (4th Cir. 2007). In these situations, the Fourth Circuit stated, "a court is obliged to accept the executive branch's claim of privilege without further demand." *Id.* at 306.

Judicial Competence. The remarks above by both the district court and the Fourth Circuit in *El-Masri* imply that in national security matters the federal judiciary lacks the competence to independently judge the merits of state secrets assertions. The *El-Masri* district court cited this language from a 1948 Supreme Court decision: "The President, both as Commander-in-Chief and as the Nation's organ for foreign affairs, has available intelligence services whose reports are not and ought not to be published to the world. It would be intolerable that courts, without the relevant information, should review and perhaps nullify actions of the Executive taken on information properly held secret." 437 F.Supp.2d at 536 n.7, quoting *C. & S. Air Lines v. Waterman S.S. Corp.* 333 U.S. 103, 111 (1948).

We object to this notion that the federal courts lack the competence to assess state secrets claims. First, nothing in state secrets cases involves publishing information "to the world." Second, the capacity of the Supreme Court in 1948 to independently examine and assess classified documents has been vastly enhanced over the past half-century by the 1958 amendments to the Housekeeping Statute, the 1974 amendments to the Freedom of Information Act (FOIA), the 1978 creation of the Foreign Intelligence Surveillance Act (FISA) Court, and the Classified Information Procedures Act (CIPA) of 1980. Louis Fisher, In the Name of National Security 124–64 (2006). Third, long before those enactments, federal courts have always retained an independent role in assuring that the rights of defendants are not nullified by claims of "state secrets." The 1807 trial of Aaron Burr illustrates this point. The court understood that Burr, having been publicly accused of treason on the basis of certain letters in the hands of the Jefferson administration, and therefore facing the death sentence if convicted, had every right to gain access to those documents to defend himself. *Id.* at 212–20. Thus, courts are fully competent to review and evaluate the evidence supporting a claim of state secrets. If in such a case the government decides that the documents are too sensitive to release, even to the trial judge, the appropriate consequence in a criminal trial is for the government to drop the charges.

The Deference Standard. Another ground upon which courts have erroneously relied in upholding government claims of state secrets has been the deference standard from administrative law. In this context, the Supreme Court's 1984 decision in *Chevron* adopted the principle that when a federal court reviews an agency's construction of a statute, and the law is silent or ambiguous about the issue being litigated, agency regulations are to be "given controlling weight unless they are arbitrary, capricious, or manifestly contrary to the statute." *Chevron v. Natural Resources Defense Council*, 467 U.S. 837, 844 (1984). If the agency's interpretation is reasonable it is "entitled to deference." *Id*. at 865.

The *Chevron* model has no application to the state secrets privilege. When application of the state secrets doctrine is litigated in court, this is not a situation in which Congress has delegated broad authority to an agency. Nor is there any opportunity, as there is in administrative law, for Congress to reenter the picture by enacting legislation that overrides an agency interpretation or by passing restrictive appropriations riders. Moreover, agency rulemaking invites broad public participation through the notice-and-comment procedure. By definition, the public is barred from reviewing executive claims of state secrets. Agency rulemaking is subject to public congressional hearings, informal private and legislative pressures, and the restrictive force of legislative history. Those mechanisms are absent from litigation involving state secrets. When the state secrets privilege is invoked, the sole check on arbitrary and possibly illegal executive action is the federal judiciary.

***Ex Parte* Review**. The deference standard is poorly suited for state secrets cases for another reason. When the executive branch agrees to release a classified or secret document to a federal judge, it will be read not only in private but *ex parte*, without an opportunity for private litigants to examine the document. The judge may decide to release the document to the private parties, in whole or in redacted form, but the initial review will be by the judge. This procedure already presents the appearance of serious bias toward the executive branch and its asserted prerogatives. To add to that advantage the standard of "deference," "utmost deference," or treating the state secrets privilege as an "absolute" makes the federal judiciary look like an arm of the Executive. It undermines judicial independence, the adversary process, and fairness to private litigants. When the state secrets privilege is initially invoked, no federal judge can know whether it is being asserted for legitimate reasons or to conceal embarrassment, illegality, or constitutional violations.

Who Decides a Privilege? In his classic 1940 treatise on evidence, John Henry Wigmore recognized that a state secrets privilege exists covering "matters whose disclosure would endanger the Nation's governmental requirements or its relations of friendship and profit with other nations." 8 Wigmore, EVIDENCE § 2212a (3d ed. 1940). Yet he cautioned that this privilege "has been so often improperly invoked and so loosely misapplied that a strict definition of its legitimate limits must be made." *Id.* When he asked who should determine the necessity for secrecy—the executive or the judiciary—he concluded it must be the court: "Shall every subordinate in the department have access to the secret, and not the presiding officer of justice? Cannot the constitutionally coördinate body of government share the confidence? . . . The truth cannot be escaped that a Court which abdicates its inherent function of determining the facts upon which the admissibility of evidence depends will furnish to bureaucratic officials too ample opportunities for abusing the privilege . . . Both principle and policy demand that the determination of the privilege shall be for the Court." § 2378.

When the Third Circuit decided the *Reynolds* case in 1951, it warned that recognizing a "sweeping privilege" against the disclosure of sensitive or confidential documents is "contrary to sound public policy" because it "is but a small step to assert a privilege against any disclosure of records merely because they might prove embarrassing to government officers." 192 F.2d at 995. The district judge directed the government to produce the B-29 documents for his personal examination, stating that the government was "adequately protected" from the disclosure of any privileged matter. *Id.* at 996. To permit the executive branch to conclusively determine the government's claim of privilege "is to abdicate the judicial function and permit the executive branch of the Government to infringe the independent province of the judiciary as laid down by the Constitution." *Id.* at 997. Moreover: "Neither the executive nor the legislative branch of the Government may constitutionally encroach upon the field which the Constitution has reserved for the judiciary by transferring to itself the power to decide justiciable questions which arise in cases or controversies submitted to the judicial branch for decision. . . . The judges of the United States are public officers whose responsibility under the Constitution is just as great as that of the heads of the executive departments." *Id.*

Judges are entrusted with the duty to secure the rights of litigants in court cases. Beyond this protection to individual parties, however, lies a broader institutional interest. Final say on the claim of a state secret must involve more parties than just the executive branch. Unchecked and unexamined assertions of presidential power have done great damage to the public interest and to constitutional principles.

From Rule 509 to 501. In the late 1960s and early 1970s, there were efforts to statutorily define the state secrets privilege. An advisory committee appointed by Chief Justice Earl Warren completed a preliminary draft of proposed rules of evidence in December 1968. Among the proposed rules was Rule 5-09, later renumbered 509. It defined a secret of state as "information not open or theretofore officially disclosed to the public concerning the national defense or the international relations of the United States." Here "disclosure" meant release to the public. Nothing in that definition prevented the executive branch from releasing state secrets to a judge to be read in chambers. Louis Fisher, "State Your Secrets," *Legal Times*, June 26, 2006, at 68; Fisher, IN THE NAME OF NATIONAL SECURITY, at 140–45.

The advisory committee concluded that if a judge sustained a claim of privilege for a state secret involving the government as a party, the court would have several options. If the claim deprived a private party of material evidence, the judge could make "any further orders which the interests of justice require, including striking the testimony of a witness, declaring a mistrial, finding against the government upon an issue as to which the evidence is relevant, or dismissing the action." The Justice Department vigorously opposed the draft and wanted the proposed rule changed to recognize that the executive's classification of information as a state secret was final and binding on judges. A revised rule was released in March 1972, eliminating the definition of "a secret of state" but keeping final control with the judge. A third version was presented to Congress the next year, along with other rules of evidence. Congress concluded that it lacked time to thoroughly review all the rules within 90 days and vote to disapprove particular ones. It passed legislation to prevent any of the proposed rules from taking effect.

When Congress passed the rules of evidence in 1975, it included Rule 501 on privileges. It does not recognize any authority on the part of the executive branch to dictate the reach of a privilege and makes no mention of state secrets. Rule 501 expressly grants authority to the courts to decide privileges. The rule, still in effect, states: "Except as otherwise required by the Constitution of the United States or provided by Act of Congress or in rules prescribed by the Supreme Court pursuant to statutory authority, the privilege of a witness, person, government, State, or political subdivision thereof *shall be governed by the principles of the common law as they may be interpreted by the courts of the United States* in the light of reason and experience" (emphasis added). One exception expressly stated in Rule 501 concerns civil actions at the state level where state law supplies the rule of decision. Advocates of executive power might read the language "[e]xcept as otherwise required by the Constitution" to open the door to claims of inherent presidential power under Article II. However, even if this interpretation supports the existence of a state secrets privilege, it cannot overcome the rule that courts must assess and determine whether the privilege applies in a given case.

Agency Claims. The principle of judicial authority over rules of evidence included in Rule 501 appeared in a dispute that reached the Court of Federal Claims in *Barlow v. United States*, 2000 U.S. Claims LEXIS 156 (2000). On February 10, 2000, then-CIA Director George Tenet signed a formal claim of state-secrets privilege, but added: "I recognize it is the Court's decision rather than mine to determine whether requested material is relevant to matters being addressed in litigation." Tenet's statement reflects executive subordination to the rule of law and undergirds the constitutional principle of judicial independence. Most agency claims and declarations, however, simply assert the state secrets privilege without recognizing any superior judicial authority in deciding matters of relevancy and evidence. When an agency head signs a declaration invoking the privilege, is there any reason to believe the agency has complied with the procedural safeguard discussed in *Reynolds* that the official has actually examined the document with any thoroughness and reached an independent, informed decision? Agencies should not be permitted to police themselves in determining whether the state secrets privilege properly applies in a given case. As Tenet recognized, it is for the courts to decide whether the requested materials should be disclosed.

Aftermath of Reynolds. In its 1953 decision, the Court referred to the secret equipment on the B-29: "On the record before the trial court it appeared that this accident occurred to a military plane which had gone aloft to test secret electronic equipment. Certainly there was a reasonable danger that the accident investigation report would contain references to the secret electronic equipment which was the primary concern of the mission." In fact, the report was never given to the district court and there were no grounds for concluding that the report made any reference to secret electronic equipment. The Court was content to rely on what "appeared" to be the case, based on government assertions in a highly ambiguous statement by Secretary of the Air Force Thomas K. Finletter. His statement referred to the secret equipment and to the accident report, but never said clearly or conclusively that the report actually mentioned or discussed the equipment.

The Air Force declassified the accident report in the 1990s. Judith Loether, daughter of one of the civilian engineers who died on the plane, located the report during an Internet search in February 2000. Indeed the report does not discuss the secret equipment. As a result, the three families returned to court in 2003 on a petition for *coram nobis*. Under this procedure, they charged that the judiciary had been misled by the government and there had been fraud against the courts. As recounted in Fisher, IN THE NAME OF NATIONAL SECURITY, the families lost in district court and in the Third Circuit. On May 1, 2006, the Supreme Court denied *certiorari*. The Third Circuit decided solely on the ground of "judicial finality." That is certainly an important principle. Not every case can be relitigated. However, the Third Circuit gave no attention to another fundamental value. The judiciary cannot allow litigants to mislead a court so that it decides in a manner it would not have if in possession of correct information. Especially is that true when the litigant is the federal government, which is in court more than any other party.

On the basis of the ambiguous Finletter statement produced by the executive branch, the Supreme Court assumed that the claim of state secrets had merit. By failing to examine the document, the Court risked being fooled. As it turned out, it was. Examination of the declassified accident report reveals no military secrets. It contained no discussion of the secret equipment being tested. The government had motives other than protecting national security, which may have ranged from withholding evidence of negligence about a military accident to using the B-29 case as a test vehicle for establishing the state secrets privilege.

What happened in *Reynolds* raises grave questions about the capacity and willingness of the judiciary to function as a separate, trusted branch in the field of national security. Courts must take care to restore and preserve the integrity of the courtroom. To protect its independent status, the judiciary must have the capacity and determination to examine executive claims. Otherwise there is no system of checks and balances, private litigants will have no opportunity to successfully contest government actions, and it will appear that the executive and judicial branches are forming a common front against the public on national security cases. The fact that the documents in the B-29 case, once declassified, contained no state secrets produced a stain on the Court's reputation and a loss of confidence in the judiciary's ability to exercise an independent role.

Options Available to Judges. As with the district court and the Third Circuit in the original *Reynolds* case, federal courts can present the government with a choice: either surrender a requested document to the district judge for *in camera* inspection, or lose the case. That is an option when private litigants sue the government, as with the B-29 case. When the government sues a private individual or company, assertion of the state secrets privilege can also come at a cost to the government. In criminal cases, it has long been recognized that if federal prosecutors want to charge someone with a crime, the defendant has a right to documents needed to establish innocence. The judiciary should not defer to executive departments and allow the suppression of documents that might tend to exculpate. As noted by the Second Circuit in 1946, when the government "institutes criminal procedures in which evidence, otherwise privileged under a statute or regulation, becomes importantly relevant, it abandons the privilege." *United States v. Beekman*, 155 F.2d 580, 584 (2d Cir. 1946).

When the government initiates a civil case, defendants also seek access to federal agency documents. Lower courts often tell the government that when it brings a civil case against a private party, it must be prepared to either surrender documents to the defendant or drop the charges. Once a government seeks relief in a court of law, the official "must be held to have waived any privilege, which he otherwise might have had, to withhold testimony required by the rules of pleading or evidence as a basis for such relief." *Fleming v. Bernardi*, 4 F.R.D. 270, 271 (D. Ohio 1941).

If the government fails to comply with a court order to produce documents requested by defendants, the court can dismiss the case. The government "cannot hide behind a self-erected wall [of] evidence adverse to its interest as a litigant." *NLRB v. Capitol Fish Co.*, 294 F.2d 868, 875 (5th Cir. 1961). Responsibility for deciding questions of privilege rests with an impartial independent judiciary, not the party claiming the privilege, and certainly not when the party is the executive branch.

Whether the government initiates the suit or is sued by a private party, the procedure followed *in camera* to evaluate claims of state secrets should be the same. Federal courts should receive and review the entire document, unredacted. They should not be satisfied with a redacted document or with classified affidavits, statements, and declarations that are intended to be substitutes for the disputed document. If the entire document contains names, places, or other information that might jeopardize sources and methods or present other legitimate reasons for withholding the full document from the private party, the judge should decide the redaction and editing needed to permit the balance to be released to the private litigants.

Qualified, Not Absolute. The state secrets privilege should be treated as qualified, not absolute. Otherwise there is no adversary process in court, no exercise of judicial independence over available evidence, and no fairness accorded to private litigants who challenge the government. These concerns were well stated by the U.S. Court of Appeals for the D.C. Circuit in a 1971 case in which the court ordered the government to produce documents for *in camera* review to assess a claim of executive privilege. The D.C. Circuit argued that "[a]n essential ingredient of our rule of law is the authority of the courts to determine whether an executive official or agency has complied with the Constitution and with the mandates of Congress which define and limit the authority of the executive." Claims of executive power "cannot override the duty of the court to assure than an official has not exceeded his charter or flouted the legislative will." The court proceeded to lay down this warning: "no executive official or agency can be given absolute authority to determine what documents in his possession may be considered by the court in its task. Otherwise the head of an executive department would have the power on his own say so to cover up all evidence of fraud and corruption when a federal court or grand jury was investigating malfeasance in office, and this is not the law." *Committee for Nuclear Responsibility, Inc. v. Seaborg*, 463 F.2d 783, 794 (D.C. Cir. 1971). See Louis Fisher, "State Secrets Privilege: Invoke It at a Cost," NATIONAL LAW JOURNAL, July 31, 2006, at 23.

Legislative Action. We recommend that the responsible oversight committees in Congress, such as those handling issues relating to intelligence, judiciary, government reform and homeland security, conduct public hearings and craft statutory language designed to clarify judicial authority over civil litigation involving alleged state secrets. In the past, as with the 1974 amendments to FOIA, the creation of the FISA Court, and enactment of CIPA in 1980, Congress has recognized major responsibilities of federal judges in the area of national security. Judges now regularly review and evaluate highly classified information and documents to a degree that would have been unheard of even a half century ago. To maintain our constitutional system of checks and balances, and especially to assure that fairness in the courtroom is accorded to private civil litigants, Congress should adopt legislation clarifying that civil litigants have the right to reasonably pursue claims in the wake of the invocation of the state secrets privilege. These hearings are important to restore and strengthen the basic rights and liberties provided by our constitutional system of government.

Conclusion. For the reasons outlined above, application of the "state secrets doctrine" should be strictly limited. We urge that Congress enact legislation to clarify the narrow scope of this doctrine and safeguard the interests of private parties. In addition, courts should carefully assess any executive claims of state secrets, and treat this doctrine as a qualified privilege, not an absolute one. Such reforms are critical to ensure the independence of our judiciary and to provide a necessary check on executive power.

*Created out of the belief that we must cast aside the labels that divide us in order to keep our democracy strong, **The Constitution Project** brings together policy experts and legal practitioners from across the political spectrum to foster consensus-based solutions to the most difficult constitutional challenges of our time.

Members of the Constitution Project's Liberty and Security Committee & Coalition to Defend Checks and Balances: Endorsing the Statement on Reforming the State Secrets Privilege

Floyd Abrams, partner, Cahill Gordon & Reindel LLP

Azizah al-Hibri, professor, the T. C. Williams School of Law, University of Richmond; president, Karamah: Muslim Women Lawyers for Human Rights

Bob Barr, former member of Congress (R-GA); CEO, Liberty Strategies LLC; the 21st Century Liberties Chair for Freedom and Privacy at the American Conservative Union; chairman of Patriots to Restore Checks and Balances; practicing attorney; consultant on privacy matters for the ACLU

David E. Birenbaum, of Counsel, Fried, Frank, Harris, Shriver & Jacobson LLP; Senior Scholar, Woodrow Wilson International Center for Scholars; U.S. ambassador to the UN for UN Management and Reform, 1994–96

Christopher Bryant, professor of law, University of Cincinnati; assistant to the Senate legal counsel, 1997–99

David Cole, professor, Georgetown University Law Center

Phillip J. Cooper, professor, Mark O. Hatfield School of Government, Portland State University

John W. Dean, counsel to President Richard Nixon

Mickey Edwards, lecturer at the Woodrow Wilson School of Public and International Affairs, Princeton University; former member of Congress (R-OK) and chairman of the House Republican Policy Committee

Richard Epstein, James Parker Hall Distinguished Service Professor of Law, the University of Chicago; Peter and Kirsten Bedford Senior Fellow, the Hoover Institution

Bruce Fein, Constitutional lawyer and international consultant, Bruce Fein & Associates and the Lichfield Group; associate deputy attorney general, Reagan administration

Eugene R. Fidell, president, National Institute of Military Justice; partner, Feldesman Tucker Leifer Fidell LLP

Louis Fisher, specialist in constitutional law, Law Library, Library of Congress

Michael German, policy counsel, American Civil Liberties Union; adjunct professor, National Defense University School for National Security Executive Education; special agent, Federal Bureau of Investigation, 1988–2004

Melvin A. Goodman, senior fellow and director of the National Security Project, Center for International Policy

Morton H. Halperin, director of U.S. Advocacy, Open Society Institute; senior vice president, Center for American Progress; director of the Policy Planning Staff, Department of State, Clinton administration

Philip Heymann, James Barr Ames Professor of Law, Harvard Law School; deputy attorney general, Clinton administration

David Kay, former head of the Iraq Survey Group and special adviser on the Search for Iraqi Weapons of Mass Destruction to the director of Central Intelligence

David Keene, chairman, American Conservative Union

Christopher S. Kelley, visiting assistant professor of political science, Miami University (Ohio)

David Lawrence Jr., president, Early Childhood Initiative Foundation; former publisher, *Miami Herald* and *Detroit Free Press*

Joseph Margulies, deputy director, MacArthur Justice Center; associate clinical professor, Northwestern University School of Law

Kate Martin, director, Center for National Security Studies

Norman Ornstein, resident scholar, the American Enterprise Institute

Thomas R. Pickering, undersecretary of state for political affairs, 1997–2000; United States ambassador and representative to the United Nations, 1989–92

John Podesta, president and CEO, Center for American Progress; White House chief of staff, Clinton administration

Jack N. Rakove, W. R. Coe Professor of History and American Studies and professor of political science, Stanford University

Peter Raven Hansen, professor of law and Glen Earl Weston Research Professor, George Washington University Law School

William S. Sessions, former director, Federal Bureau of Investigation; former chief judge, United States District Court for the Western District of Texas

Jerome J. Shestack, partner, Wolf, Block, Schorr and Solis-Cohen LLP; former president, American Bar Association

John Shore, founder and president, noborg LLC; former senior adviser for science and technology to Senator Patrick Leahy

David Skaggs, executive director, Colorado Commission on Higher Education; former member of Congress (D-CO)

Neal Sonnett, chair, American Bar Association Task Force on Treatment of Enemy Combatants and Task Force on Domestic Surveillance in the Fight against Terrorism

Suzanne E. Spaulding, principal, Bingham Consulting Group; former chief counsel, Senate and House Intelligence Committees; former executive director, National Terrorism Commission; former assistant general counsel, CIA

Geoffrey R. Stone, Harry Kalven Jr. Distinguished Service Professor of Law, the University of Chicago

John F. Terzano, vice president, Veterans for America

James A. Thurber, director and Distinguished Professor, Center for Congressional and Presidential Studies, American University

Charles Tiefer, general counsel (acting), 1993–94, solicitor and deputy general counsel, 1984–95, U.S. House of Representatives

Don Wallace Jr., professor, Georgetown University Law Center; chairman, International Law Institute, Washington, DC

John W. Whitehead, president, the Rutherford Institute

Roger Wilkins, Clarence J. Robinson Professor of History and American Culture, George Mason University; director of U.S. Community Relations Service, Johnson administration

The Constitution Project's Liberty and Security Committee & Coalition to Defend Checks and Balances. "Reforming the State Secrets Privilege." Washington, DC: The Constitution Project. May 31, 2007.

Used by permission.

Views of the Department of Justice on S.2533, the "State Secrets Protection Act"

by Michael Mukasey*

March 31, 2008

The Honorable Patrick J. Leahy
Chairman
Committee on the Judiciary
United States Senate
Washington, D.C. 20510

Dear Mr. Chairman:

This letter presents the views of the Department of Justice on the Manager's Amendment to S. 2533, the "State Secrets Protection Act." We strongly oppose this legislation. If the legislation were presented to the President in its current form, his senior advisors would recommend that he veto it.

The Constitution and settled Supreme Court precedent define the law governing the state secrets privilege, and this well-developed and well-tested body of law already strikes the appropriate balance between the need to protect the national security in civil litigation and the need to protect the rights of litigants in cases that implicate national security information. For the reasons set forth below, the Manager's Amendment would needlessly and improperly interfere with the appropriate constitutional role of both the Judicial and Executive branches in state secrets cases; would alter decades of settled case law; and would likely result in the harmful disclosure of national security information that would not be disclosed under current doctrine.

1. The state secrets privilege has a long and well-established pedigree.

The state secrets privilege long has been recognized by United States courts as a method of allowing the Executive branch to safeguard information regarding the Nation's security or diplomatic relations. *See Totten v. United States,* 92 U.S. 105, 107 (1875) (dismissing contract claim to protect civil war era espionage relationship). Over fifty years ago, in *United States v. Reynolds,* 345 U.S. 1 (1953), the Supreme Court articulated the basic contours of the state secrets privilege. The Supreme Court held that the United States may prevent the disclosure of information in a judicial proceeding if "there is a reasonable danger" that such disclosure "will expose military matters which, in the interest of national security, should not be divulged." *Id.* at 10. The Supreme Court recognized the imperative of protecting such information when it further held that even where a litigant has a strong need for that information, the privilege is absolute: "Where there is a strong showing of necessity, the claim of privilege should not be lightly accepted, but even the most compelling necessity cannot overcome the claim of privilege if the court is ultimately satisfied that military secrets are at stake." *Id.*[1]

2. Several procedural and substantive requirements preclude the state secrets privilege from being lightly invoked or accepted.

Reynolds also imposes procedural and substantive requirements that preclude the state secrets privilege from being lightly invoked or accepted. As an initial matter, *Reynolds* requires that the privilege be formally asserted by (a) the head of the agency or Department that has control over the matter (b) after actual personal consideration. *See* 345 U.S. at 7–8. Mere invocation of the privilege is not enough. Rather, the privilege is not to be "lightly accepted," *id.* at 11, and the Judicial branch must decide whether invocation of the privilege is proper and should be upheld, *see id.* at 9–10.

Once the privilege is upheld, a court still must decide what impact exclusion of the protected information will have on the case. For example, the court may decide that the privileged information is peripheral and that the case can proceed without it. Thus, assertion of the state secrets privilege does not necessarily result in dismissal of a lawsuit. But where the privileged information goes to the core of the case, where the plaintiff would need the information to establish a prima facie case, or where the defendant would need the information to present a defense, the case must be dismissed because there is no way to proceed without disclosing the information.

Dismissal of civil lawsuits to protect state secrets seemingly may impose a "harsh remedy" on individual plaintiffs, but the state secrets privilege is premised upon the conclusion that "the greater public good—ultimately the less harsh remedy"—is dismissal in order to protect the interests of all Americans in the security of the nation. *See Bareford v. General Dynamics Corp.*, 973 F.2d 1138, 1141 (5th Cir. 1992).

3. It is highly questionable that Congress has the authority to alter the state secrets privilege, which is rooted in the Constitution and is not merely a common law privilege.

It is far from clear that Congress has the constitutional authority to alter the terms and conditions of the state secrets privilege, as the bill purports to do. Congress, of course, cannot alter the President's constitutional authorities and responsibilities by statute. The state secrets privilege is not a mere common law privilege, but instead, as the courts have long recognized, is a privilege with a firm foundation in the Constitution. Any doubt that the privilege is rooted in the Constitution was dispelled in *United States v. Nixon*, 418 U.S. 683 (1974), in which the Supreme Court explained that, to the extent a claim of privilege "relates to the effective discharge of the President's powers, it is constitutionally based." *Id.* at 711. The Court went on to recognize expressly that a "claim of privilege on the ground that [information constitutes] military or diplomatic secrets"—that is, the state secrets privilege—necessarily involves "areas of Art. II duties" assigned to the President. *Id.* at 710; *see Department of Navy v. Egan*, 484 U.S. 518, 527 (1988) (President's "authority to classify and control access to information bearing on national security . . . flows primarily from" his constitutional authority under Article II as Commander in Chief "and exists quite apart from any explicit congressional grant"); *El-Masri v. United States*, 479 F.3d 296, 303–04 (4th Cir. 2007) (holding that state secrets privilege "has a firm foundation in the Constitution").

4. The Manager's Amendment would inappropriately shift the responsibility for making national security judgments away from the Executive and to the courts, which have neither the constitutional authority nor the institutional expertise to assume such functions.

We strongly object to the Manager's Amendment upon the ground that it allocates to the courts a responsibility that rests with the President under the Constitution: the authority to make independent and controlling determinations respecting the extent of harm to national security that would result from the disclosure of certain information. Under the bill's proposed new 28 U.S.C. § 4054(e), a court would decide whether the Executive branch's invocation of the state secrets privilege is "valid," based upon a determination that disclosure of the information would "cause significant harm to the national defense or foreign relations of the United States." Furthermore, proposed new 28 U.S.C. §§ 4053–4055 would impose wholly new procedures in civil litigation that would permit courts to require that the Executive branch attempt to segregate classified information or substitute non-classified information—the effect of which would be to have the courts, rather than the Executive branch, determine whether such segregation or substitution was possible without harm to national security. The bill's treatment of national security determinations in proposed sections 4053–4055 raises separation of powers concerns, because the provisions purport to transfer to the Judiciary through legislation authorities that the Constitution commits to the President. *See, e.g., Egan*, 484 U.S. at 527, 530; *Chicago & S. Air Lines, Inc. v. Waterman S.S. Corp.*, 333 U.S. 103, 111 (1948) (noting limited judicial role with respect to "information properly held in secret").

To be sure, under current law it is the province of the Judicial branch to determine whether the state secrets privilege has been invoked properly. It is well settled, however, that the courts should make that determination by according the "utmost deference" to the expertise and judgment of national-security officials. *E.g., Halkin v. Helms*, 598 F.2d 1, 9 (D.C. Cir. 1978) ("Courts should accord the 'utmost deference' to executive assertions of privilege upon grounds of military or diplomatic secrets.") (quoting *Nixon*, 418 U.S. at 710). As many courts have recognized, the "utmost deference" to the judgment of the Executive branch is appropriate not only for constitutional reasons, but also for practical reasons, because national security officials "occupy a position superior to that of the courts in evaluating the consequences of a release of sensitive information." *El-Masri*, 479 F.3d at 305; *see also Al-Haramain Islamic Foundation, Inc. v. Bush*, 507 F.3d 1190, 1203 (9th Cir. 2007) ("[W]e acknowledge the need to defer to the Executive on matters of foreign policy and national security and surely cannot legitimately find ourselves second guessing the Executive in this arena."). As the courts have recognized, "[t]he significance of one item of information may frequently depend upon knowledge of many other items of information," and "[w]hat may seem trivial to the uninformed, may appear of great moment to one who has a broad view of the scene and may put the questioned item of information in its proper context." *United States v. Marchetti*, 466 F.2d 1309, 1318 (4th Cir. 1972). "[C]ourts are not," and should not be, "required to play with fire and chance further disclosure—inadvertent, mistaken, or even intentional—that would defeat the very purpose for which the privilege exists." *Sterling v. Tenet*, 416 F.3d 338, 344 (4th Cir. 2005).

5. The Manager's Amendment would raise other serious constitutional concerns.

Several provisions in the Manager's Amendment, such as proposed new 28 U.S.C. §§ 4054(c) (requiring the Executive branch to submit sensitive and classified national security information to Federal courts) and 4058(a)(2) & (3) (requiring the Executive branch to submit classified affidavits asserting, and classified information relating to, the state secrets privilege to several congressional committees), would infringe upon the Executive's constitutional authority under Article II to control access to national security information. *See, e.g., Department of Navy v. Egan*, 484 U.S. 518 at 527 (1988). These provisions are incompatible with the President's constitutionally based privilege to withhold national security information. *See id.* at 527, 530; *Chicago & S. Air Lines*, 333 U.S. at 111; *Whistleblower Protections for Classified Disclosures*, 22 Op. O.L.C. 92, 95 (1998) (President has "the right . . . to decide to withhold national security information from Congress under extraordinary circumstances"); *id.* at 100 (President has the authority "to decide, based on the national interest, how, when and under what circumstances particular classified information should be discussed [*sic*] to Congress"). Of course, by well-established practice with respect to the Federal courts and pursuant to bipartisan traditions and the requirements of the National Security Act of 1947, the Executive branch keeps both the Article III judiciary and Congress appropriately informed of pending national security matters.

Proposed new 28 U.S.C. § 4052(c)(1) also could be construed to authorize courts to demand that the Executive branch grant security clearances to private plaintiffs' counsel and other attorneys to enable them to access classified information. Furthermore, proposed section 4052(c)(3) appears to authorize Federal courts to second-guess the Executive branch's reasons for denying a security clearance or, in the court's eyes, for taking too long to decide whether to issue a security clearance. These provisions raise the same constitutional concerns noted in the preceding paragraph. In *Egan*, the Supreme Court explained that security-clearance determinations "must be made by those with the necessary expertise in protecting classified information," and declared that "it is not reasonably possible for an outside nonexpert body to review the substance of such a judgment and to decide whether the agency should have been able to make the necessary affirmative prediction with confidence. Nor can such a body determine what constitutes an acceptable margin of error in assessing the potential risk." 484 U.S. at 529–30. In addition to raising the constitutional concerns noted above with respect to the disclosure of national security information to courts and to Congress, requiring disclosure of the Nation's secrets to numerous private civil litigants and their lawyers could harm national security.

Finally, proposed new 28 U.S.C. § 4058(b)(1), which requires the Attorney General to file a report with Congress that includes "suggested amendments to this chapter," would infringe upon the President's constitutional authority under the Recommendations Clause of the Constitution, U.S. CONST. art. II, § 3. The Recommendations Clause grants the President the authority to recommend for legislative consideration "such Measures as he shall judge necessary and expedient. . . ." The President's authority to formulate and to present his own recommendations includes the power to decline to offer any recommendation. Legislative provisions that would require the President's subordinates to provide Congress with assistance in developing particular legislation, regardless of the President's judgment as to whether such legislation is necessary and expedient, infringe on the powers reserved to the President by the Recommendations Clause. This provision is objectionable unless it is revised to eliminate language requiring the submission of Executive branch proposals or recommendations to Congress.

6. The Manager's Amendment would alter the state secrets privilege in ways detrimental to national security.

The Manager's Amendment would alter the state secrets privilege in ways that could harm national security. As an initial matter, S. 2533 would supplant the existing standard under *Reynolds*—that information is protected by the privilege if there is a reasonable danger that its disclosure could harm national security—in favor of a higher threshold that disclosure of the information must be reasonably likely to cause "*significant* harm" to national security. *See* proposed new 28 U.S.C. § 4051 (emphasis added). The existing standard has been held to include within its scope information that would result in "impairment of the nation's defense capabilities, disclosure of intelligence-gathering methods or capabilities, and disruption of diplomatic relations with foreign governments." *Black v. United States*, 62 F.3d 1115, 1118 (8th Cir. 1995) (quoting *Ellsberg v. Mitchell*, 709 F.2d 51, 57 (D.C. Cir. 1983)). On its face, the bill would impose a heightened "significant harm" requirement and, although the bill is not entirely clear on this point, it would appear to permit a court to determine on its own whether a particular harm was significant or not.

This change has the potential to expose to disclosure a wide range of classified national security information. For example, information may be classified at the "confidential" level if its unauthorized disclosure "reasonably could be expected to cause damage to the national security." Executive Order No. 12958, § 1.2, 60 Fed. Reg. 19825 (Apr. 17, 1995), as amended by Executive Order No. 13292, 68 Fed. Reg. 15315 (Mar. 25, 2003). This change also could expose information classified at the secret level, for which the standard is "serious damage" because of the uncertain distinction between "serious" and "significant."

There are other reasons to believe that the Manager's Amendment would make it more likely that national security information would be disclosed through litigation. For example, proposed new 28 U.S.C. § 4055(2) would permit courts to dismiss a case only where "dismissal of the claim or counterclaim would not harm national security." This provision would appear to give a judge wide discretion to reject the Government's security concerns simply because the judge believes that it is important to have a public determination of the legality of the challenged conduct.

Similarly, the legislation would permit courts to dismiss a case only if removing the privileged information "would substantially impair the ability of a party to pursue a valid defense to the claim or counterclaim." *See* proposed new 28 U.S.C. § 4055(3). This would narrow significantly the standard for dismissal under existing law, which requires dismissal in three essential circumstances: 1) if "the plaintiff cannot prove the *prima facie* elements of her claim with non-privileged evidence"; 2) "if the privilege deprives the defendant of information that would otherwise give the defendant a valid defense to the claim"; and 3) "if the 'very subject matter of the action' is a state secret." *Kasza v. Browner*, 133 F.3d 1159, 1166 (9th Cir. 1998) (internal quotations omitted).

At the same time, the legislation would create extremely difficult standards for the Executive branch to meet: The Executive branch would be required to show it was "impossible" to segregate or redact classified information from the case, proposed new 28 U.S.C. § 4055(1), or that there were "no possible means" of proceeding with segregable information, proposed new 28 U.S.C. § 4054(e)(1). If the Executive branch believed that redactions or substitutions were not possible, courts would be authorized to resolve a disputed issue of fact against the Government—penalizing the Government for protecting national security information. *See* proposed new 28 U.S.C. § 4054(g).

Other provisions of the Manager's Amendment would prohibit courts from ruling on a motion to dismiss until the completion of pretrial discovery hearings required in the legislation. The risk of disclosure of national security information in the course of discovery proceedings is one of the very things that the state secrets privilege is designed to avoid. Therefore, these provisions of the Manager's Amendment would put the Nation's secrets at risk of disclosure.

While purporting to apply principles of the Classified Information Procedures Act to civil proceedings, the Manager's Amendment would depart radically from CIPA proceedings—which apply solely in criminal settings—because, in the criminal context, the United States maintains the discretion to protect classified information by dropping a prosecution if necessary. The United States does not have that option in civil cases filed against it and, thus, the Manager's Amendment would put the United States to the Hobson's Choice of either disclosing classified activities or losing cases.

The Manager's Amendment also would permit a court to decide whether any opinions or orders may be sealed or redacted to the extent that a court, rather than the Executive branch, decided that doing so was or was not to protect the national security. *See* proposed new 28 U.S.C. § 4052(e). This provision too would arrogate to the Judiciary determinations that are constitutionally vested in the Executive branch.

7. Additional Concerns

We note that the Manager's Amendment could affect important, ongoing litigation, particularly because the legislation would be immediately applicable to pending cases.

Additionally, the Department of Defense and elements of the intelligence community currently have guidance on what constitutes classified information, the level of classification, and when and how classified information can be released. The Manager's Amendment does not clarify whether it would make these requirements applicable to a court that handled any classified information, as opposed to information for which the state secrets privilege has been invoked.

* * *

For all of the foregoing reasons, the legislation raises serious constitutional questions concerning the ability of the Executive branch to protect national security information under the well-established standards articulated by the Supreme Court in *Reynolds* and would effect a significant departure from decades of well-settled case law, likely resulting in the disclosure of national security information. In attempting to reallocate national security decision making to the Judicial from the Executive branch, the Manager's Amendment also would impose new duties upon the Judiciary that it is ill-equipped to shoulder. Therefore, we strongly oppose the Manager's Amendment to S. 2533.

Thank you for the opportunity to present our views. The Office of Management and Budget has advised us that from the perspective of the Administration's program, there is no objection to submission of this letter.

Sincerely,

Michael B. Mukasey
Attorney General

cc: The Honorable Arlen Specter
Ranking Minority Member

NOTE

1. It has been claimed that the privileged documents at issue in *Reynolds* (concerning the investigation of a B-29 crash) did not actually contain any sensitive national security information. However, the Court of Appeals for the Third Circuit rejected a claim that the United States had committed a fraud on the court in *Reynolds* and reaffirmed that disclosure of the information over which the United States had asserted the privilege in *Reynolds* indeed could have caused harm to national security. *See Herring* v. *United States*, 424 F.3d 384 (3rd Cir. 2005).

*__Michael Mukasey__ is the former chief judge of the District Court for the Southern District of New York who served as the 81st attorney general of the United States. He is currently a partner at the law firm Debevoise & Plimpton.

Michael Mukasey to the Honorable Patrick J. Leahy, March 31, 2008. http://www.justice.gov/archive/ola/views-letters/110-2/03-31-08-ag-ltr-re-s2533-state-secrets.pdf.

The Brennan Center for Justice on S.2533, the "State Secrets Protection Act"

*by Aziz Huq and Emily Berman**

MEMORANDUM FROM AZIZ HUQ & EMILY BERMAN, BRENNAN CENTER FOR JUSTICE, RESPONDING TO ATTORNEY GENERAL MICHAEL MUKASEY'S LETTER EXPRESSING THE DEPARTMENT OF JUSTICE'S OBJECTIONS TO THE STATE SECRETS PROTECTION ACT OF 2008 S. 2533 (APRIL 3, 2008).

This memorandum addresses the constitutional power of Congress to enact the State Secrets Protection Act, [S.2533] ("SSPA"), establishing rules regulating the invocation of the state secrets privilege, and addresses some of the points made by Attorney General Michael Mukasey in his letter of March 31, 2008, to Hon. Patrick Leahy. Such regulation falls well within Congress's authority, would not be an unconstitutional infringement on Article II powers, and need not compromise national security.[1]

1. CONGRESS HAS AUTHORITY TO REGULATE COURTS' HANDLING OF SECURITY-RELATED MATERIALS

As a threshold matter, there is no dispute that Congress has the power to prescribe regulations for the taking of evidence in the federal courts.[2] Congress has exercised this authority to enact rules governing sensitive evidence in many contexts, including the Classified Information Procedures Act[3] ("CIPA"), the Foreign Intelligence Surveillance Act[4] ("FISA"), and the Freedom of Information Act ("FOIA").[5] Significantly, no serious question has arisen as to the constitutionality of any of these statutes. Nor has the operation of these statutes compromised national security information.[6]

The "long and well-established pedigree"[7] of the state secrets privilege mentioned by the Attorney General does not undermine Congress's power to regulate the use and admissibility of evidence in the courts. As an initial matter, this pedigree is simply not that well-established. The Court only articulated a "state secrets" privilege in 1953, even though dicta implying some kind of privilege goes back earlier.[8] It is implausible to suggest that a tradition that is barely fifty years old is sacrosanct and immune from legislation. And in the nineteen year period following *United States v. Reynolds*, courts saw only six state secrets assertions.[9] There is no deep-rooted tradition or reliance on the specific form of the privilege that would counsel against action now. In any event, Congress frequently reverses or revises rules announced by the courts, including in the national security arena.[10] Legislation on state secrets would be both legitimately within Congress's powers and permissible insofar as it would not disrupt any settled expectations.

II. State Secrets Legislation Would Not Trench on Article II Authority

Assuming *arguendo* that the state secrets privilege is constitutionally based, its constitutional complexion does not translate automatically into unfettered executive discretion to determine the manner in which it operates.

Only in cases "where the Constitution by explicit text commits the power at issue to the exclusive control of the President" have the courts refused to acknowledge a role for the legislature.[11] But since responsibility for the national security of the United States is not textually committed exclusively to the President, but shared between the political branches, the control of national security information is a matter properly determined by both of those branches.

Article II contains no express textual grant of nondisclosure. The Commander-in-Chief Clause does not convey this power: "Aside from the president's prerogative of superintendence over the armed forces and the federally conscripted militia, the evidence does not reveal an original understanding that the Commander in Chief enjoyed preclusive authority over matters pertaining to war making."[12]

Instead, as the courts have recognized time and again, the Constitution assigns *shared* responsibility in the area of national security and military controls both to the executive and to Congress.[13] In this area, the Supreme Court has rejected the proposition that the President has unilateral prerogatives even when it comes to core questions of battlefield conduct and the treatment of individuals seized on a battlefield.[14] This is hardly a novel development. Reaching back to the early 1800s, the federal courts have regulated the conduct of military and security affairs whenever Congress has set forth a relevant statute establishing boundaries to the President's authority.[15] If Congress has the authority to determine the metes and bounds of military conduct attendant to the battlefield, it *a fortiori* has the authority to regulate how military actions will be regulated for the purposes of loss allocations. And in the case of state secrets, which usually are invoked in circumstances having nothing to do with the battlefield,[16] we have moved even farther away from any area committed solely to the executive's control.

Unsurprisingly, therefore, the D.C. Circuit has held in *United States v. AT&T*, that the executive branch does not have an absolute discretion with respect to the flow of information in the national security area.[17]

A contrary result would rest on a unilateral executive authority to withhold information—even from another branch of government. This would indeed be surprising because it would have significant repercussions across a spectrum of national security questions: It would at least cast into shadow Congress's authority to promulgate rules concerning classification, security clearance, and disclosure. It would also arguably mean that congressional investigations into national security matters—and indeed any legislative actions resting on information from the executive—would proceed at the sufferance of the executive. And it would cast into constitutional doubt a host of long-standing statutes, including FISA, FOIA, and CIPA, as unconstitutional trenching on the authority of the executive branch.

Nor do the two principal cases relied on by the Attorney General in his constitutional analysis[18]—*Chicago and Southern Airlines v. Waterman S.S. Corporation*[19] and *Department of Navy v. Egan*[20]—dictate a contrary result. Neither case supports the executive branch's expansive claims to unilateral authority. Both cases trained on judicial interpretations of a *statutory* scheme that vested review of agency decisions in an administrative review board. Although both cases suggested in dicta that the executive had some Article II authority respecting national security matters, in neither case did the Court confront a situation in which Congress and the President were acting at cross-purposes regarding the dissemination of national security information. Under the famous *Youngstown*[21] framework, that is, *Egan* and *Waterman* involved situations at which the executive's authority was at its highest mark—supported by Congress. Here—where Congress would have stepped in to *remove* the President's authority—the executive's power is at its lowest ebb.

At a minimum, *Egan* and *Waterman* do not remotely stand for the broad proposition of unilateral executive control of information that the Attorney General claims. More directly, a host of Founding era precedent—renewed and reaffirmed by the Supreme Court in 2004 and 2006—confirm that the President lacks unilateral and preclusive authority in this situation.[22]

III. The SSPA Does Not Alter Existing Law in Dangerous, Novel, Or Unmanageable Ways

The Attorney General's letter argues that the consequences of the SSPA are novel, unfair, and unwise. Yet the manner in which the SSPA resolves the tension between justice and secrecy is neither new nor unfair to the government. To the contrary, it embodies a longstanding means of both preserving secrecy and also preventing the unfair distribution of costs from national security activities.

With respect to the content of the pending SSPA, the Attorney General's letter overstates the bill's modest effect.[23] The SSPA does not meaningfully change the definition of what qualifies as a state secret. The SSPA's application hinges on whether public disclosure "would be reasonably likely to cause significant harm" to national defense or foreign relations. This basically tracks the standard established in *Reynolds* and recognized throughout subsequent case law.[24]

The Attorney General's letter argues that the word "significant" alters the substantive standard.[25] But whether or not the significance of the harm is reviewed by the court or simply asserted by the government, this would not in our view constitute a substantial change in the legislative scheme. The executive has never—to our knowledge—argued that an insignificant harm warrants nondisclosure, and it would be a remarkable departure for courts to grant the privilege if the harm were not substantial.

Nor does any provision of the SSPA compel disclosure or authorize a court to compel disclosure. Rather, "the court shall resolve the disputed issue of fact or law to which the evidence pertains in the non-government party's favor" in suits against the government.[26] To be sure, this *may* lead to a judgment against the government. But it may not. Even if it does, the government *still* will not be forced to make any disclosure: Any constitutional privilege will remain unstained.

The Attorney General also argues that the bill puts the government to a "Hobson's choice."[27] Perhaps it is true that, at times, the government might have to choose between submitting evidence it prefers to keep secret and a court finding against it on a particular question of law or fact. In effect, that finding against the government—and any possible resulting damages judgment—is the cost of maintaining secrecy. But using this as an argument against the SSPA is flawed in two respects. First, it seems to assume that, under the current state of the law, there is no cost of government secrecy. And this is not the case. Under the status quo, the cost of secrecy falls on injured plaintiffs who, for want of non-confidential evidence, cannot prove their case. Thus, in essence, the true

Hobson's choice is a choice about who should bear the cost of secrecy—the government or those who are injured? And if the need for secrecy must exact a toll, it seems more just to let the cost of that secrecy fall upon the government than upon injured individuals. Second, the executive itself will never bear a direct cost as a result of the SSPA for maintaining secrecy. The only potential cost is to the government's coffers. And the question whether the government should risk a damages judgment against it as a result of a decision to maintain secrecy is exactly the sort of decision about the use of the public fisc that falls squarely within Congress's jurisdiction.

A related point is that the SSPA does not mark an innovation from previous schemes to deal with secrecy. Rather than "depart[ing] radically" from the model of CIPA, as the Attorney General suggests,[28] this statutory scheme is the exact analog of CIPA. Just as CIPA sometimes requires the executive to choose between dropping a prosecution and disclosing information, the SSPA might require the executive to choose between disclosure and a finding against it on a question of fact or of law. Arguably, the costs imposed by CIPA—permitting a possibly guilty criminal to go free—exceed the costs contemplated by the SSPA—paying damages to a plaintiff possibly injured by the government's national security policy.

Finally, the Attorney General insists that the executive's supposed expertise on national security matters necessitates complete executive control over decisions regarding the danger of disclosing a particular piece of information. There is no reason to believe that the SSPA would lead judges to disregard this expertise. The bill does not alter the degree of deference a judge gives to the executive's argument that a specific piece of information would cause national security harms if disclosed. As a practical matter, federal judges are and remain very deferential to executive claims of national security. This trait is unlikely to diminish or change any time soon.

The SSPA simply provides judges with a mechanism for sifting true expertise-based claims from situations of abuse or malfeasance. There is good reason to leave the judiciary in control of this final decision. Both history and logic teach that overreliance on the executive's expertise in the area of national security can lead down undesirable paths. As Justice Souter recently noted,

[f]or reasons of inescapable human nature, the branch of the Government asked to counter a serious threat is not the branch on which to rest the Nation's entire reliance in striking the balance between the will to win and the cost in liberty on the way to victory; the responsibility for security will naturally amplify the claim that security legitimately raises.[29]

And indeed there are examples of such amplified security concerns leading to disastrous results.[30]

Through the SSPA, Congress is simply attempting to recalibrate this balance. Aiding in the vindication of the rights of those who may have been injured by the executive's well-meaning efforts to protect the security of the homeland is well within Congress's constitutional powers. It is also consistent with the ideals and principles that make that homeland worth protecting.

Notes

1. Because the constitutional issues raised by the executive's use and release of national security information are complex, the Brennan Center is currently engaged in researching a comprehensive report on the topic. This memo therefore is necessarily a brief sketch of a complex topic.

2. See, e.g., Act to Establish Rules of Evidence for Certain Courts and Proceedings, Pub L. No. 93-595, 88 Stat. 1926 (1975) (enacting the Federal Rules of Evidence); see also Art. I, § 8 (Congress has the power "[t]o constitute Tribunals inferior to the supreme Court"); Art. III, § 2 ("[T]he supreme Court shall have appellate Jurisdiction, both as to Law and Fact, with such Exceptions, and under such Regulations as the Congress shall make.").

3. 18 U.S.C. app. 3.

4. 50 U.S.C. § 1806(f).

5. 5 U.S.C. § 552(a)(4)(B).

6. Claims that the use of CIPA has compromised national security are baseless. See Serrin Turner & Stephen J. Schulhofer, THE SECRECY PROBLEM IN TERRORISM TRIALS (2006).

7. Letter from Attorney General Michael Mukasey to the Honorable Patrick J. Leahy, Chairman of the Judiciary Committee of the United States Senate 1 (Mar. 31, 2008) (hereinafter "Attorney General Mukasy Letter").

8. United States v. Reynolds, 345 U.S. 1 (1953).

9. Robert M. Chesney, State Secrets and the Limits of National Security Litigation, 75 GEO. WASH. L. REV. 1249, 1297 (2007).

10. For example, the Congress enacted the Military Commissions Act of 2006, Pub. L. No. 109-366, 120 Stat. 2600, in response to the Supreme Court's decision invalidating the President's use of military commissions in Hamdan v. Rumsfeld, 548 U.S. 557 (2006). And the Court's decision in City of Boerne v. Flores, 521 U.S. 507 (1997), was the direct impetus for the passage of the Religious Land Use and Institutionalized Persons Act of 2000, Pub. L. No. 106-274, 114 Stat. 803.

11. Public Citizen v. U.S. Dep't of Justice, 491 U.S. 440, 485 (1989) (Kennedy, J., concurring).

12. Barron & Lederman, The Commander in Chief at the Lowest Ebb—a Constitutional History, 121 HARV. L. REV. 941, 946 (2008).

13. See U.S. Const., art. I (Conferring on Congress the powers to declare war, to raise and support armed forces and, in the case of the Senate, to consent to treaties and the appointment of ambassadors).

14. See, e.g., Hamdi v. Rumsfeld, 542 U.S. 507, 536 (2004); accord Hamdan v. Rumsfeld, 126 S. Ct. 2749, 2799 (2006); see also id. at 2774 n.23 ("Whether or not the President has independent power, absent congressional authorization, to convene military commissions, he may not disregard limitations that Congress has, in proper exercise of its own war powers, placed on his powers.").

15. See, e.g., Little v. Barreme, 6 U.S. (2 Cranch) 170 (1804); see also Bas v. Tinguy, 4 U.S. (4 Dall.) 37 (1800). Little and Bas concerned the scope of statutory grants of authority to conduct captures overseas.

16. See, e.g., El-Masri v. United States, 479 F.3d 296 (4th Cir. 2007) (rendition program); Al-Haramain Islamic Found., Inc. v. Bush, 507 F.3d 1190 (9th Cir. 2008) (warrantless surveillance program).

17. *United States v. AT&T*, 567 F.2d 121, 128 (D.C. Cir. 1977) ("While the Constitution assigns to the President a number of powers relating to national security, . . . it confers upon Congress other powers equally inseparable from the national security. . . . More significant, perhaps, is the fact that the Constitution is largely silent on the question of allocation of powers associated with foreign affairs and national security. These powers have been viewed as falling within a "zone of twilight" in which the President and Congress share authority or in which its distribution is uncertain.") (citing *Youngstown Sheet &Tube Co. v. Sawyer*, 343 U.S. 579 (1952)).

18. *See* Attorney General Mukasey Letter, *supra*, at 3–4.

19. 333 U.S. 103 (1948).

20. 484 U.S. 518 (1988).

21. *Youngstown Sheet & Tube Co. v. Sawyer*, 343 U.S. 579 (1952).

22. *See supra* notes 14 and 15.

23. Attorney General Mukasey Letter, *supra*, at 5–6.

24. Under presently applied case law, information is a state secret if "there is a reasonable danger" that disclosure of the information "will expose military matters which, in the interest of national security, should not be divulged." *El-Masri v. United States*, 479 F.3d 296, 302 (4th Cir. 2007) (quoting *Reynolds*, 345 U.S. at 10).

25. Attorney General Mukasey Letter, *supra*, at 5.

26. SSPA § 4054(g).

27. Attorney General Mukasey Letter, *supra*, at 6.

28. *Id.*

29. *Hamdi v. Rumsfeld*, 542 U.S. 507, 545 (2004) (Souter, J., concurring).

30. *See, e.g., Korematsu v. United States*, 323 U.S. 214 (1944) (Deferring to executive's determination that security concerns justified the discriminatory treatment of Japanese Americans during World War II).

*The Brennan Center for Justice at New York University School of Law is a nonpartisan law and policy institute that seeks to improve America's systems of democracy and justice by holding political institutions and laws accountable to the twin American ideals of democracy and equal justice for all. The center's work ranges from voting rights to campaign finance reform, from racial justice in criminal law to constitutional protection in the fight against terrorism.

Aziz Huq is an assistant professor of law at the University of Chicago Law School.

Emily Berman is a visiting assistant professor of law at Brooklyn Law School.

Berman Center for Justice. State Secrets Protection Act. Memorandum. April 3, 2008. http://www.brennancenter.org/sites/default/files/legacy/Justice/Constitutionality_of_State_Secrets_Protection_Act.pdf.

Used by permission.

Excerpts of Judicial Opinions Regarding State Secrets

The following are excerpts from judicial opinions in which courts dismissed plaintiffs' claims on the grounds that litigating those claims would risk harm to the national security by exposing state secrets. The cases illustrate just how much can be at stake—these plaintiffs have alleged not only significant injuries to themselves but also egregious government misconduct. A successful claim of state secrets therefore potentially results not only in the denial of justice for an injured party but also undermines government accountability and denies to the public information about what actions the government has taken in its name. As the opinions make clear, judges faced with claims of state secrets do not fail to recognize the significance of their decisions. In fact, these particular opinions stress the courts' awareness of the import of their decisions, recognize the gravity of the plaintiffs' claims, and insist they have carefully scrutinized the government's privilege claim. Note that all of the allegations made by the plaintiffs in these cases remain just that—allegations. Had their suits been permitted to continue, the plaintiffs would have had to convince a judge or jury that their allegations were in fact true. But because the cases were terminated by state secrets claims, the accuracy of the allegations was never tested in court.

Mohamed v. Jeppesen Dataplan, Inc.

This case requires us to address the difficult balance the state secrets doctrine strikes between fundamental principles of our liberty, including justice, transparency, accountability and national security. Although as judges we strive to honor *all* of these principles, there are times when exceptional circumstances create an irreconcilable conflict between them. On those rare occasions, we are bound to follow the Supreme Court's admonition that "even the most compelling necessity cannot overcome the claim of privilege if the court is ultimately satisfied that [state] secrets are at stake." *United States v. Reynolds*, 345 U.S. 1, 11, 73 S.Ct. 528, 97 L.Ed. 727 (1953). After much deliberation, we reluctantly conclude this is such a case, and the plaintiffs' action must be dismissed.

[...]

A. Factual Background

1. The Extraordinary Rendition Program

Plaintiffs allege that the Central Intelligence Agency ("CIA"), working in concert with other government agencies and officials of foreign governments, operated an extraordinary rendition program to gather intelligence by apprehending foreign nationals suspected of involvement in terrorist activities and transferring them in secret to foreign countries for detention and interrogation by United States or foreign officials. According to plaintiffs, this program has allowed agents of the U.S. government "to employ interrogation methods that would [otherwise have been] prohibited under federal or international law." Relying on documents in the public domain, plaintiffs, all foreign nationals, claim they were each processed through the extraordinary rendition program. They also make the following individual allegations.

Plaintiff Ahmed Agiza, an Egyptian national who had been seeking asylum in Sweden, was captured by Swedish authorities, allegedly transferred to American custody and flown to Egypt. In Egypt, he claims he was held for five weeks "in a squalid, windowless, and frigid cell," where he was "severely and repeatedly beaten" and subjected to electric shock through electrodes attached to his ear lobes, nipples and genitals. Agiza was held in detention for two and a half years, after which he was given a six-hour trial before a military court, convicted and sentenced to 15 years in Egyptian prison. According to plaintiffs, "[v]irtually every aspect of Agiza's rendition, including his torture in Egypt, has been publicly acknowledged by the Swedish government."

Plaintiff Abou Elkassim Britel, a 40-year-old Italian citizen of Moroccan origin, was arrested and detained in Pakistan on immigration charges. After several months in Pakistani detention, Britel was allegedly transferred to the custody of American officials. These officials dressed Britel in a diaper and a torn t-shirt and shackled and blindfolded him for a flight to Morocco. Once in Morocco, he says he was detained incommunicado by Moroccan security services at the Temara prison, where he was beaten, deprived of sleep and food and threatened with sexual torture, including sodomy with a bottle and castration. After being released and re-detained, Britel says he was coerced into signing a false confession, convicted of terrorism-related charges and sentenced to 15 years in a Moroccan prison.

Plaintiff Binyam Mohamed, a 28-year-old Ethiopian citizen and legal resident of the United Kingdom, was arrested in Pakistan on immigration charges. Mohamed was allegedly flown to Morocco under conditions similar to those described above, where he claims he was transferred to the custody of Moroccan security agents. These Moroccan authorities allegedly subjected Mohamed to "severe physical and psychological torture," including routinely beating him and breaking his bones. He says they cut him with a scalpel all over his body, including on his penis, and poured "hot stinging liquid" into the open wounds. He was blindfolded and handcuffed while being made "to listen to extremely loud music day and night." After 18 months in Moroccan custody, Mohamed was allegedly transferred back to American custody and flown to Afghanistan. He claims he was detained there in a CIA "dark prison" where he was kept in "near permanent darkness" and subjected to loud noise, such as the recorded screams of women and children, 24 hours a day. Mohamed was fed sparingly and irregularly and in four months he lost between 40 and 60 pounds. Eventually, Mohamed was transferred to the U.S. military prison at Guantanamo Bay, Cuba, where he remained for nearly five years. He was released and returned to the United Kingdom during the pendency of this appeal.[1]

Plaintiff Bisher al-Rawi, a 39-year-old Iraqi citizen and legal resident of the United Kingdom, was arrested in Gambia while traveling on legitimate business. Like the other plaintiffs, al-Rawi claims he was put in a diaper and shackles and placed on an airplane, where he was flown to Afghanistan. He says he was detained in the same "dark prison" as Mohamed and loud noises were played 24 hours per day to deprive him of sleep. Al-Rawi alleges he was eventually transferred to Bagram Air Base, where he was "subjected to humiliation, degradation, and physical and psychological torture by U.S. officials," including being beaten, deprived of sleep and threatened with death. Al-Rawi was eventually transferred to Guantanamo; in preparation for the flight, he says he was "shackled and handcuffed in excruciating pain" as a result of his beatings. Al-Rawi was eventually released from Guantanamo and returned to the United Kingdom.

Plaintiff Farag Ahmad Bashmilah, a 38-year-old Yemeni citizen, says he was apprehended by agents of the Jordanian government while he was visiting Jordan to assist his ailing mother. After a brief detention during which he was "subject[ed] to severe physical and psychological abuse," Bashmilah claims he was given over to agents of the U.S. government, who flew him to Afghanistan in similar fashion as the other plaintiffs. Once in Afghanistan, Bashmilah says he was placed in solitary confinement, in 24-hour darkness, where he was deprived of sleep and shackled in painful positions. He was subsequently moved to another cell where he was subjected to 24-hour light and loud noise. Depressed by his conditions, Bashmilah attempted suicide three times. Later, Bashmilah claims he was transferred by airplane to an unknown CIA "black site" prison, where he "suffered sensory manipulation through constant exposure to white noise, alternating with deafeningly loud music" and 24-hour light. Bashmilah alleges he was transferred once more to Yemen, where he was tried and convicted of a trivial crime, sentenced to time served abroad and released.

2. Jeppesen's Alleged Involvement in the Rendition Program

Plaintiffs contend that publicly available information establishes that defendant Jeppesen Dataplan, Inc., a U.S. corporation, provided flight planning and logistical support services to the aircraft and crew on all of the flights transporting each of the five plaintiffs among the various locations where they were detained and allegedly subjected to torture. The complaint asserts "Jeppesen played an integral role in the forced" abductions and detentions and "provided direct and substantial services to the United States for its so-called 'extraordinary rendition' program," thereby "enabling the clandestine and forcible transportation of terrorism suspects to secret overseas detention facilities." It also alleges that Jeppesen provided this assistance with actual or constructive "knowledge of the objectives of the rendition program," including knowledge that the plaintiffs "would be subjected to forced disappearance, detention, and torture" by U.S. and foreign government officials.[2]

[...]

C. Procedural History

Before Jeppesen answered the complaint, the United States moved to intervene and to dismiss plaintiffs' complaint under the state secrets doctrine. The then-Director of the CIA, General Michael Hayden, filed two declarations in support of the motion to dismiss, one classified, the other redacted and unclassified. The public declaration states that "[d]isclosure of the information covered by this privilege assertion reasonably could be expected to cause serious—and in some instances, exceptionally grave—damage to the national security of the United States and, therefore, the information should be excluded from any use in this case." It further asserts that "because highly classified information is central to the allegations and issues in this case, the risk is great that further litigation will lead to disclosures harmful to U.S. national security and, accordingly, this case should be dismissed."

[...]

[W]e assume without deciding that plaintiffs' prima facie case and Jeppesen's defenses may not inevitably depend on privileged evidence. Proceeding on that assumption, we hold that dismissal is nonetheless required under *Reynolds* because there is no feasible way to litigate Jeppesen's alleged liability without creating an unjustifiable risk of divulging state secrets. *See El-Masri*, 479 F.3d at 312 (coming to the same conclusion in a related and comparable case), cert. denied, 552 U.S. 947, 128 S.Ct. 373, 169 L.Ed.2d 258 (2007).[3]

We reach this conclusion because all seven of plaintiffs' claims, even if taken as true, describe Jeppesen as providing logistical support in a broad, complex process, certain aspects of which, the government has persuaded us, are absolutely protected by the state secrets privilege. Notwithstanding that some information about that process has become public, Jeppesen's alleged role and its attendant liability cannot be isolated from aspects that are secret and protected. Because the facts underlying plaintiffs' claims are so infused with these secrets, *any* plausible effort by Jeppesen to defend against them would create an unjustifiable risk of revealing state secrets, even if plaintiffs could make a prima facie case on one or more claims with nonprivileged evidence. *See Kasza*, 133 F.3d at 1170; *Black*, 62 F.3d at 1118 ("[P]roof of 'the factual allegations in the Amended Complaint are so tied to the privileged information that further litigation will constitute an undue threat that privileged information will be disclosed.'") (quoting and affirming the district court); *Bareford*, 973 F.2d at 1144 ("[T]he danger that witnesses might divulge some privileged material during cross-examination is great because the privileged and non-privileged material are inextricably linked. We are compelled to conclude that the trial of this case would inevitably lead to a significant risk that highly sensitive information concerning this defense system would be disclosed."); *Fitzgerald*, 776 F.2d at 1243 ("In examining witnesses with personal knowledge of relevant military secrets, the parties would have every incentive to probe dangerously close to the state secrets themselves. In these circumstances, state secrets could be compromised even without direct disclosure by a witness."); *Farnsworth Cannon*, 635 F.2d at 281 ("[T]he plaintiff and its lawyers would have every incentive to probe as close to the core secrets as the trial judge would permit. Such probing in open court would inevitably be revealing. It is evident that any attempt on the part of the plaintiff to establish a prima facie case would so threaten disclosure of state secrets that the overriding interest of the United States and the preservation of its state secrets precludes any further attempt to pursue this litigation."); *see also In re Sealed Case*, 494 F.3d at 152–54 (acknowledging the appropriateness of dismissal when unprivileged and privileged matters are so entwined that the risk of disclosure of privileged material is unacceptably high, although concluding that the case before the court did not fall within that category).

Here, further litigation presents an unacceptable risk of disclosure of state secrets no matter what legal or factual theories Jeppesen would choose to advance during a defense. Whether or not Jeppesen provided logistical support in connection with the extraordinary rendition and interrogation programs, there is precious little Jeppesen could say about its relevant conduct and knowledge without revealing information about how the United States government does *or does not* conduct covert operations. Our conclusion holds no matter what protective procedures the district court might employ. Adversarial litigation, including pretrial discovery of documents and witnesses and the presentation of documents and testimony at trial, is inherently complex and unpredictable. Although district courts are well equipped to wall off isolated secrets from disclosure, the challenge is exponentially greater in exceptional cases like this one, where the relevant secrets are difficult or impossible to isolate and even efforts to define a boundary between privileged and unprivileged evidence would risk disclosure by implication. In these rare circumstances, the risk of disclosure that further proceedings would create cannot be averted through the use of devices such as protective orders or restrictions on testimony.

[...]

V. OTHER REMEDIES

Our holding today is not intended to foreclose—or to pre-judge—possible *nonjudicial* relief, should it be warranted for any of the plaintiffs. Denial of a judicial forum based on the state secrets doctrine poses concerns at both individual and structural levels. For the individual plaintiffs in this action, our decision forecloses at least one set of judicial remedies, and deprives them of the opportunity to prove their alleged mistreatment and obtain damages. At a structural level, terminating the case eliminates further judicial review in this civil litigation, one important check on alleged abuse by government officials and putative contractors. Other remedies may partially mitigate these concerns, however, although we recognize each of these options brings with it its own set of concerns and uncertainties.

First, that the judicial branch may have deferred to the executive branch's claim of privilege in the interest of national security does not preclude the government from honoring the fundamental principles of justice. The government, having access to the secret information, can determine whether plaintiffs' claims have merit and whether misjudgments or mistakes were made that violated plaintiffs' human rights. Should that be the case, the government may be able to find ways to remedy such alleged harms while still maintaining the secrecy national security demands. For instance, the government made reparations to Japanese Latin Americans abducted from Latin America for internment in the United States during World War II. *See Mochizuki v. United States*, 43 Fed. Cl. 97 (1999).[4]

Second, Congress has the authority to investigate alleged wrongdoing and restrain excesses by the executive branch.[5] "The power of the Congress to conduct investigations is inherent in the legislative process." *Watkins v. United States*, 354 U.S. 178, 187, 77 S.Ct. 1173, 1 L.Ed.2d 1273 (1957); *accord Eastland v. U.S. Servicemen's Fund*, 421 U.S. 491, 504, 95 S.Ct. 1813, 44 L.Ed.2d 324 (1975). "Congress unquestionably has . . . broad authority to investigate, to inform the public, and, ultimately, to legislate against suspected corruption and abuse of power in the Executive Branch." *Nixon v. Adm'r of Gen. Servs.*, 433 U.S. 425, 498, 97 S.Ct. 2777, 53 L.Ed.2d 867 (1977) (Powell, J., concurring); *see also Branzburg v. Hayes*, 408 U.S. 665, 741, 92 S.Ct. 2646, 33 L.Ed.2d 626 (1972) (Stewart, J., dissenting) ("We have long recognized the value of the role played by legislative investigations. . . .").

Third, Congress also has the power to enact private bills. *See Nixon v. Fitzgerald*, 457 U.S. 731, 762 n. 5, 102 S.Ct. 2690, 73 L.Ed.2d 349 (1982) (Burger, C.J., concurring) ("For uncompensated injuries Congress may in its discretion provide separate nonjudicial remedies such as private bills."); *Plaut v. Spendthrift Farm, Inc.*, 514 U.S. 211, 239 n.9, 115 S.Ct. 1447, 131 L.Ed.2d 328 (1995) ("Private bills in Congress are still common, and were even more so in the days before establishment of the Claims Court."); *Office of Pers. Mgmt. v. Richmond*, 496 U.S. 414, 431, 110 S.Ct. 2465, 110 L.Ed.2d 387 (1990) ("Congress continues to employ private legislation to provide remedies in individual cases of hardship."). Because as a general matter the federal courts are better equipped to handle claims, *see Kosak v. United States*, 465 U.S. 848, 867–69, 104 S.Ct. 1519, 79 L.Ed.2d 860 (1984) (Stevens, J., dissenting), Congress can refer the case to the Court of Federal Claims to make a recommendation before deciding whether to enact a private bill, *see* 28 U.S.C. § 1492; *see also Banfi Prods. Corp. v. United States*, 40 Fed. Cl. 107, 109 (1997), although Congress alone will make the ultimate decision. When national security interests deny alleged victims of wrongful governmental action meaningful access to a judicial forum, private bills may be an appropriate alternative remedy.[6]

Fourth, Congress has the authority to enact remedial legislation authorizing appropriate causes of action and procedures to address claims like those presented here. When the state secrets doctrine "compels the subordination of appellants' interest in the pursuit of their claims to the executive's duty to preserve our national security, this means that remedies for . . . violations that cannot be proven under existing legal standards, if there are to be such remedies, must be provided by Congress. That is where the government's power to remedy wrongs is ultimately reposed." *Halkin v. Helms*, 690 F.2d at 1001 (footnote omitted).

VI. Conclusion

We, like the dissent, emphasize that it should be a rare case when the state secrets doctrine leads to dismissal at the outset of a case. Nonetheless, there are such cases—not just those subject to *Totten's* per se rule, but those where the mandate for dismissal is apparent even under the more searching examination required by *Reynolds*. This is one of those rare cases.

For all the reasons the dissent articulates—including the impact on human rights, the importance of constitutional protections and the constraints of a judge-made doctrine—we do not reach our decision lightly or without close and skeptical scrutiny of the record and the government's case for secrecy and dismissal. We expect our decision today to inform district courts that *Totten* has its limits, that every effort should be made to parse claims to salvage a case like this using the *Reynolds* approach, that the standards for peremptory dismissal are very high and it is the district court's role to use its fact-finding and other tools to full advantage before it concludes that the rare step of dismissal is justified. We also acknowledge that this case presents a painful conflict between human rights and national security. As judges, we have tried our best to evaluate the competing claims of plaintiffs and the government and resolve that conflict according to the principles governing the state secrets doctrine set forth by the United States Supreme Court.

For the reasons stated, we hold that the government's valid assertion of the state secrets privilege warrants dismissal of the litigation, and affirm the judgment of the district court.[7] The government shall bear all parties' costs on appeal.

Fazaga v. FBI

[...]

I. Introduction

The present case involves a group of counterterrorism investigations by the Federal Bureau of Investigation ("FBI"), dubbed "Operation Flex," in which the FBI engaged a covert informant to help gather information on certain, unidentified individuals from 2006 to 2007. Although some of the general facts about Operation Flex, including the identity of one informant, Craig Monteilh, have been disclosed to the public, much of the essential details of the operation remain classified. [. . .] Plaintiffs allege that Defendants conducted an indiscriminate "dragnet" investigation and gathered personal information about them and other innocent Muslim Americans in Southern California based on their religion. In doing so, Plaintiffs allege that Defendants violated their constitutional and civil rights. [. . .] Defendants argue that all of Plaintiffs' claims [. . .] must be dismissed because litigation of those claims would risk or require disclosure of certain evidence properly protected by the Attorney General's assertion of the state secrets privilege.

The Attorney General's privilege claim in this action requires the Court to wrestle with the difficult balance that the state secrets doctrine strikes between the fundamental principles of liberty, including judicial transparency, and national security. Although, as the Ninth Circuit aptly opined, "as judges we strive to honor *all* of these principles, there are times when exceptional circumstances create an irreconcilable conflict between them." *Mohamed v. Jeppesen Dataplan, Inc.*, 614 F.3d 1070, 1073 (9th Cir. 2010), *cert. denied*, 131 S.Ct. 2442, 179 L.Ed.2d 1235 (2011). "On those rare occasions, we are bound to follow the Supreme Court's admonition that 'even the most compelling necessity cannot overcome the claim of privilege if the court is ultimately satisfied that [state] secrets are at stake.'" *Id.* (quoting *United States v. Reynolds*, 345 U.S. 1, 11, 73 S.Ct. 528, 97 L.Ed. 727 (1953)). Such is the case here.

[...]

II. Background

The central subject matter of this case is a group of counterterrorism investigations by the FBI, known as "Operation Flex," which focused on fewer than 25 individuals and "was directed at detecting and preventing possible terrorist attacks." (Pub. Giuliano Decl. ¶ 11.) During the investigations, the FBI utilized Craig Monteilh as a confidential informant from 2006 to 2007. (*Id.* ¶¶ 6, 11.) "The goal of Operation Flex was to determine whether particular individuals were involved in the recruitment and training of individuals in the United States or overseas for possible terrorist activity." (*Id.* ¶ 11.) Plaintiffs allege that as part of Operation Flex, Defendants directed Monteilh to infiltrate mosques and indiscriminately collect information about Plaintiffs and other members of the Los Angeles and Orange County Muslim community because of their adherence to and practice of the religion of Islam from July 2006 to October 2007. (First Amended Complaint ("FAC") ¶¶ 1–3, 86, 167.)

The FBI has only acknowledged that Monteilh engaged in confidential source work and disclosed limited information concerning Monteilh's actions. (Pub. Giuliano Decl. ¶ 6.) For example, in an unrelated criminal proceeding in this district, *United States v. Niazi*, Case No. 8:09-cr-28-CJC(ANx), the FBI disclosed to the defendant Ahmadullah Niazi the content of the audio and video recordings containing conversations between him and Monteilh and others. (*Id.* ¶ 12.) The FBI also acknowledged in the *Niazi* case that Monteilh provided handwritten notes to the FBI and that it produced certain notes provided by Monteilh concerning Niazi. (*Id.*)[8] However, essential details regarding Operation Flex and Monteilh's activities have not been disclosed, and the Government asserts that this information "remains highly sensitive information concerning counterterrorism matters that if disclosed reasonably could be expected to cause significant harm to national security." (*Id.* ¶ 6.) The allegedly privileged information includes (i) the identities of the specific individuals who have or have not been the subject of counterterrorism investigations, (ii) the reasons why individuals were subject to investigation, including in Operation Flex, and their status and results, and (iii) the particular sources and methods used in obtaining information for counterterrorism investigations, including in Operation Flex. (Holder Decl. ¶ 4; Pub. Giuliano Decl. ¶ 6.) The Government provides a more fulsome discussion of the nondisclosed matters in its *ex parte, in camera* materials that include two classified declarations and a classified supplemental memorandum. (Dkt. Nos. 35, 36, 56.)

[...]

B. Operation Flex[9]

Plaintiffs allege many disturbing facts about Operation Flex and wrongdoing by Defendants. Sometime prior to July 2006, Plaintiffs allege that the FBI hired Monteilh to be a paid informant to covertly gather information about Muslims in the Irvine area. (FAC ¶ 48.) Monteilh became a Muslim convert, began to attend the ICOI and five of the other largest mosques in Orange County, and assumed the name Farouk al-Aziz. (*Id.* ¶¶ 49–50, 92.) Monteilh interacted with many members of the Muslim community in Southern California during the relevant time period, including Plaintiffs, as part of a "broader pattern of dragnet surveillance program that Monteilh engaged in at the behest of his FBI handlers," known as "Operation Flex," which referenced Monteilh's cover as a fitness instructor. (*Id.* ¶¶ 54–85, 86, 88.) Armstrong and Allen, who supervised all of Monteilh's work, informed Monteilh that Operation Flex was part of a broader surveillance program that went beyond his work. (*Id.* ¶ 88.) Defendants did not limit Monteilh to specific targets on which they wanted information, but "repeatedly made clear that they were interested simply in Muslims" and that he should gather "as much information on as many people in the Muslim community as possible," with heightened attention to particularly religious members and those who attracted Muslim youths. (*Id.* ¶¶ 89, 90, 98.) Plaintiffs allege that "[t]he central feature of the FBI agents' instructions to Monteilh was their directive that he gather information on Muslims, without any further specification," and indiscriminately gather information about them under the maximum [*sic*] that "everybody knows somebody" who may have some connection with the [terrorist organizations] Taliban, Hezbollah, and Hamas. (*Id.* ¶¶ 89, 117.)

Over the course of Operation Flex, Plaintiffs allege that Armstrong and Allen sent Monteilh to conduct surveillance and audio recording in approximately ten mosques in Los Angeles and Orange County. (*Id.* ¶ 92.) Defendants provided Monteilh with surveillance tools, including sophisticated audio and video recording devices, such as key fobs with audio recording capability and a hidden camera outfitted to his shirt, to conduct an "indiscriminate surveillance" of Muslims, who were targeted "solely due to their religion." (*Id.* ¶¶ 86, 122, 124, 128.) Defendants gathered information about Plaintiffs and other members of the Muslim community through these devices and from extensive review of Monteilh's handwritten notes about all aspects of his daily interactions with Muslims. (*Id.* ¶ 122.) Plaintiffs allege that Armstrong and Allen were well aware that many of the surveillance tools they had given Monteilh were being used illegally without warrants. (*Id.* ¶ 136.)

[...]

Plaintiffs allege that through Monteilh, Defendants gathered information on Muslims and their associates consisting of hundreds of phone numbers and thousands of email addresses; background information on hundreds of individuals; hundreds of hours of video recordings that captured the interiors of mosques, homes, businesses, and the associations of Muslims; and thousands of hours of audio recordings of conversations as well as recordings of religious lectures, discussion groups, classes, and other Muslim religious and cultural events occurring in mosques. (*Id.* ¶¶ 2, 137.) Plaintiffs allege that the FBI's "dragnet investigation did not result in even a single conviction related to counterterrorism" because, unsurprisingly, "the FBI did not gather the information based on suspicion of criminal activity, but instead gathered the information simply because the targets were Muslim." (*Id.* ¶ 3.) Plaintiffs allege Monteilh discontinued working for Defendants as an informant around September 2007. (*Id.* ¶ 151.)

[...]

IV. Application of the State Secrets Doctrine

The Government requests dismissal of all of Plaintiffs' claims against Defendants, aside from the FISA and Fourth Amendment claims, under the *Reynolds* privilege. The Government argues that dismissal of these claims under the state secrets privilege is appropriate because it has satisfied the procedural requirements for invoking the privilege and further litigation of the action would risk or require the disclosure of state secrets related to Operation Flex. More specifically, the Government contends that because Plaintiffs' claims are premised on their core allegation that Defendants conducted an indiscriminate religion-based investigation, any rebuttal against this allegation would risk or require disclosure of privileged information—whom and what the FBI was investigating under Operation Flex and why—in order to establish that the investigation was properly predicated and focused. (Gov't Br., at 5–6, 45–53.) The Court agrees. As discussed more fully below, because further litigation of this action would require or, at the very least, create an unjustifiable risk of disclosure of state secrets, the Court finds that dismissal of Plaintiffs' claims, aside from their FISA claim, is required under the *Reynolds* privilege.

[...]

The Court has thoroughly and skeptically examined the Government's public and classified submissions. In particular, the Court has critically scrutinized the Attorney General's classified declarations and the classified memorandum—which are comprehensive and detailed—since they were submitted for the Court's *ex parte*, *in camera* review in August and November 2011. The Court is convinced that the subject matter of this action, Operation Flex, involves intelligence that, if disclosed, would significantly compromise national security. The Court is further convinced that litigation of this action would certainly require or, at the very least, greatly risk disclosure of secret information, such that dismissal at this stage of the proceeding is required.[...]

V. Conclusion

The state secrets privilege strives to achieve a difficult compromise between the principles of national security and constitutional freedoms. The state secrets privilege can only be invoked and applied with restraint, in narrow circumstances, and infused with judicial skepticism. Yet, when properly invoked, it is absolute—the interest of protecting state secrets cannot give way to any other need or interest. Navigating through the narrow straits of the state secrets privilege has not been an easy or enviable task for the Court. In the context of the Executive's counterterrorism efforts engendered by 9/11, the Court has been confronted with the difficult task of balancing its obligation to defer to the Executive in matters of national security with its duty to promote open judicial inquiry. Too much deference would short-circuit constitutional liberties while too much judicial inquiry would risk disclosure of information that would jeopardize national security. In struggling with this conflict, the Court is reminded of the classic dilemma of Odysseus, who faced the challenge of navigating his ship through a dangerous passage, flanked by a voracious six-headed monster, on the one side, and a deadly whirlpool, on the other.

Odysseus opted to pass by the monster and risk a few of his individual sailors, rather than hazard the loss of his entire ship to the sucking whirlpool. Similarly, the proper application of the state secrets privilege may unfortunately mean the sacrifice of individual liberties for the sake of national security. *El-Masri*, 479 F.3d at 313 ("[A] plaintiff suffers this reversal not through any fault of his own, but because his personal interest in pursuing his civil claim is subordinated to the collective interest in national security."); *Sterling*, 416 F.3d at 348 ("[T]here can be no doubt that, in limited circumstances . . . the fundamental principle of access to court must bow to the fact that a nation without sound intelligence is a nation at risk."); *Fitzgerald v. Penthouse Int'l, Ltd.*, 776 F.2d 1236, 1238 n.3 (4th Cir. 1985) ("When the state secrets privilege is validly asserted, the result is unfairness to individual litigants—through the loss of important evidence or dismissal of a case—in order to protect a greater public value.")

The Court recognizes the weight of its conclusion that Plaintiffs must be denied a judicial forum for their claims. The Court does not reach its decision today lightly, but does so only reluctantly, after months of careful review of the parties' submissions and arguments, particularly the Government's *in camera* materials upon which the Court heavily relies. Plaintiffs raise the specter of *Korematsu v. United States*, 323 U.S. 214, 65 S.Ct. 193, 89 L.Ed. 194 (1944), and protest that dismissing their claims based upon the state secrets privilege would permit a "remarkable assertion of power" by the Executive, and that any practice, no matter how abusive, may be immunized from legal challenge by being labeled as "counterterrorism" and "state secrets." (Pls. Opp'n to Gov't, at 20, 41–42.) But such a claim assumes that courts simply rubber stamp the Executive's assertion of the state secrets privilege. That is not the case here. The Court has engaged in rigorous judicial scrutiny of the Government's assertion of privilege and thoroughly reviewed the public and classified filings with a skeptical eye. The Court firmly believes that after careful examination of all the parties' submissions, the present action falls squarely within the narrow class of cases that require dismissal of claims at the outset of the proceeding on state secret grounds. Accordingly, all of Plaintiffs' causes of action against Defendants, aside from their FISA claim, are DISMISSED.

Sterling v. Tenet

[...]

Jeffrey Sterling, an African American, was an Operations Officer in the CIA's Near East and South Asia division from 1993 to 2001. He alleges that during this time he experienced unlawful discriminatory practices at the hands of CIA management. For instance, Sterling believes that the expectations for him were "far above those required of non-African-American Operations Officers." He says his superiors repeatedly denied him advantageous opportunities, subjected him to disparate treatment, and gave him Advanced Work Plans that contained more rigorous requirements than those given to non-African Americans.

He also alleges retaliation for utilizing the internal Equal Employment Opportunity ("EEO") process. He claims that he was scheduled to undergo security processing earlier than he should have been. According to him, security processing is an "arbitrary regime within the CIA that is utilized more for its nature as a tool for intimidation than any substantive security implications." He also asserts that management vandalized his personal property.

[...]

As a covert operative, Sterling's position and responsibilities inherently involved state secrets. We hardly need defend the proposition that CIA personnel, activities, and objectives must be protected from prying eyes. The Supreme Court has noted in the context of discussing the Freedom of Information Act (FOIA) "that Congress intended to give the Director of Central Intelligence broad power to protect the secrecy and integrity of the intelligence process. The reasons are too obvious to call for enlarged discussion; without such protections the Agency would be virtually impotent." *CIA v. Sims*, 471 U.S. 159, 170, 105 S.Ct. 1881, 85 L.Ed.2d 173 (1985).

This national security concern is particularly acute here because as a covert operative, the nature of Sterling's duties may well have involved recruiting foreign sources of intelligence. Congress has imbued the Director with "very broad authority to protect all sources of intelligence information from disclosure." *Id.* at 168–69, 105 S.Ct. 1881 (discussing FOIA). "'The continued availability of intelligence sources depends upon the CIA's ability to guarantee the security of information that might compromise them and even endanger their personal safety.'" *Id.* at 175–76, 105 S.Ct. 1881 (quoting *Snepp v. United States*, 444 U.S. 507, 512, 100 S.Ct. 763, 62 L.Ed.2d 704 (1980) (per curiam)) (alterations omitted).

There is no way for Sterling to prove employment discrimination without exposing at least some classified details of the covert employment that gives context to his claim. [. . .]

[...]

We recognize that our decision places, on behalf of the entire country, a burden on Sterling that he alone must bear. "When the state secrets privilege is validly asserted, the result is unfairness to individual litigants—through the loss of important evidence or dismissal of a case—in order to protect a greater public value." *Fitzgerald*, 776 F.2d at 1238 n. 3. Yet there can be no doubt that, in limited circumstances like these, the fundamental principle of access to court must bow to the fact that a nation without sound intelligence is a nation at risk. *See Reynolds*, 345 U.S. at 11, 73 S.Ct. 528.

We take comfort in the fact that Sterling and those similarly situated are not deprived of all opportunity to press discrimination claims. The CIA provides, and Sterling has utilized, an internal EEO process where his claims may be heard and resolved. While the state secrets privilege is not contingent on the availability of such internal or administrative process, invocation of the privilege in federal court must not operate to discourage the CIA's own efforts to provide a working environment that honors our nation's bedrock commitment to nondiscrimination and fair treatment.

NOTES FOR MOHAMED V. JEPPESEN DATAPLAN, INC.

Notes have been renumbered for this edition.

1. Mohamed's allegations have been discussed in other litigation in both the United States and the United Kingdom. *See Mohammed v. Obama*, 689 F.Supp.2d 38 (D.D.C. 2009); *R (Mohamed) v. Secretary of State for Foreign and Commonwealth Affairs*, [2010] EWCA (Civ) 65 (decision of the United Kingdom Court of Appeal).

2. Among the materials plaintiffs filed in opposition to the government's motion to dismiss is a former Jeppesen employee's declaration, which plaintiffs assert demonstrates this knowledge. *See* Dissent at 1095 n.3.

3. In *El-Masri*, the Supreme Court declined to review the Fourth Circuit's dismissal of similar claims against the various United States government and corporate actors alleged to be more directly responsible for the rendition and interrogation programs at issue here. Nothing in the Supreme Court's state secrets jurisprudence suggests that plaintiffs' claims here, against an alleged provider of logistical support to those programs, should proceed where claims against the government and corporate actors who plaintiffs allege were primarily responsible failed.

   As the dissent correctly notes, we have previously disapproved of *El-Masri* for conflating the *Totten* bar's "very subject matter" inquiry with the *Reynolds* privilege. *See Al-Haramain*, 507 F.3d at 1201. We adhere to that approach today by maintaining a distinction between the *Totten* bar on the one hand and the *Reynolds* privilege on the other. *See Tenet*, 544 U.S. at 9, 125 S.Ct. 1230 (explaining that *Reynolds* "in no way signaled our retreat from *Totten's* broader holding that lawsuits premised on alleged espionage agreements are altogether forbidden"). Maintaining that distinction, however, does not mean that the *Reynolds* privilege can never be raised prospectively or result in a dismissal at the pleading stage. As we explained in *Al-Haramain* (as do we in the text), the *Totten* bar and the *Reynolds* privilege form a "continuum of analysis." 507 F.3d at 1201. A case may fall outside the *Totten* bar because its "very subject matter" is not a state secret, and yet it may become clear in conducting a *Reynolds* analysis that plaintiffs cannot establish a prima facie case, that defendants are deprived of a valid defense or that the case cannot be litigated without presenting either a certainty or an unacceptable risk of revealing state secrets. When that point is reached, including, if applicable, at the pleading stage, dismissal is appropriate under the *Reynolds* privilege. Notwithstanding its erroneous conflation of the *Totten* bar and the *Reynolds* privilege, we rely on *El-Masri* because it properly concluded—with respect to allegations comparable to those here—that "virtually any conceivable response to [plaintiffs'] allegations would disclose privileged information," and, therefore, that the action could not be litigated "without threatening the disclosure" of state secrets. *El-Masri*, 479 F.3d at 308, 310.

4. Other governments have committed to doing this. *See, e.g.*, Prime Minister David Cameron, A Statement Given by the Prime Minister to the House of Commons on the Treatment of Terror Suspects (July 6, 2010), http://www.number10.gov.uk/news/statements-and-articles/2010/07/statement-on-detainees-52943 ("[W]e are committed to mediation with those who have brought civil claims about their detention in Guantanamo. And wherever appropriate, we will offer compensation.").

5. In addition, Congress has constituted independent investigatory bodies within the executive branch. *See, e.g.*, 50 U.S.C. § 403q (establishing the Office of Inspector General in the Central Intelligence Agency "to initiate and conduct independently inspections, investigations, and audits relating to programs and operations of the Agency"); *see also* Office of Inspector General, Central Intelligence Agency, Special Review: Counterterrorism Detention and Interrogation Activities (September 2001–October 2003), May 7, 2004 (partially redacted), *available at* http://graphics8.nytimes.com/packages/pdf/politics/20090825-DETAIN/2004CIAIG.pdf.

6. Proceedings in the Court of Federal Claims following congressional referral may pose some of the same problems that require dismissal here—the Court of Federal Claims must avoid disclosure of state secrets too. The referral proceedings might be less problematic than this lawsuit, however, because, for example, the question of third-party liability would not be the focus: a private bill addresses compensation by the government, not by third parties. In addition, Congress might tailor its referral to protect state secrets, by, for example, requiring the Court of Federal Claims to make its recommendation based solely on the plaintiffs' own testimony and nonprivileged documents in the public domain. Moreover, Congress presumably possesses the power to restrict application of the state secrets privilege in the referral proceedings. *Cf. Al-Haramain*, 507 F.3d at 1205–06 (remanding to the district court to consider whether the Foreign Intelligence Surveillance Act, 50 U.S.C. § 1806(f), preempts the state secrets privilege).

7. We do not share the dissent's confidence that the present proceedings come within Federal Rule of Civil Procedure 12(b)(6). Dissent 1093–95, 1097. *Reynolds* necessarily entails consideration of materials outside the pleadings: at minimum, the *Reynolds* analysis requires the court to review the government's formal claim of privilege. That fact alone calls into question reliance on Rule 12(b)(6). *See Lee v. City of Los Angeles*, 250 F.3d 668, 688 (9th Cir. 2001).

NOTES FOR *FAZAGA V. FBI*

[...]

8. With regard to these materials obtained by Monteilh, the FBI states that is it "presently assessing whether additional audio, video, or notes can be disclosed without risking disclosure of the privileged information . . . and [risking] significant harm to national security interests in protecting counterterrorism investigations." (Pub. Giuliano Decl. ¶ 12.)

9. The Court emphasizes that the facts regarding Operation Flex are only *allegations* from the FAC and do not constitute established facts or disclosures by Defendants. The FBI has neither confirmed nor denied that Monteilh collected information specifically in connection with any of the Plaintiffs or the putative class members.

Mohamed v. Jeppesen Dataplan, Inc., 614 F.3d 1070 (9th Cir. 2010) (en banc).

Fazaga v. FBI, 884 F.Supp.2d 1022 (C.D.Cal. 2012).

Sterling v. Tenet, 416 F.3d 338 (4th Cir. 2005).

Part 5: Unauthorized Disclosure: Leakers, Whistle-Blowers, and Spies

---

Given that the United States has constructed an elaborate legal regime designed to keep government secrets secret, the question arises of what to do when that regime fails—in other words, what to do about *unauthorized* disclosures of information. The Obama administration has been particularly aggressive in this arena, prosecuting more than twice as many alleged leakers as all previous presidential administrations combined. The Justice Department has even scrutinized the private communications of members of the press in the course of its investigations, a highly controversial act. This aggressive approach may be in part a response to twenty-first-century technology. Leaks have always been an issue, but never before could such vast amounts of information be stored, transferred, and disseminated anywhere around the world with such speed and lack of expense. But vigorous pursuit of leakers also chills the dissemination of information routinely provided to the press by government officials—a significant source of information for the American people. After all, the government's "leaker" or "spy" might be the public's "whistle-blower" or a journalist's source. Extensive leaks to the media by former government contractor Edward Snowden have highlighted the competing interests in this area like never before. Snowden's exposure of multiple, highly classified programs run by the National Security Agency have led some to hail him as a hero and others to condemn him as a traitor.

Asking "Has the *New York Times* Violated the Espionage Act?" Gabriel Schoenfeld argues that media outlets that publish classified information leaked to them by government officials should be criminally prosecuted for doing so. In "The Publication of National Security Information in the Digital Age," Mary-Rose Papandrea answers Schoenfeld's question with a resounding no. She asserts that leaks to the media are such a crucial tool for exposing illegal or immoral government action that media entities should not be subject to criminal liability for disclosing national security information unless they did so with the intent to harm the United States. "The Secret Sharer," by Jane Mayer, looks at the issue from the perspective of government employees, asking what such an individual should do when he finds himself in possession of classified information that he believes implicates government wrongdoing or waste.

As you read the selections, consider the following questions:

• How should newspapers and other media outlets decide whether to decline to print something because it endangers the national security? Do journalists have sufficient expertise to judge the level of harm publication will cause?

• Should the media be criminally liable for printing classified information? Or should prosecutions continue to be focused on the leakers themselves? Papandrea argues that publication of classified information by the media should be prosecuted only if the media entity had the intent to harm the United States. Does that rule provide sufficient protection for government secrets? Should there be a special, more permissive rule that applies to the media?

• Should traditional media outlets like the *New York Times* be treated differently from more contemporary sources of information such as WikiLeaks or blogs? If so, how do we decide who fits into the category of "traditional media"? Who should make that decision?

• Subsequent to the original publication of Schoenfeld's article, the AIPAC espionage case against Rosen and Weissman was dropped after a judge decided that, to prevail, the prosecution would have to show beyond a reasonable doubt that Rosen and Weissman *knew* the information they disclosed would potentially harm the United States, and disclosed that information with the *purpose* of disobeying or disregarding the law. In other words, the judge imposed an "intent" requirement more stringent than the government could prove. Is that strict intent requirement appropriate? Or should the courts have permitted the government to prosecute an individual who received and passed along classified information even if there was no intent to break the law or harm the nation?

• What mechanisms should we have for government employees to report fraud, waste, or abuse when the problematic behavior relates to classified information? Is relying on federal employees to leak to the media information about government misconduct appropriate? Can we rely on government employees to disclose only non-harmful information to the media or the public? And if not, how do we ensure proper oversight of executive policy implementation?

• Subsequent to the publication of Jane Mayer's article, the government's felony case against Thomas Drake collapsed upon closer scrutiny of the evidence. Drake ultimately pleaded guilty to the misdemeanor crime of "exceeding authorized use of a government computer." Does that vindicate Drake's allegations of mismanagement? How will Drake's experience affect other potential whistle-blowers?

• If government employees are limited in their ability to report problems through official channels, such as conveying information to Congress, are they more likely to seek out unofficial channels, such as leaks to the press?

Has the *New York Times* Violated the Espionage Act?

*by Gabriel Schoenfeld**

"Bush Lets U.S. Spy on Callers Without Courts." Thus ran the headline of a front-page news story whose repercussions have roiled American politics ever since its publication last December 16 in the *New York Times*. The article, signed by James Risen and Eric Lichtblau, was adapted from Risen's then-forthcoming book, *State of War*.[1]

In it, the *Times* reported that shortly after September 11, 2001, President Bush had "authorized the National Security Agency [NSA] to eavesdrop on Americans and others inside the United States . . . without the court-approved warrants ordinarily required for domestic spying."

Not since Richard Nixon's misuse of the CIA and the IRS in Watergate, perhaps not since Abraham Lincoln suspended the writ of habeas corpus, have civil libertarians so hugely cried alarm at a supposed law-breaking action of government. People for the American Way, the Left-liberal interest group, has called the NSA wiretapping "arguably the most egregious undermining of our civil liberties in a generation." The American Civil Liberties Union has blasted Bush for "violat[ing] our Constitution and our fundamental freedoms."

Leading Democratic politicians, denouncing the Bush administration in the most extreme terms, have spoken darkly of a constitutional crisis. Former Vice President Al Gore has accused the Bush White House of "breaking the law repeatedly and insistently" and has called for a special counsel to investigate. Senator Barbara Boxer of California has solicited letters from four legal scholars inquiring whether the NSA program amounts to high crimes and misdemeanors, the constitutional standard for removal from office. John Conyers of Michigan, the ranking Democrat on the House Judiciary Committee, has demanded the creation of a select panel to investigate "those offenses which appear to rise to the level of impeachment."

The President, for his part, has not only stood firm, insisting on both the legality and the absolute necessity of his actions, but has condemned the *disclosure* of the NSA surveillance program as a "shameful act." In doing so, he has implicitly raised a question that the *Times* and the President's foes have conspicuously sought to ignore—namely, what is, and what should be, the relationship of news-gathering media to government secrets in the life-and-death area of national security. Under the protections provided by the First Amendment of the Constitution, do journalists have the right to publish whatever they can ferret out? Such is certainly today's working assumption, and it underlies today's practice. But is it based on an informed reading of the Constitution and the relevant statutes? If the President is right, does the December 16 story in the *Times* constitute not just a shameful act, but a crime?

II

Ever since 9/11, U.S. intelligence and law-enforcement authorities have bent every effort to prevent our being taken once again by surprise. An essential component of that effort, the interception of al-Qaeda electronic communications around the world, has been conducted by the NSA, the government arm responsible for signals intelligence. The particular NSA program now under dispute, which the *Times* itself has characterized as the U.S. government's "most closely guarded secret," was set in motion by executive order of the President shortly after the attacks of September 11. Just as the *Times* has reported, it was designed to track and listen in on a large volume of calls and e-mails *without* applying for warrants to the Foreign Intelligence Security Act (FISA) courts, whose procedures the administration deemed too cumbersome and slow to be effective in the age of cell phones, calling cards, and other rapidly evolving forms of terrorist telecommunication.

Beyond this, all is controversy. According to the critics, many of whom base themselves on a much-cited study by the officially nonpartisan Congressional Research Service, Congress has never granted the President the authority to bypass the 1978 FISA Act and conduct such surveillance. In doing so, they charge, the Bush administration has flagrantly overstepped the law, being guilty, in the words of the *New Republic*, of a "bald abuse of executive power."

Defenders answer in kind. On more than twelve occasions, as the administration itself has pointed out, leaders of Congress from both parties have been given regularly scheduled, classified briefings about the NSA program. In addition, the program has been subject to internal executive-branch review every 45 days, and cannot continue without explicit presidential reauthorization (which as of January had been granted more than 30 times). Calling it a "domestic surveillance program" is, moreover, a misnomer: the communications being swept up are international in nature, confined to those calls or e-mails one terminus of which is abroad and at one terminus of which is believed to be an al-Qaeda operative.

Defenders further maintain that, contrary to the Congressional Research Service, the law itself is on the President's side.[2] In addition to the broad wartime powers granted to the executive in the Constitution, Congress, immediately after September 11, empowered the President "to take action to deter and prevent acts of international terrorism against the United States." It then supplemented this by authorizing the President to "use all necessary and appropriate force against those nations, organizations, or persons he determines planned, authorized, committed, or aided the terrorist attacks." The NSA surveillance program is said to fall under these specified powers.[3]

The debate over the legality of what the President did remains unresolved, and is a matter about which legal minds will no doubt continue to disagree, largely along partisan lines. What about the legality of what the *Times* did?

III

Although it has gone almost entirely undiscussed, the issue of leaking vital government secrets in wartime remains of exceptional relevance to this entire controversy, as it does to our very security. There is a rich history here that can help shed light on the present situation.

One of the most pertinent precedents is a newspaper story that appeared in the *Chicago Tribune* on June 7, 1942, immediately following the American victory in the battle of Midway in World War II. In a front-page article under the headline, "Navy Had Word of Jap Plan to Strike at Sea," the *Tribune* disclosed that the strength and disposition of the Japanese fleet had been "well known in American naval circles several days before the battle began." The paper then presented an exact description of the imperial armada, complete with the names of specific Japanese ships and the larger assemblies of vessels to which they were deployed. All of this information was attributed to "reliable sources in . . . naval intelligence."

The inescapable conclusion to be drawn from the *Tribune* article was that the United States had broken Japanese naval codes and was reading the enemy's encrypted communications. Indeed, cracking JN-25, as it was called, had been one of the major Allied triumphs of the Pacific war, laying bare the operational plans of the Japanese Navy almost in real time and bearing fruit not only at Midway— a great turning point of the war—but in immediately previous confrontations, and promising significant advantages in the terrible struggles that still lay ahead. Its exposure, a devastating breach of security, thus threatened to extend the war indefinitely and cost the lives of thousands of American servicemen.

An uproar ensued in those quarters in Washington that were privy to the highly sensitive nature of the leak. The War Department and the Justice Department raised the question of criminal proceedings against the *Tribune* under the Espionage Act of 1917. By August 1942, prosecutors brought the paper before a federal grand jury. But fearful of alerting the Japanese, and running up against an early version of what would come to be known as graymail, the government balked at providing jurors with yet more highly secret information that would be necessary to demonstrate the damage done.

Thus, in the end, the *Tribune* managed to escape criminal prosecution. For their part, the Japanese either never got wind of the story circulating in the United States or were so convinced that their naval codes were unbreakable that they dismissed its significance. In any case, they left them unaltered, and their naval communications continued to be read by U.S. and British cryptographers until the end of the war.[4]

If the government's attempt to employ the provisions of the 1917 Espionage Act in the heat of World War II failed, another effort three decades later was no more successful. This was the move by the Nixon White House to prosecute Daniel Ellsberg and Anthony Russo for leaking the Pentagon Papers, which foundered on the rocks of the administration's gross misconduct in investigating the offense. The administration also petitioned the Supreme Court to stop the *New York Times* from publishing Ellsberg's leaked documents, in order to prevent "grave and irreparable danger" to the public interest; but it did not even mention the Espionage Act in this connection, presumably because that statute does not allow for the kind of injunctive relief it was seeking.

Things took a different turn a decade later with an obscure case known as *United States of America* v. *Samuel Loring Morison*. From 1974 to 1984, Morison, a grandson of the eminent historian Samuel Eliot Morison, had been employed as a part-time civilian analyst at the Naval Intelligence Support Center in Maryland. With the permission of his superiors, he also worked part-time as an editor of *Jane's Fighting Ships*, the annual reference work that is the standard in its field. In 1984, dissatisfaction with his government position led Morison to pursue full-time employment with *Jane's*.

In the course of his job-seeking, Morison had passed along three classified photos, filched from a colleague's desk, which showed a Soviet nuclear-powered aircraft carrier under construction. They had been taken by the KH-11 satellite system, whose electro-optical digital-imaging capabilities were the first of their kind and a guarded military secret. The photographs, which eventually appeared in *Jane's Defence Weekly*, another publication in the *Jane's* family, were traced back to Morison. Charged with violations of the Espionage Act, he was tried, convicted, and sentenced to a two-year prison term.[5]

Finally, and bearing on issues of secrecy from another direction, there is a case wending its way through the judicial process at this very moment. It involves the American Israel Public Affairs Committee (AIPAC), which lobbies Congress and the executive branch on matters related to Israel, the Middle East, and U.S. foreign policy. In the course of these lobbying activities, two AIPAC officials, Steven J. Rosen and Keith Weissman, allegedly received classified information from a Defense Department analyst by the name of Lawrence Franklin. They then allegedly passed on this information to an Israeli diplomat, and also to members of the press.

Both men are scheduled to go on trial in April for violations of the Espionage Act. The indictment, which names them as part of a "conspiracy," asserts that they used "their contacts within the U.S. government and elsewhere to gather sensitive U.S. government information, including classified information relating to national defense, for subsequent unlawful communication, delivery, and transmission to persons not entitled to receive it." As for Franklin, who admitted to his own violations of the Espionage Act and was promised leniency for cooperating in an FBI sting operation against Rosen and Weissman, he was sentenced this January to twelve-and-a-half years in prison, half of the maximum 25-year penalty.[6]

IV

Despite their disparate natures and outcomes, each of these cases bears on the NSA wiretapping story. In attempting to bring charges against the *Chicago Tribune*, both Frances Biddle, FDR's wartime attorney general, and other responsible officials were operating under the well-founded principle that newspapers do not carry a shield that automatically allows them to publish whatever they wish. In particular, the press can and should be held to account for publishing military secrets in wartime.

In the case of the *Tribune* there was no indictment, let alone a conviction; in the Pentagon Papers case, the prosecution was botched. But *Morison* was seen all the way through to conviction, and the conviction was affirmed at every level up to the Supreme Court (which upheld the verdict of the lower courts by declining to hear the case). It would thus seem exceptionally relevant to the current situation.

In appealing his conviction, Morison argued along lines similar to those a newspaper reporter might embrace—namely, that the Espionage Act did not apply to him because he was neither engaged in "classic spying and espionage activity" nor transmitting "national-security secrets to agents of foreign governments with intent to injure the United States." In rejecting both of these contentions, the appeals court noted that the law applied to "whoever" transmits national-defense information to "a person not entitled to receive it." The Espionage Act, the court made clear, is not limited to spies or agents of a foreign government, and contains no exemption "in favor of one who leaks to the press."

But if the implication of *Morison* seems straightforward enough, it is also clouded by the fact that Morison's status was so peculiar: was he convicted as a miscreant government employee (which he was) or, as he maintained in his own defense, an overly zealous journalist? In the view of the courts that heard his case, the answer seemed to be more the former than the latter, leaving unclear the status of a journalist engaged in the same sort of behavior today.

The AIPAC case presents another twist. In crucial respects, the status of the two defendants does resemble that of journalists. Unlike Morison but like James Risen of the *New York Times*, the AIPAC men were not government employees. They were also involved in a professional activity—attempting to influence the government by means of lobbying—that under normal circumstances enjoys every bit as much constitutional protection as publishing a newspaper. Like freedom of the press, indeed, the right to petition the government is explicitly stipulated in the First Amendment. Yet for allegedly taking possession of classified information and then passing such information along to others, including not only a representative of the Israeli government but also, as the indictment specifies, a "member of the media," Rosen and Weissman placed themselves in legal jeopardy.

The AIPAC case thus raises an obvious question. If Rosen and Weissman are now suspended in boiling hot water over alleged violations of the Espionage Act, why should persons at the *Times* not be treated in the same manner?

To begin with, there can be little argument over whether, in the case of the *Times*, national-defense material was disclosed in an unauthorized way. The *Times*'s own reporting makes this plain; the original December 16 article explicitly discusses the highly secret nature of the material, as well as the *Times*'s own hesitations in publishing it. A year before the story actually made its way into print, the paper (by its own account) told the White House what it had uncovered, was warned about the sensitivity of the material, and was asked not to publish it. According to Bill Keller, the *Times*'s executive editor, the administration "argued strongly that writing about this eavesdropping program would give terrorists clues about the vulnerability of their communications and would deprive the government of an effective tool for the protection of the country's security." Whether because of this warning or for other reasons, the *Times* withheld publication of the story for a year.[7]

Nor does James Risen's *State of War* hide this aspect of things. To the contrary, one of the book's selling points, as its subtitle indicates, is that it is presenting a "secret history." In his acknowledgements, Risen thanks "the many current and former government officials who cooperated" with him, adding that they did so "sometimes at great personal risk." In an age when government officials are routinely investigated by the FBI for leaking classified information, and routinely charged with a criminal offense if caught in the act, what precisely would that "great personal risk" entail if not the possibility of prosecution for revealing government secrets?

The real question is therefore not whether secrets were revealed but whether, under the espionage statutes, the elements of a criminal act were in place. This is a murkier matter than one might expect.

Thus, one subsection of the Espionage Act requires that the country be in a state of war, and one might argue that this requirement was not present. Although President Bush and other leading officials speak of a "war on terrorism," there has been no formal declaration of war by Congress. Similarly, other subsections demand evidence of a clear intent to injure the United States. Whatever the motives of the editors and reporters of the *New York Times*, it would be difficult to prove that among them was the prospect of causing such injury.

True, several sections of the Act rest on neither a state of war nor on intent to injure, instead specifying a lower threshold: to be found guilty, one must have acted "willfully." Yet this key term is itself ambiguous—"one of the law's chameleons," as it has been called. Does it mean merely acting with awareness? Or does it signify a measure of criminal purposiveness? In light of these and other areas of vagueness in the statutes, it is hardly surprising that, over the decades, successful prosecution of the recipients and purveyors of leaked secret government information has been as rare as leaks of such information have been abundant.

V

But that does not end the matter. Writing in 1973, in the aftermath of the Pentagon Papers muddle, two liberal-minded law professors, Harold Edgar and Benno C. Schmidt, Jr., undertook an extensive study of the espionage statutes with the aim of determining the precise degree to which "constitutional principles limit official power to prevent or punish public disclosure of national-defense secrets."[8] Their goal proved elusive. The First Amendment, Edgar and Schmidt found, despite providing "restraints against grossly sweeping prohibitions" on the press, did not deprive Congress of the power to pass qualifying legislation "reconciling the conflict between basic values of speech and security." Indeed, the Espionage Act of 1917 was just such a piece of law-making, and Edgar and Schmidt devote many pages to reviewing the discussion that led up to its passage.

What they show is a kind of schizophrenia. On the one hand, a "series of legislative debates, amendments, and conferences" preceding the Act's passage can "fairly be read as *excluding* criminal sanctions for well-meaning publication of information no matter what damage to the national security might ensue and regardless of whether the publisher knew its publication would be damaging" (emphasis added). On the other hand, whatever the "apparent thrust" of this legislative history, the statutes themselves retain plain meanings that cannot be readily explained away. The "language of the statute," the authors concede, "has to be bent somewhat to exclude publishing national-defense material from its [criminal] reach, and tortured to exclude from criminal sanction preparatory conduct necessarily involved in almost every conceivable publication" of military secrets.

Thus, in the Pentagon Papers case, four members of the Court—Justices White, Stewart, Blackmun, and Chief Justice Burger—suggested that the statutes can impose criminal sanctions on newspapers for retaining or publishing defense secrets. Although finding these pronouncements "most regrettable," a kind of "loaded gun pointed at newspapers and reporters," Edgar and Schmidt are nevertheless compelled to admit that, in this case as in many others in modern times, the intent of the espionage statutes is indisputable:

> If these statutes mean what they seem to say and are constitutional, public speech in this country since World War II has been rife with criminality. The source who leaks defense information to the press commits an offense; the reporter who holds onto defense material commits an offense; and the retired official who uses defense material in his memoirs commits an offense.

For Edgar and Schmidt, the only refuge from this (to them) dire conclusion is that Congress did not understand the relevant sections of the Espionage Act "to have these effects when they were passed, or when the problem of publication of defense information was considered on other occasions."

Edgar and Schmidt may or may not be right about Congress's incomprehension. But even if they are right, would that mean that newspapers can indeed publish whatever they want whenever they want, secret or not, without fear of criminal sanction?

Hardly. For in 1950, as Edgar and Schmidt also note, in the wake of a series of cold-war espionage cases, and with the *Chicago Tribune* episode still fresh in its mind, Congress added a very clear provision to the U.S. Criminal Code dealing specifically with "communications intelligence"—exactly the area reported on by the *Times* and James Risen. Here is the section in full, with emphasis added to those words and passages applicable to the conduct of the *New York Times*:

§798. DISCLOSURE OF CLASSIFIED INFORMATION.

(a) *Whoever* knowingly and willfully communicates, furnishes, transmits, or otherwise makes available to an unauthorized person, or *publishes,* or uses in any manner prejudicial to the safety or interest of the United States or for the benefit of any foreign government to the detriment of the United States *any classified information*—

(1) concerning the nature, preparation, or use of any code, cipher, or cryptographic system of the United States or any foreign government; or

(2) concerning the design, construction, use, maintenance, or repair of any device, apparatus, or appliance used or prepared or planned for use by the United States or any foreign government for cryptographic or communication intelligence purposes; or

(3) *concerning the communication intelligence activities of the United States* or any foreign government; or

(4) obtained by the processes of communication intelligence from the communications of any foreign government, knowing the same to have been obtained by such processes—

Shall be fined not more than $10,000 or imprisoned not more than ten years, or both.

(b) As used in this subsection (a) of this section—

The term "classified information" means information which, at the time of a violation of this section, is, for reasons of national security, specifically designated by a United States Government agency for limited or restricted dissemination or distribution;

The terms "code," "cipher," and "cryptographic system" include in their meanings, in addition to their usual meanings, any method of secret writing and any mechanical or electrical device or method used for the purpose of disguising or concealing the contents, significance, or meanings of communications;

The term "foreign government" includes in its meaning any person or persons acting or purporting to act for or on behalf of any faction, party, department, agency, bureau, or military force of or within a foreign country, or for or on behalf of any government or any person or persons purporting to act as a government within a foreign country, whether or not such government is recognized by the United States;

The term "communication intelligence" means all procedures and methods used in the interception of communications and the obtaining of information from such communications by other than the intended recipients;

The term "unauthorized person" means any person who, or agency which, is not authorized to receive information of the categories set forth in subsection (a) of this section, by the President, or by the head of a department or agency of the United States Government which is expressly designated by the President to engage in communication intelligence activities for the United States.

Not only is this provision completely unambiguous, but Edgar and Schmidt call it a "model of precise draftsmanship." As they state, "the use of the term 'publishes' makes clear that the prohibition is intended to bar public speech," which clearly includes writing about secrets in a newspaper. Nor is a motive required in order to obtain a conviction: "violation [of the statute] occurs on knowing engagement of the proscribed conduct, without any additional requirement that the violator be animated by anti-American or pro-foreign motives." The section also does not contain any requirement that the U.S. be at war.

One of the more extraordinary features of Section 798 is that it was drawn with the very purpose of *protecting* the vigorous public discussion of national-defense material. In 1946, a joint committee investigating the attack on Pearl Harbor had urged a blanket prohibition on the publication of government secrets. But Congress resisted, choosing instead to carve out an exception in the special case of cryptographic intelligence, which it described as a category "both vital and vulnerable to an almost unique degree."

With the bill narrowly tailored in this way, and "with concern for public speech having thus been respected" (in the words of Edgar and Schmidt), Section 798 not only passed in Congress but, perhaps astonishingly in hindsight, won the support of the American Society of Newspaper Editors. At the time, the leading editors of the *New York Times* were active members of that society.

VI

If prosecuted, or threatened with prosecution, under Section 798, today's *New York Times* would undoubtedly seek to exploit the statute's only significant loophole. This revolves around the issue of whether the information being disclosed was improperly classified as secret. In all of the extensive debate about the NSA program, no one has yet convincingly made such a charge.

The *Times* would also undoubtedly seek to create an additional loophole. It might assert that, unlike in the *Chicago Tribune* case or in *Morison*, the disclosure at issue is of an *illegal* governmental activity, in this case warrantless wiretapping, and that in publishing the NSA story the paper was fulfilling a central aspect of its public-service mission by providing a channel for whistleblowers in government to right a wrong. In this, it would assert, it was every bit as much within its rights as when newspapers disclosed the illegal "secret" participation of the CIA in Watergate.

But this argument, too, is unlikely to gain much traction in court. As we have already seen, congressional leaders of both parties have been regularly briefed about the program. Whether or not legal objections to the NSA surveillance ever arose in those briefings, the mere fact that Congress has been kept informed shows that, whatever legitimate objections there might be to the program, this is not a case, like Watergate, of the executive branch running amok. Mere allegations of illegality do not, in our system of democratic rule, create any sort of terra firma—let alone a presumption that one is, in turn, entitled to break the law.

As for whistleblowers unhappy with one or another government program, they have other avenues at their disposal than splashing secrets across the front page of the *New York Times*. The Intelligence Community Whistleblower Protection Act of 1998 shields employees from retribution if they wish to set out evidence of wrongdoing. When classified information is at stake, the complaints must be leveled in camera, to authorized officials, like the inspectors general of the agencies in question, or to members of congressional intelligence committees, or both. Neither the *New York Times* nor any other newspaper or television station is listed as an authorized channel for airing such complaints.

Current and former officials who choose to bypass the provisions of the Whistleblower Protection Act and to reveal classified information directly to the press are unequivocally lawbreakers. This is not in dispute. What Section 798 of the Espionage Act makes plain is that the same can be said about the press itself when, eager to obtain classified information however it can, and willing to promise anonymity to leakers, it proceeds to publish the government's communications-intelligence secrets for all the world to read.

VII

If the *Times* were indeed to run afoul of a law once endorsed by the American Society of Newspaper Editors, it would point to a striking role reversal in the area of national security and the press.

Back in 1942, the *Chicago Tribune* was owned and operated by Colonel Robert R. McCormick. In the 1930's, as Hitler plunged Europe into crisis, his paper, pursuing the isolationist line of the America First movement, tirelessly editorialized against Franklin Roosevelt's "reckless" efforts to entangle the U.S. in a European war. Once war came, the *Tribune* no less tirelessly criticized Roosevelt's conduct of it, lambasting the administration for incompetence and much else.

In its campaign against the Roosevelt administration, one of the *Tribune's* major themes was the evils of censorship; the paper's editorial page regularly defended its publication of secrets as in line with its duty to keep the American people well informed. On the very day before Pearl Harbor, it published an account of classified U.S. plans for fighting in Europe that came close to eliciting an indictment.[9]

The subsequent disclosure of our success in breaking the Japanese codes was thus by no means a singular or accidental mishap but an integral element in an ideological war that called for pressing against the limits.

During World War II, when the *Chicago Tribune* was recklessly endangering the nation by publishing the most closely guarded cryptographic secrets, the *New York Times* was by contrast a model of wartime rectitude. It is inconceivable that in, say, June 1944, our leading newspaper would have carried a (hypothetical) dispatch beginning: "A vast Allied invasion force is poised to cross the English Channel and launch an invasion of Europe, with the beaches of Normandy being the point at which it will land."

In recent years, however, under very different circumstances, the *Times* has indeed reversed roles, embracing a quasi-isolationist stance. If it has not inveighed directly against the war on terrorism, its editorial page has opposed almost every measure taken by the Bush administration in waging that war, from the Patriot Act to military tribunals for terrorist suspects to the CIA renditions of al-Qaeda operatives to the effort to depose Saddam Hussein. "Mr. Bush and his attorney general," says the *Times*, have "put in place a strategy for a domestic anti-terror war that [has] all the hallmarks of the administration's normal method of doing business: a Nixonian obsession with secrecy, disrespect for civil liberties, and inept management." Of the renditions, the paper has argued that they "make the United States the partner of some of the world's most repressive regimes"; constitute "outsourcing torture"; and can be defended only on the basis of "the sort of thinking that led to the horrible abuses at prisons in Iraq." The *Times*'s opposition to the Patriot Act has been even more heated: the bill is "unconstitutionally vague"; "a tempting bit of election-year politics"; "a rushed checklist of increased police powers, many of dubious value"; replete with provisions that "trample on civil liberties"; and plain old "bad law."

In pursuing its reflexive hostility toward the Bush administration, the *Times*, like the *Chicago Tribune* before it, has become an unceasing opponent of secrecy laws, editorializing against them consistently and publishing government secrets at its own discretion. So far, there has been only a single exception to this pattern. It merits a digression, both because it is revealing of the *Times*'s priorities and because it illustrates how slender is the legal limb onto which the newspaper has climbed.

The exception has to do with Valerie Plame Wilson. The wife of a prominent critic of the administration's decision to go to war in Iraq, Plame is a CIA officer who, despite her ostensible undercover status, was identified as such in July 2003 by the press. That disclosure led to a criminal investigation, in the course of which the *Times* reporter Judith Miller was found in contempt of court and jailed for refusing to reveal the names of government officials with whom she had discussed Plame's CIA status. In the end, Miller told what she knew to the special prosecutor, leading him to indict I. Lewis "Scooter" Libby, an aide to Vice President Cheney, for allegedly lying under oath about his role in the outing of Plame.

The *Times* has led the pack in deploring Libby's alleged leak, calling it "an egregious abuse of power" equivalent to "the disclosure of troop movements in wartime," and blowing it up into a kind of conspiracy on the part of the Bush administration to undercut critics of the war. That its hysteria over the leak of Plame's CIA status sits oddly with its own habit of regularly pursuing and publishing government secrets is something the paper affects not to notice. But if the Plame case reveals a hypocritical or partisan side to the *Times*'s concern for governmental secrecy, it also shows that neither the First Amendment nor any statute passed by Congress confers a shield allowing journalists to step outside the law.

The courts that sent Judith Miller to prison for refusing to reveal her sources explicitly cited the holding in *Branzburg v. Hayes* (1972), a critical case in the realm of press freedom. In *Branzburg*, which involved not government secrets but narcotics, the Supreme Court ruled that "it would be frivolous to assert . . . that the First Amendment, in the interest of securing news or otherwise, confers a license on . . . the reporter to violate valid criminal laws," and that "neither reporter nor source is immune from conviction for such conduct, whatever the impact on the flow of news."

The Plame affair extends the logic of *Branzburg*, showing that a journalist can be held in contempt of court when the unauthorized disclosure of intelligence-related information is at stake.[10]

Making this episode even more relevant is the fact that the classified information at issue—about which Judith Miller gathered notes but never published a single word, hence doing no damage herself to the public interest—is of trivial significance in comparison with disclosure of the NSA surveillance program, which tracks the surreptitious activities of al-Qaeda operatives in the U.S. and hence involves the security of the nation and the lives of its citizens. If journalists lack immunity in a matter as narrow as Plame, they also presumably lack it for their role in perpetrating a much broader and deadlier breach of law.

"Unauthorized disclosures can be extraordinarily harmful to the United States national-security interests and . . . far too many such disclosures occur," said President Clinton on one occasion, adding that they "damage our intelligence relationships abroad, compromise intelligence gathering, jeopardize lives, and increase the threat of terrorism." To be sure, even as he uttered these words, Clinton was in the process of vetoing a bill that tightened laws against leaking secrets. But, his habitual triangulating aside, he was right and remains right. In recent years a string of such devastating leaks has occurred, of which the NSA disclosure is at the top of the list.

By means of that disclosure, the *New York Times* has tipped off al Qaeda, our declared mortal enemy, that we have been listening to every one of its communications that we have been able to locate, and have succeeded in doing so even as its operatives switch from line to line or location to location. Of course, the *Times* disputes that its publication has caused any damage to national security. In a statement on the paper's website, Bill Keller asserts complacently that "we satisfied ourselves that we could write about this program . . . in a way that would not expose any intelligence-gathering methods or capabilities that are not already on the public record." In his book, James Risen goes even further, ridiculing the notion that the NSA wiretapping "is critical to the global war on terrorism." Government officials, he writes, "have not explained why any terrorist would be so naïve as to assume that his electronic communication was impossible to intercept."

But there are numerous examples of terrorists assuming precisely that. Prior to September 11, Osama bin Laden regularly communicated with top aides using satellite telephones whose signals were being soaked up by NSA collection systems. After a critical leak in 1998, these conversations immediately ceased, closing a crucial window into the activities of al Qaeda in the period running up to September 11.

Even after September 11, according to Risen and Eric Lichtblau in their December story, terrorists continued to blab on open lines. Thus, they wrote, NSA eavesdropping helped uncover a 2003 plot by Iyman Faris, a terrorist operative, who was apprehended and sentenced to 20 years in prison for providing material support and resources to al Qaeda and conspiring to supply it with information about possible U.S. targets. Another plot to blow up British pubs and subways stations using fertilizer bombs was also exposed in 2004, "in part through the [NSA] program." This is the same James Risen who blithely assures us that terrorists are too smart to talk on the telephone.

For its part, the *New York Times* editorial page remains serenely confident that the problem is not our national security but the overreaching of our own government. Condescending to notice that the "nation's safety is obviously a most serious issue," the paper wants us to focus instead on how "that very fact has caused this administration and many others to use it as a catch-all for any matter it wants to keep secret." If these are not the precise words used by Colonel McCormick's *Tribune* as it gave away secrets that could have cost untold numbers of American lives, the self-justifying spirit is exactly the same.

We do not know, in our battle with al Qaeda, whether we have reached a turning point like the battle of Midway (whose significance was also not fully evident at the time). Ongoing al-Qaeda strikes in the Middle East, Asia, and Europe suggest that the organization, though wounded, is still a coordinated and potent force. On January 19, after having disappeared from view for more than a year, Osama bin Laden surfaced to deliver one of his periodic threats to the American people, assuring us in an audio recording that further attacks on our homeland are "only a matter of time. They [operations] are in the planning stages, and you will see them in the heart of your land as soon as the planning is complete." Bin Laden may be bluffing; but woe betide the government that proceeds on any such assumption.

The 9/11 Commission, in seeking to explain how we fell victim to a surprise assault, pointed to the gap between our foreign and domestic intelligence-collection systems, a gap that over time had grown into a critical vulnerability. Closing that gap, in the wake of September 11, meant intercepting al-Qaeda communications all over the globe. This was the purpose of the NSA program—a program "essential to U.S. national security," in the words of Jane Harman, the ranking Democratic member of the House Intelligence Committee—the disclosure of which has now "damaged critical intelligence capabilities."

One might go further. What the *New York Times* has done is nothing less than to compromise the centerpiece of our defensive efforts in the war on terrorism. If information about the NSA program had been quietly conveyed to an al-Qaeda operative on a microdot, or on paper with invisible ink, there can be no doubt that the episode would have been treated by the government as a cut-and-dried case of espionage. Publishing it for the world to read, the *Times* has accomplished the same end while at the same time congratulating itself for bravely defending the First Amendment and thereby protecting us—from, presumably, ourselves. The fact that it chose to drop this revelation into print on the very day that renewal of the Patriot Act was being debated in the Senate—the bill's reauthorization beyond a few weeks is still not assured—speaks for itself.

The Justice Department has already initiated a criminal investigation into the leak of the NSA program, focusing on which government employees may have broken the law. But the government is contending with hundreds of national-security leaks, and progress is uncertain at best. The real question that an intrepid prosecutor in the Justice Department should be asking is whether, in the aftermath of September 11, we as a nation can afford to permit the reporters and editors of a great newspaper to become the unelected authority that determines for all of us what is a legitimate secret and what is not. Like the Constitution itself, the First Amendment's protections of freedom of the press are not a suicide pact. The laws governing what the *Times* has done are perfectly clear; will they be enforced?

NOTES

1. *State of War: The Secret History of the CIA and the Bush Administration.* Free Press, 240 pp., $26.00.

2. The non-partisan status of the Congressional Research Service has been called into question in this instance by the fact that the study's author, Alfred Cumming, donated $1,250 to John Kerry's presidential campaign, as was reported by the *Washington Times*.

3. What the U.S. government was doing, furthermore, differed little if at all from what it had done in the past in similar emergencies. "For as long as electronic communications have existed," as Attorney General Alberto Gonzalez has pointed out, "the United States has conducted surveillance of [enemy] communications during wartime—all without judicial warrant."

4. David Kahn concludes in *The Codebreakers* (1967) that in part, "the Japanese trusted too much to the reconditeness of their language for communications security, clinging to the myth that no foreigner could ever learn its multiple meanings well enough to understand it properly. In part they could not envision the possibility that their codes might be read."

5. In January 2001, a decade-and-a-half after his release, and following a campaign on his behalf by Senator Daniel Patrick Moynihan, Morison was granted a full pardon by President Bill Clinton on his final day in office.

6. If Franklin continues to cooperate with the authorities, his sentence will be reviewed and probably reduced after the trial of Rosen and Weissman.

7. According to Jon Friedman's online Media Web, the *Times*'s publisher, Arthur Sulzberger, Jr., also met with President Bush before the NSA story was published.

8. The Espionage Statutes and Publication of Defense Information," *Columbia Law Review*, Vol. 73., No. 5., May 1973.

9. If the Japanese were not paying close attention to American newspapers, the Germans were. Within days of Pearl Harbor, Hitler declared war on the United States, indirectly citing as a *casus belli* the American war plans revealed in the *Tribune*.

10. Whether Plame was in fact a secret agent—according to *USA Today*, she has worked at CIA headquarters in Langley, Virginia since 1997—remains an issue that is likely to be explored fully if the Libby case proceeds to trial.

*Gabriel Schoenfeld is a senior fellow at the Hudson Institute in Washington, D.C., and a resident scholar at the Witherspoon Institute in Princeton, New Jersey. He was senior editor at *Commentary* from 1994 to 2008 and holds a PhD in political science from Harvard University.

Schoenfeld, Gabriel. "Has the *New York Times* Violated the Espionage Act?" *Commentary* (March 2006).

Reprinted from COMMENTARY, March 2006, by permission; © 2006 by Commentary, Inc.

The Publication of National Security Information in the Digital Age

by Mary-Rose Papandrea*

In one of her speeches on Internet freedom, Secretary of State Hillary Rodham Clinton said that "[t]he fact that WikiLeaks used the internet is not the reason we criticized its actions."[1] Although Clinton is correct that it is essential to separate the technology WikiLeaks uses from its actions, the digital age has raised new concerns about the unauthorized dissemination of sensitive national security information. New technology has made it much easier to leak and otherwise disseminate national security information. At the same time, leaks continue to play an essential role in checking governmental power and often make invaluable contributions to our public debate. WikiLeaks has prompted renewed debate concerning when the disclosure of national security information by nongovernmental actors should be protected, both as a policy matter and as a matter of constitutional law.

One dominant theme in the discussion of how to strike the balance between an informed public and the need to protect legitimate national security secrets is whether new media entities like WikiLeaks are part of "the press" and whether Julian Assange and his cohorts are engaging in "journalism."[2] As the gathering and distribution of news and information becomes more widely dispersed, and the act of informing the public more participatory and collaborative, however, determining who is engaging in journalism and what constitutes the press has become increasingly difficult. It is not possible to draw lines based on the medium of communication, the journalistic background of the publisher, the editing process, the size of the audience, or the methods used to obtain the information.

Rather than attempt to define who is a journalist or what is the press, Congress and courts should give careful consideration to the relevant scienter requirements that would apply in cases involving nongovernmental actors. In such cases, the relevant laws should require that the offender acted with a subjective intent to harm the United States or with reckless indifference to any such harm. Such a test provides a means of protecting those who disseminate national security information responsibly and with a good-faith purpose to inform the public debate. This intent requirement would be in addition to proof of imminent and serious harm to U.S. interests.[3]

1. The Importance of Leaks

Throughout our nation's history, democratic principles of open government have often clashed with the asserted need for secrecy in diplomatic and military affairs. The executive branch enjoys virtually unbridled authority to control the flow of national security information to the public. The primary means by which the executive branch exercises this power is the classification system.[4] The Freedom of Information Act (FOIA)[5] and whistleblower protection laws[6] are ineffective checks on this power. FOIA provides a cumbersome and limited mechanism for obtaining national security information.[7] Whistleblower protection laws can be confusing, and they provide minimal protection to employees who reveal national security information.[8] Although it might be possible to provide better statutory checks on executive classification authority, it is doubtful that any statutory fix could resolve the endemic problem of overclassification.[9]

As a result of the tension between the executive branch's asserted need for secrecy and the democratic requirements of openness and transparency, the government and the media have engaged in a game of leaks. Although the media is often criticized for publishing national security information, its access to information frequently is the result of a planned strategy by a government official to advance or promote a particular policy, sabotage the plans or policies of rival agencies or political parties, discredit opponents, float a public opinion trial balloon, or expose corruption or illegal activities. Indeed, leaks have been part of this nation's history since its founding and are an important way in which government officials promote their agendas and attempt to persuade the public.[10] As the saying goes, the ship of state is the only known vessel that leaks from the top. Thus, it is important to keep in mind that the executive branch does not want to end all leaks; it simply wants to end the leaks that it does not like.[11] This is not to deny that some leaks come from self-styled patriots or disgruntled employees. Regardless of the motivation of the leaker, however, these leaks also can make valuable contributions to the public debate.

Leaks have played a key role in exposing illegal or morally reprehensible government practices, such as the treatment of prisoners in Abu Ghraib, extraordinary rendition, and the NSA warrantless wiretapping program. Relying on leaks is hardly a perfect way of making sure the public receives essential information or of checking excessive government power; it does not guarantee that improperly classified information will come to light, or that genuinely sensitive information will remain secret.[12] Nevertheless, this imperfect system is the best we have for checking the virtually unbridled power of the government to control the dissemination of national security information.

For at least the last century, it has generally been mainstream media out-lets—especially the nation's leading newspapers—that have published sensitive national security information. For the most part, these entities have been both cooperative and responsible in their publication decisions. They routinely ask the government for guidance on the ramifications of the national security in-formation in their possession and frequently have withheld stories or limited their scope in order to soften their impact. For example, at President Kennedy's request, *The New York Times* agreed to delay publishing a story about nuclear weapons in Cuba.[13] During the Iran hostage crisis, the press withheld stories that might have harmed the hostages or undermined secret negotiations for their release.[14] In 1986, *The Washington Post* acceded to the White House's re-quest to refrain from publishing information about an underwater spy project in Russian waters called "Ivy Bells."[15] Famed journalist Benjamin Bradlee has said that while he was editor at the *Post*, he "kept many stories out of the paper because I felt—without any government pressure—that the national security would be harmed by their publication."[16] More recently, the *Times* sat on its NSA wiretapping story for a year while government officials argued for the ne-cessity of keeping the program secret.[17] Similarly, when the *Post* published an article revealing the existence of "black sites," where terrorist suspects were se-cretly detained and interrogated[18] it agreed to the government's request to with-hold the names of the Eastern European countries that were participating in the program. To be sure, the government has not always agreed with the publication decisions of the mainstream media. But newspapers and other news outlets in possession of national security information have generally made a serious effort to take the administration's concerns seriously, and there is little evidence that any of their publication decisions have actually caused the United States seri-ous harm.

For decades this country has lived in a state of "benign indeterminancy" re-garding the constitutionality of prosecutions for the receipt and dissemination of national security information.[19] On the one hand, this state of affairs has served us well. Major media outlets generally have been responsible in exer-cising a "gate-keeping" function, disseminating sensitive national security in-formation only when the benefits of that dissemination outweigh the harm. If anything, there has been more concern that the established press has not been as willing as new media to challenge government orthodoxy.[20] On the other hand, we cannot assume that all journalists—whether professional or belonging to the new "citizen media" class—will continue to act responsibly.

II. NEW CHALLENGES

The evolution of the Internet and the dispersal of the newsgathering and dissemination functions traditionally exercised by major media outlets have the potential to undermine this system of leaks that has been working rather well since the development of mass media over a century ago.

Prior to the Internet, those in possession of national security information who wanted to reveal it to the public had to go through a traditional media outlet to accomplish that goal. Thus, when Daniel Ellsberg was in possession of the Pentagon Papers, he went to several major newspapers as well as the three major television networks in an effort to find an outlet.[21] Today's leakers can deposit a treasure trove of information on any number of websites around the world designed to receive confidential information. Admittedly, Julian Assange of WikiLeaks cooperated with some of the world's most influential newspapers in order to assure that the information he had collected would be noticed. Nevertheless, the government has good reason to be concerned that its enemies will not limit their reading to *The New York Times* and *The Washington Post* and instead will be searching the Internet for valuable information. The Internet makes it easy to search vast databases with little effort.

The government has never prosecuted the press for publishing national security information and has instead traditionally pursued the government employees or contractors who leaked the information in the first place.[22] Although the government has arrested Bradley Manning, the person identified as primarily responsible for the leak of U.S. classified information to WikiLeaks, it may not be so easy to identify leakers in the future. Technology has developed to make it possible for individuals to exchange information anonymously, making it impossible for the government to subpoena the identity of leakers from the website that received the information. Technology has given rise to the development of intermediaries like WikiLeaks that can serve as a conduit of information between the original sources and the public. As Jay Rosen has noted, sources no longer have to meet a reporter in a dark parking garage.[23]

Although new technology threatens the old way of doing things, we have to keep in mind that the traditional media outlets do not have a monopoly on the ability to inform the public in a responsible way. Nonprofessional journalists have provided valuable information to the public debate that the mainstream media either missed or ignored.[24] WikiLeaks itself has uncovered valuable information about human rights abuses and other atrocities in countries around the globe; in fact, in 2009, WikiLeaks won an award from Amnesty International for its release of documents concerning the extra-judicial killings and disappearances in Kenya.[25] Rather than condemning non-traditional media websites, we need to begin to recognize that new technology allows non-professionals to play an important role in informing the public.

One common justification for distinguishing WikiLeaks from the traditional media is that it does not engage in the traditional journalistic practice of carefully analyzing and giving context to the material that it publishes.[26] As a factual matter, it is inaccurate to argue that WikiLeaks does not engage in any editorial practices. Although initially WikiLeaks did not filter the electronic files it obtained, it no longer simply publishes every bit of information it receives.[27] In addition, it has sought government guidance on what names and identifying information it should redact from its materials in order to avoid a significant risk of harm to individuals.[28] Furthermore, regardless of how WikiLeaks itself operates, it certainly is not the case that every website would function in the same way. WikiLeaks was not the first website committed to transparency, and it is almost certainly not the last.[29]

It is also true that the traditional media is capable of making irresponsible publication decisions and publishing national security information without due care and consideration. Indeed, during the debates leading to the passage of the Espionage Act of 1917, Congress was concerned about "disloyal papers" that had loyalties to Germany or other enemies.[30] In 1973, long before the Internet was developed, Harold Edgar and Benno Schmidt noted in their seminal article on the Espionage Act that "some underground newspaper stands ready to publish anything that the Times deems too sensitive to reveal."[31] Outrage over the publication of the identities of American operatives in books and magazines prompted the passage of the Intelligence Identities Protection Act of 1982.[32] In other words, concerns about publications with bad motives existed long before WikiLeaks came on the scene; these concerns do not depend on the medium of communication or whether "professional" journalists are the ones making the publication decisions.

Another common argument for distinguishing WikiLeaks from the traditional media is that WikiLeaks stole its information, or solicited or encouraged sources to leak sensitive information. In her speech on Internet freedom, Secretary of State Clinton maintained that "the WikiLeaks incident began with a theft, just as if it had been executed by smuggling papers in a briefcase."[33] The problem is that there is no evidence that WikiLeaks stole any documents. Vice President Joseph Biden similarly argued that there was a difference between WikiLeaks' solicitation of classified information and the manner in which the traditional press acquires its information.[34] This distinction does not hold up, especially given the absence of any public evidence that WikiLeaks or Julian Assange actively solicited classified information. Indeed, it appears that *The New York Times*, taking a page from WikiLeaks' playbook, is considering establishing a virtual "drop box" where members of the public could deposit documents anonymously.[35] Several other organizations have already established portals for leaked information, including *The Wall Street Journal*[36] and *Al Jazeera*.[37]

The publication of national security secrets in a newspaper, magazine, or website may be as damaging to our national security interests as the transfer of secrets in the traditional espionage setting.[38] We must assume that our enemies consume our public media just as we do theirs; given this, publication of a national security secret in a newspaper might cause even more harm because the whole world potentially can learn about it. Nevertheless, Congress has traditionally been concerned with the dilemma of protecting legitimate national security secrets without undermining the sort of public debate that is essential in a democracy. Thus, when it was debating legislation that would become the Espionage Act of 1917, Congress rejected President Wilson's proposal for broad authority to punish the publication of national defense information.[39] The legislative history of the Espionage Act of 1917 "is replete with concern that these criminal statutes make use of appropriate standards of culpability to distinguish the morally innocent from the guilty."[40]

Congress has repeatedly recognized the importance of protecting legitimate criticism and examination of government actions every time it has amended the Espionage Act and related statutes.[41] Although recognizing the need to protect national security secrets, Congress has been concerned about passing laws that would unduly restrict the media's well-intentioned disclosures.[42] Thus, for example, in the debates surrounding the passage of the Intelligence Identities Protection Act of 1982, Congress repeatedly expressed concerns that any prohibitions on the disclosure of the identities of American agents should not cover academic studies of government programs and policies, or news media reporting of intelligence failures.[43] Recognizing that even the disclosure of an agent's identity could be valuable, Congress provided that such disclosures are not actionable unless made with "reason to believe" that the disclosure would harm the United States, and that the disclosures were part of a "pattern or practice" of disclosure.[44]

Although Congress has historically appeared interested in protecting the freedom of the press and limiting executive power to control the debate on national security and military affairs, the plain language of the Espionage Act points a "loaded gun" at those who report on such topics.[45] For example, Section

793(e) prohibits the dissemination or retention of national security information by those in "unauthorized possession" of it, and the only applicable *mens rea* requirement in cases involving tangible materials is that the dissemination or retention be "willful."[46] With respect to the dissemination or retention of nontangible "information pertaining to the national defense," the government must prove that the offender has "reason to believe [the information] could be used to the injury of the United States or advantage a foreign nation."[47] Exactly what this provision requires is unclear. Some lower courts have held that the government must show that the offender had a "bad faith purpose either to harm the United States or aid a foreign government,"[48] but this construction is difficult to derive from the actual statutory language and arises from concerns that the phrase "national security information" would be unconstitutionally vague without it.

III. Suggestions for Reform

Given that national security leaks play an important role in our democracy, Congress is faced with the difficult task of deciding under what circumstances the disclosure of national security information should be protected. The foregoing section illustrated the difficulties of line-drawing based on the medium of communication, the journalistic background of the publisher, or complicity in the leak itself. Instead of drawing lines on any of these bases, Congress should consider authorizing criminal sanctions against nongovernmental actors only in cases where the disclosure is made with an intent to harm the United States or with reckless indifference to any harm the disclosure would have.

At the outset, Congress must make a clear distinction between government employees (and contractors) and those who do not have a position of trust and confidentiality with the government. Very different policy considerations—as well as weaker First Amendment protections—apply in cases where individuals have obtained national security information as a result of a trusted relationship. It may well be that even in such cases there should be protection for the disclosure of information that has been improperly classified, or for the exposure of illegal or fraudulent activity.[49] In addition, it is appropriate to distinguish between the traditional espionage setting, where a government employee exposes secrets to a foreign power, and other circumstances in which the employee acts with the purpose of revealing information to the general public.[50]

Very different considerations come into play when deciding whether to criminalize the disclosure of national security information by third parties who did not obtain national security information as a result of a trusted relationship with the government. Although the legal landscape is unclear, the First Amendment arguably provides protection for the dissemination of any information that does not threaten grave, direct, and unavoidable harm to the United States.[51]

First, Congress should consider amending the Espionage Act to make clear what kind of information is covered by its provisions. Currently some of the Act's provisions apply to "information relating to the national defense." This category is vague and encompasses a potentially limitless universe of information. Instead, with respect to third parties who obtain unauthorized access to information, Congress should be specific about what information is subject to criminal sanctions. This has been the approach Congress has taken in more recent legislation, such as the Intelligence Identities Protection Act of 1982, which prohibits the identification of covert agents.[52]

Second, once Congress has identified specific topics that are especially sensitive, it should include rigorous culpability requirements. Determining the requisite level of intent is essential in drafting any criminal statute. In the criminal law context, the very same conduct may face dramatically different sanctions depending upon the intent of the actor. The same is true in the context of prosecutions based on the dissemination of national security information. The Espionage Act and related statutes contain a hodge-podge of intent standards that are hard to understand and difficult to apply.

The dissemination of information by nongovernment actors should be punishable only if the offender acted with the intent to harm the United States or with reckless indifference to such harm. This sort of intent standard would provide protection for all responsible publishers acting in good faith, no matter who they are or what medium they use for communication. Such a standard is similar to the "actual malice" standard the Supreme Court adopted in *New York Times Co. v. Sullivan*.[53] There, the Court held that given "a profound national commitment to the principle that debate on public issues should be uninhibited, robust, and wide-open,"[54] strict liability for the publication of false defamatory information about public officials would have a severe chilling effect on the press, which would be sure to make only statements that "steer far wider of the unlawful zone."[55] While recognizing that false defamatory speech can cause real harm to reputation, the Court determined that a public official can recover only if he demonstrates that the defendant published "with knowledge that [the speech] was false or with reckless disregard of whether it was false or not."[56] Just as the damage to our national security interests is the same regardless of the intent of the disseminator, the damage to a public official's reputation occurs regardless of the motivation of a defendant in a defamation action. Nevertheless, an intent requirement in both circumstances serves as an important way of promoting vigorous public debate while preserving the government's ability to act in the most egregious situations.

To be clear, this intent requirement does not turn on the motivation for disclosure. Even the most esteemed newspapers are driven in part by profit-seeking motives to increase circulation, just as some government employees engaged in traditional espionage do it for the money, not to harm the United States. Of course these sorts of pecuniary motivations might make it more difficult for a defendant to demonstrate that he was not recklessly indifferent to the harm the disclosure might cause, but they do not by themselves constitute intent to harm the United States or to aid our enemies.

Furthermore, the inclusion of a robust scienter requirement should not replace other important necessary elements. Proof of imminent and serious harm to U.S. interests must be demonstrated in addition to subjective intent to harm the United States. As Geoffrey Stone has persuasively argued, it would be inconsistent with the First Amendment to permit nongovernmental actors to be punished for the dissemination of national security information that does not in fact threaten imminent and serious harm.[57]

Conclusion

When considering whether and how to amend the Espionage Act and related statutes, Congress must keep in mind the important role that the press has played in our democracy throughout its history. In order to protect this vital function, it will be necessary at times to permit the publication of sensitive national security information that causes real harm. What is not necessary, however, is to protect the publication of such information if it is done with the intent to harm the United States—or aid its enemies—or with reckless disregard to any harm the publication will cause. To be sure, an intent requirement will not give the government the sort of control it might like over the information that is disseminated in the media, professional or otherwise. It is true that a stringent intent requirement would permit the press to publish information that might be useful to our enemies. But, as Congress has noted in its prior debates, this is the price we must pay in order to protect free debate. This approach places the burden squarely on the government to work harder to prevent and isolate leaks of national security information for which secrecy is essential.

Notes

1. Hillary Rodham Clinton, U.S. Sec'y of State, Internet Rights and Wrongs: Choices and Challenges in a Networked World, Address at George Washington University (Feb. 15, 2011), *available at* http://www.state.gov/secretary/rm/2011/02/156619.htm.

2. *See* Jonathan Peters, *WikiLeaks, the First Amendment, and the Press*, HARVARD LAW AND POLICY REVIEW, Apr. 18, 2011, *available at* http://hlpronline.com/2011/04/wikileaks-the-first-amendment-and-the-press/. For a thorough summary of the government's and mainstream media's disdain for WikiLeaks and Julian Assange, see Yochai Benckler, *A Free Irresponsible Press: WikiLeaks and the Battle Over the Soul of the Networked Fourth Estate*, HARV. C.R.-C.L. L. REV. (forthcoming 2011), *available at* http://www.benkler.org/Benkler_Wikileaks_current.pdf.

3. *See* Geoffrey R. Stone, *WikiLeaks, the Proposed SHIELD Act, and the First Amendment*, 5 J. NAT'L SECURITY L. & POL'Y 105 (2011).

4. For an excellent overview of the classification system and the problem of overclassification, see Heidi Kitrosser, *Classified Information Leaks and Free Speech*, U. ILL. L. REV. 881, 888–896 (2008).

5. 5 U.S.C. §552 (2006), *amended by* OPEN Government Act of 2007, Pub. L. No. 110-175, 121 Stat. 2524.

6. Intelligence Community Whistleblower Protection Act of 1998, Pub. L. No. 105-272, 112 Stat. 2413 (codified as amended at 50 U.S.C. §403(q) (2006)); Whistleblower Protection Act of 1989, Pub. L. No. 101-12, 103 Stat. 16 (codified as amended at 5 U.S.C. § 2302 (2006)); Military Whistleblower Protection Act of 1988, Pub. L. No. 100-456, 102 Stat. 2027 (codified as amended at 10 U.S.C. §1034 (2006)).

7. Kitrosser, *supra* note 4, at 894.

8. *See* Mary-Rose Papandrea, *Lapdogs, Watchdogs, and Scapegoats: The Press and National Security Information*, 83 INDIANA L. J. 233, 246–248 (2008).

9. Kitrosser, *supra* note 4, at 896.

10. For a thorough discussion of the history of intentional, strategic leaks, see Papandrea, *supra* note 8, at 249–262.

11. *See* Tom Wicker, *Leak On, O Ship of State!*, N.Y. TIMES, Jan. 26, 1982, at A15; *see also* LEON V. SIGAL, REPORTERS AND OFFICIALS: THE ORGANIZATION AND POLITICS OF NEWSMAKING 145 (1973) (quoting aide to President Johnson as saying that "the people at 1600 Pennsylvania Avenue are not really worried about all leaks—only those that originate outside the White House").

12. *See* Louis Henkin, *The Right To Know and the Duty To Withhold: The Case of the Pentagon Papers*, 120 U. PA. L. REV. 271, 278 (1971).

13. MAX FRANKEL, HIGH NOON IN THE COLD WAR: KENNEDY, KHRUSHCHEV, AND THE CUBAN MISSILE CRISIS 108–110 (2004).

14. DEBORAH HOLMES, GOVERNING THE PRESS: MEDIA FREEDOM IN THE U.S. AND GREAT BRITAIN 61–62 (1986).

15. Richard Zoglin, *Questions of National Security*, TIME, June 2, 1986, at 67.

16. BENJAMIN BRADLEE, A GOOD LIFE: NEWSPAPERING AND OTHER ADVENTURES 474 (1995).

17. James Risen & Eric Lichtblau, *Bush Lets U.S. Spy on Callers Without Courts*, N.Y. TIMES, Dec. 16, 2005, at A1.

18. Dana Priest, *CIA Holds Terror Suspects in Secret Prisons*, WASH. POST, Nov. 2, 2005, at A1.

19. Harold Edgar & Benno C. Schmidt, Jr., *The Espionage Act and Publication of Defense Information*, 73 COLUM. L. REV. 929, 936 (1973). *See also* William H. Freivogel, *Publishing National Security Secrets: The Case for Benign Indeterminacy*, 3 J. NAT'L SECURITY L. & POL'Y 95 (2010).

20. For a lengthier discussion of the failures of the mainstream media in recent years, see Mary-Rose Papandrea, *Citizen Journalism and the Reporter's Privilege*, 91 MINN. L. REV. 515, 524–528 (2007).

21. DAVID RUDENSTINE, THE DAY THE PRESSES STOPPED: THE STORY OF THE PENTAGON PAPERS CASE 127, 248 (1998). Unlike the major newspapers, the networks were unwilling to publish the Pentagon Papers because they feared retaliation from the Federal Communications Commission. *Id.* at 127.

22. *See* Scott Shane, *Obama Takes a Hard Line Against Leaks to Press*, N.Y. TIMES, June 12, 2010, at A1, *available at* nytimes.com/2010/06/12/us/politics/12leak.html. From time to time the government has also subpoenaed reporters to obtain the identity of individuals who leaked classified information. *See, e.g.*, Adam Liptak & Maria Newman, *New York Times Reporter Jailed for Keeping Source Secret*, N.Y. TIMES, July 6, 2005 (describing subpoenas for identities of confidential sources to reporters Matt Cooper and Judith Miller,

and Miller's being jailed for contempt of court for her refusal to comply), *available at* https://www.nytimes.com/2005/07/06/politics/06cnd-leak.html?_r=1&pagewanted=2.

23. Jay Rosen, *Jay Rosen on WikiLeaks: "The Watchdog Press Died; We Have This Instead,"* VIMEO, Dec. 2, 2010, http://vimeo.com/17393373?utm_source=www.twitter.com%2Fstkonrath&utm_medium=twitter&utm_campaign=future-of-journalism.

24. *See* Papandrea, *supra* note 20, at 524–528 (summarizing some of the contributions of bloggers and other online media outlets to the public discourse).

25. *See* Amnesty International, *Amnesty International Media Awards 2009: Winners and Shortlist* (2009), http://www.amnesty.org.uk/uploads/documents/doc_20539.pdf.

26. *See, e.g.,* David Rivkin & Bruce Brown, *Prosecute Assange with Espionage Act,* USA TODAY, Dec. 14, 2010, *available at* http://www.usatoday.com/news/opinion/forum/2010-12-15-column15_ST1_N.htm.

27. For a summary of the evolving modus operandi of WikiLeaks, see Yochai Benckler, *supra* note 2, at 4–14.

28. Letter from Julian Assange to U.S. Ambassador Louis B. Susman (Nov. 26, 2010), *available at* http://www.foreignpolicy.com/files/fp_uploaded_documents/101129_plugin-Letter-to-US-Ambassador-from-Julian-Assange-26-November-2010.pdf. State Department Legal Advisor Harold Koh wrote a stern letter to WikiLeaks flatly refusing to have any discussions about the sensitive material WikiLeaks possessed and demanding the immediate return of all documents that it possessed. Letter from Harold Hongju Koh to Jennifer Robinson, Attorney for Julian Assange (Nov. 27, 2010), *available at* http://media.washingtonpost.com/wp-srv/politics/documents/Dept_of_State_Assange_letter.pdf.

29. Cryptome was a predecessor to WikiLeaks. *See* Andrew Orlowski, *WikiLeaks Are For-Hire Mercenaries—Cryptome,* REGISTER, Dec. 7, 2010, http://www.theregister.co.uk/2010/12/07/cryptome_on_wikileaks/. GreenLeaks.com, GreenLeaks.org, and OpenLeaks.org are considered by some to be successors to WikiLeaks. *See* Mark Hosenball, *Exclusive: The Next Generation of WikiLeaks,* REUTERS, Jan. 28, 2011, http://www.reuters.com/article/2011/01/28/us-wikileaks-idUSTRE70R5A120110128.

30. *See* Edgar & Schmidt, *supra* note 19, at 965–966.

31. *Id.* at 1077.

32. 50 U.S.C. §§421–426 (2006).

33. Clinton, *supra* note 1.

34. Interview by David Gregory, host of Meet the Press, with Vice President Joseph Biden, NBC NEWS (Dec. 19, 2010), *available at* http://www.msnbc.msn.com/id/40720643/ns/meet_the_press-transcripts/ns/meet_the_press-transcripts.

35. Michael Calderone, *NY Times Considers Creating an "EZ Pass Lane for Leakers,"* YAHOO! NEWS, Jan. 25, 2011, http://news.yahoo.com/s/yblog_thecutline/20110125/ts_yblog_thecutline/ny-times-considers-creating-an-ez-pass-lane-for-leakers.

36. *See* SafeHouse, https://www.wsjsafehouse.com/.

37. *See About the Transparency Unit,* http://transparency.aljazeera.net/.

38. Edgar & Schmidt, *supra* note 19, at 934.

39. *Id.* at 940–941.

40. *Id.* at 1039.

41. *Id.* at 937 (noting that the Act's "legislative debates, amendments and conferences . . . may fairly be read as excluding criminal sanctions for well-meaning publication of information no matter what damage to the national security might ensue and regardless of whether the publisher knew its publication would be damaging").

42. *Id.* at 939.

43. Jerry J. Berman & Morton H. Halperin, *The Agents Identities Protection Act: A Preliminary Analysis of the Legislative History,* in FIRST AMENDMENT AND NATIONAL SECURITY 41, 51–52 (Paul Stephen ed., 1984).

44. *Id.* at 51–52.

45. Edgar & Schmidt, *supra* note 19, at 936.

46. 18 U.S.C. §793(e) (2006).

47. *Id.*

48. *See, e.g.*, United States v. Rosen, 445 F. Supp. 2d 602, 626 (E.D. Va. 2006).

49. *See* Geoffrey R. Stone, *Government Secrecy v. Freedom of the Press*, 1 Harv. L. & Pol. Rev. 185, 196 (2007).

50. The leading case involving a government employee who disclosed classified information to the press is *United States v. Morison*, in which the court rejected the defendant's argument that the Espionage Act is limited to the classic spying scenario but noted that the Act does permit heavier penalties for traditional espionage. *See* 844 F.2d 1057, 1065 (4th Cir. 1988).

51. *See* Stone, *supra* note 49, at 202.

52. 50 U.S.C. §§421–426 (2006).

53. 376 U.S. 254 (1964).

54. *Id.* at 270.

55. *Id.* at 279.

56. *Id.* at 279–280.

57. *See* Stone, *supra* note 3, at 114–115.

*Mary-Rose Papandrea is a professor at Boston College Law School.

Papandrea, Mary-Rose. "Publication of National Security Information in the Digital Age." *Journal of National Security Law and Policy* 5, no. 1 (2011): 119–130. This article is also available at jnslp.com.

Used by permission.

The Secret Sharer

*by Jane Mayer**

IS THOMAS DRAKE AN ENEMY OF THE STATE?

On June 13th, a fifty-four-year-old former government employee named Thomas Drake is scheduled to appear in a courtroom in Baltimore, where he will face some of the gravest charges that can be brought against an American citizen. A former senior executive at the National Security Agency, the government's electronic-espionage service, he is accused, in essence, of being an enemy of the state. According to a ten-count indictment delivered against him in April, 2010, Drake violated the Espionage Act—the 1917 statute that was used to convict Aldrich Ames, the C.I.A. officer who, in the eighties and nineties, sold U.S. intelligence to the K.G.B., enabling the Kremlin to assassinate informants. In 2007, the indictment says, Drake willfully retained top-secret defense documents that he had sworn an oath to protect, sneaking them out of the intelligence agency's headquarters, at Fort Meade, Maryland, and taking them home, for the purpose of "unauthorized disclosure." The aim of this scheme, the indictment says, was to leak government secrets to an unnamed newspaper reporter, who is identifiable as Siobhan Gorman, of the *Baltimore Sun*. Gorman wrote a prize-winning series of articles for the *Sun* about financial waste, bureaucratic dysfunction, and dubious legal practices in N.S.A. counterterrorism programs. Drake is also charged with obstructing justice and lying to federal law-enforcement agents. If he is convicted on all counts, he could receive a prison term of thirty-five years.

The government argues that Drake recklessly endangered the lives of American servicemen. "This is not an issue of benign documents," William M. Welch II, the senior litigation counsel who is prosecuting the case, argued at a hearing in March, 2010. The N.S.A., he went on, collects "intelligence for the soldier in the field. So when individuals go out and they harm that ability, our intelligence goes dark and our soldier in the field gets harmed."

Top officials at the Justice Department describe such leak prosecutions as almost obligatory. Lanny Breuer, the Assistant Attorney General who supervises the department's criminal division, told me, "You don't get to break the law and disclose classified information just because you want to." He added, "Politics should play no role in it whatsoever."

When President Barack Obama took office, in 2009, he championed the cause of government transparency, and spoke admiringly of whistle-blowers, whom he described as "often the best source of information about waste, fraud, and abuse in government." But the Obama Administration has pursued leak prosecutions with a surprising relentlessness. Including the Drake case, it has been using the Espionage Act to press criminal charges in five alleged instances of national-security leaks—more such prosecutions than have occurred in all previous Administrations combined. The Drake case is one of two that Obama's Justice Department has carried over from the Bush years.

Gabriel Schoenfeld, a conservative political scientist at the Hudson Institute, who, in his book "Necessary Secrets" (2010), argues for more stringent protection of classified information, says, "Ironically, Obama has presided over the most draconian crackdown on leaks in our history—even more so than Nixon."

One afternoon in January, Drake met with me, giving his first public interview about this case. He is tall, with thinning sandy hair framing a domed forehead, and he has the erect bearing of a member of the Air Force, where he served before joining the N.S.A., in 2001. Obsessive, dramatic, and emotional, he has an unwavering belief in his own rectitude. Sitting at a Formica table at the Tastee Diner, in Bethesda, Drake—who is a registered Republican—groaned and thrust his head into his hands. "I actually had hopes for Obama," he said. He had not only expected the President to roll back the prosecutions launched by the Bush Administration; he had thought that Bush Administration officials would be investigated for overstepping the law in the "war on terror."

"But power is incredibly destructive," Drake said. "It's a weird, pathological thing. I also think the intelligence community coopted Obama, because he's rather naive about national security. He's accepted the fear and secrecy. We're in a scary space in this country."

The Justice Department's indictment narrows the frame around Drake's actions, focussing almost exclusively on his handling of what it claims are five classified documents. But Drake sees his story as a larger tale of political reprisal, one that he fears the government will never allow him to air fully in court. "I'm a target," he said. "I've got a bull's-eye on my back." He continued, "I did not tell secrets. I am facing prison for having raised an alarm, period. I went to a reporter with a few key things: fraud, waste, and abuse, and the fact that there were legal alternatives to the Bush Administration's 'dark side'"—in particular, warrantless domestic spying by the N.S.A.

The indictment portrays him not as a hero but as a treacherous man who violated "the government trust." Drake said of the prosecutors, "They can say what they want. But the F.B.I. can find something on anyone."

Steven Aftergood, the director of the Project on Government Secrecy at the Federation of American Scientists, says of the Drake case, "The government wants this to be about unlawfully retained information. The defense, meanwhile, is painting a picture of a public-interested whistle-blower who struggled to bring attention to what he saw as multibillion-dollar mismanagement." Because Drake is not a spy, Aftergood says, the case will "test whether intelligence officers can be convicted of violating the Espionage Act even if their intent is pure." He believes that the trial may also test whether the nation's expanding secret intelligence bureaucracy is beyond meaningful accountability. "It's a much larger debate than whether a piece of paper was at a certain place at a certain time," he says.

Jack Balkin, a liberal law professor at Yale, agrees that the increase in leak prosecutions is part of a larger transformation. "We are witnessing the bipartisan normalization and legitimization of a national-surveillance state," he says. In his view, zealous leak prosecutions are consonant with other political shifts since 9/11: the emergence of a vast new security bureaucracy, in which at least two and a half million people hold confidential, secret, or top-secret clearances; huge expenditures on electronic monitoring, along with a reinterpretation of the law in order to sanction it; and corporate partnerships with the government that have transformed the counterterrorism industry into a powerful lobbying force. Obama, Balkin says, has "systematically adopted policies consistent with the second term of the Bush Administration."

On March 28th, Obama held a meeting in the White House with five advocates for greater transparency in government. During the discussion, the President drew a sharp distinction between whistle-blowers who exclusively reveal wrongdoing and those who jeopardize national security. The importance of maintaining secrecy about the impending raid on Osama bin Laden's compound was likely on Obama's mind. The White House has been particularly bedevilled by the ongoing release of classified documents by WikiLeaks, the group led by Julian Assange. Last year, WikiLeaks began releasing a vast trove of sensitive government documents allegedly leaked by a U.S. soldier, Bradley Manning; the documents included references to a courier for bin Laden who had moved his family to Abbottabad—the town where bin Laden was hiding out. Manning has been charged with "aiding the enemy."

Danielle Brian, the executive director of the Project on Government Oversight, attended the meeting, and said that Obama's tone was generally supportive of transparency. But when the subject of national-security leaks came up, Brian said, "the President shifted in his seat and leaned forward. He said this may be where we have some differences. He said he doesn't want to protect the people who leak to the media war plans that could impact the troops." Though Brian was impressed with Obama's over-all stance on transparency, she felt that he might be misinformed about some of the current leak cases. She warned Obama that prosecuting whistle-blowers would undermine his legacy. Brian had been told by the White House to avoid any "ask"s on specific issues, but she told the President that, according to his own logic, Drake was exactly the kind of whistle-blower who deserved protection.

As Drake tells it, his problems began on September 11, 2001. "The next seven weeks were crucial," he said. "It's foundational to why I am a criminal defendant today."

The morning that Al Qaeda attacked the U.S. was, coincidentally, Drake's first full day of work as a civilian employee at the N.S.A.—an agency that James Bamford, the author of "The Shadow Factory" (2008), calls "the largest, most costly, and most technologically sophisticated spy organization the world has ever known." Drake, a linguist and a computer expert with a background in military crypto-electronics, had worked for twelve years as an outside contractor at the N.S.A. Under a program code-named Jackpot, he focussed on finding and fixing weaknesses in the agency's software programs. But, after going through interviews and background checks, he began working full time for Maureen Baginski, the chief of the Signals Intelligence Directorate at the N.S.A., and the agency's third-highest-ranking official.

Even in an age in which computerized feats are commonplace, the N.S.A.'s capabilities are breathtaking. The agency reportedly has the capacity to intercept and download, every six hours, electronic communications equivalent to the contents of the Library of Congress. Three times the size of the C.I.A., and with a third of the U.S.'s entire intelligence budget, the N.S.A. has a five-thousand-acre campus at Fort Meade protected by iris scanners and facial-recognition devices. The electric bill there is said to surpass seventy million dollars a year.

Nevertheless, when Drake took up his post the agency was undergoing an identity crisis. With the Cold War over, the agency's mission was no longer clear. As Drake puts it, "Without the Soviet Union, it didn't know what to do." Moreover, its technology had failed to keep pace with the shift in communications to cellular phones, fibre-optic cable, and the Internet. Two assessments commissioned by General Michael Hayden, who took over the agency in 1999, had drawn devastating conclusions. One described the N.S.A. as "an agency mired in bureaucratic conflict" and "suffering from poor leadership." In January, 2000, the agency's computer system crashed for three and a half days, causing a virtual intelligence blackout.

Agency leaders decided to "stir up the gene pool," Drake says. Although his hiring was meant to signal fresh thinking, he was given a clumsy bureaucratic title: Senior Change Leader/Chief, Change Leadership & Communications Office, Signals Intelligence Directorate.

The 9/11 attacks caught the U.S.'s national-security apparatus by surprise. N.S.A. officials were humiliated to learn that the Al Qaeda hijackers had spent their final days, undetected, in a motel in Laurel, Maryland—a few miles outside the N.S.A.'s fortified gates. They had bought a folding knife at a Target on Fort Meade Road. Only after the attacks did agency officials notice that, on September 10th, their surveillance systems had intercepted conversations in Afghanistan and Saudi Arabia warning that "the match begins tomorrow" and "tomorrow is Zero Hour."

Drake, hoping to help fight back against Al Qaeda, immediately thought of a tantalizing secret project he had come across while working on Jackpot. Code-named ThinThread, it had been developed by technological wizards in a kind of Skunk Works on the N.S.A. campus. Formally, the project was supervised by the agency's Signals Intelligence Automation Research Center, or SARC.

While most of the N.S.A. was reeling on September 11th, inside SARC the horror unfolded "almost like an 'I-told-you-so' moment," according to J. Kirk Wiebe, an intelligence analyst who worked there. "We knew we weren't keeping up." SARC was led by a crypto-mathematician named Bill Binney, whom Wiebe describes as "one of the best analysts in history." Binney and a team of some twenty others believed that they had pinpointed the N.S.A.'s biggest problem—data overload—and then solved it. But the agency's management hadn't agreed.

Binney, who is six feet three, is a bespectacled sixty-seven-year-old man with wisps of dark hair; he has the quiet, tense air of a preoccupied intellectual. Now retired and suffering gravely from diabetes, which has already claimed his left leg, he agreed recently to speak publicly for the first time about the Drake case. When we met, at a restaurant near N.S.A. headquarters, he leaned crutches against an extra chair. "This is too serious not to talk about," he said.

Binney expressed terrible remorse over the way some of his algorithms were used after 9/11. ThinThread, the "little program" that he invented to track enemies outside the U.S., "got twisted," and was used for both foreign and domestic spying: "I should apologize to the American people. It's violated everyone's rights. It can be used to eavesdrop on the whole world." According to Binney, Drake took his side against the N.S.A.'s management and, as a result, became a political target within the agency.

Binney spent most of his career at the agency. In 1997, he became the technical director of the World Geopolitical and Military Analysis Reporting Group, a division of six thousand employees which focusses on analyzing signals intelligence. By the late nineties, the N.S.A. had become overwhelmed by the amount of digital data it was collecting. Binney and his team began developing codes aimed at streamlining the process, allowing the agency to isolate useful intelligence. This was the beginning of ThinThread.

In the late nineties, Binney estimated that there were some two and a half billion phones in the world and one and a half billion I.P. addresses. Approximately twenty terabytes of unique information passed around the world every minute. Binney started assembling a system that could trap and map all of it. "I wanted to graph the world," Binney said. "People said, 'You can't do this—the possibilities are infinite.'" But he argued that "at any given point in time the number of atoms in the universe is big, but it's finite."

As Binney imagined it, ThinThread would correlate data from financial transactions, travel records, Web searches, G.P.S. equipment, and any other "attributes" that an analyst might find useful in pinpointing "the bad guys." By 2000, Binney, using fibre optics, had set up a computer network that could chart relationships among people in real time. It also turned the N.S.A.'s data-collection paradigm upside down. Instead of vacuuming up information around the world and then sending it all back to headquarters for analysis, ThinThread processed information as it was collected—discarding useless information on the spot and avoiding the overload problem that plagued centralized systems. Binney says, "The beauty of it is that it was open-ended, so it could keep expanding."

Pilot tests of ThinThread proved almost too successful, according to a former intelligence expert who analyzed it. "It was nearly perfect," the official says. "But it processed such a large amount of data that it picked up more Americans than the other systems." Though ThinThread was intended to intercept foreign communications, it continued documenting signals when a trail crossed into the U.S. This was a big problem: federal law forbade the monitoring of domestic communications without a court warrant. And a warrant couldn't be issued without probable cause and a known suspect. In order to comply with the law, Binney installed privacy controls and added an "anonymizing feature," so that all American communications would be encrypted until a warrant was issued. The system would indicate when a pattern looked suspicious enough to justify a warrant.

But this was before 9/11, and the N.S.A.'s lawyers deemed ThinThread too invasive of Americans' privacy. In addition, concerns were raised about whether the system would function on a huge scale, although preliminary tests had suggested that it would. In the fall of 2000, Hayden decided not to use ThinThread, largely because of his legal advisers' concerns. Instead, he funded a rival approach, called Trailblazer, and he turned to private defense contractors to build it. Matthew Aid, the author of a heralded 2009 history of the agency, "The Secret Sentry," says, "The resistance to ThinThread was just standard bureaucratic politics. ThinThread was small, cost-effective, easy to understand, and protected the identity of Americans. But it wasn't what the higher-ups wanted. They wanted a big machine that could make Martinis, too."

The N.S.A.'s failure to stop the 9/11 plot infuriated Binney: he believed that ThinThread had been ready to deploy nine months earlier. Working with N.S.A. counterterrorism experts, he had planned to set up his system at sites where foreign terrorism was prevalent, including Afghanistan and Pakistan. "Those bits of conversations they found too late?" Binney said. "That would have never happened. I had it managed in a way that would send out automatic alerts. It would have been, Bang!"

Meanwhile, there was nothing to show for Trailblazer, other than mounting bills. As the system stalled at the level of schematic drawings, top executives kept shuttling between jobs at the agency and jobs with the high-paying contractors. For a time, both Hayden's deputy director and his chief of signals-intelligence programs worked at SAIC, a company that won several hundred million dollars in Trailblazer contracts. In 2006, Trailblazer was abandoned as a $1.2-billion flop.

Soon after 9/11, Drake says, he prepared a short, classified summary explaining how ThinThread "could be put into the fight," and gave it to Baginski, his boss. But he says that she "wouldn't respond electronically. She just wrote in a black felt marker, 'They've found a different solution.'" When he asked her what it was, she responded, "I can't tell you." Baginski, who now works for a private defense contractor, recalls her interactions with Drake differently, but she declined to comment specifically.

In the weeks after the attacks, rumors began circulating inside the N.S.A.

that the agency, with the approval of the Bush White House, was violating the Foreign Intelligence Surveillance Act—the 1978 law, known as FISA, that bars domestic surveillance without a warrant. Years later, the rumors were proved correct. In nearly total secrecy, and under pressure from the White House, Hayden sanctioned warrantless domestic surveillance. The new policy, which lawyers in the Justice Department justified by citing President Bush's executive authority as Commander-in-Chief, contravened a century of constitutional case law. Yet, on October 4, 2001, Bush authorized the policy, and it became operational by October 6th. Bamford, in "The Shadow Factory," suggests that Hayden, having been overcautious about privacy before 9/11, swung to the opposite extreme after the attacks. Hayden, who now works for a security-consulting firm, declined to respond to detailed questions about the surveillance program.

When Binney heard the rumors, he was convinced that the new domestic-surveillance program employed components of ThinThread: a bastardized version, stripped of privacy controls. "It was my brainchild," he said. "But they removed the protections, the anonymization process. When you remove that, you can target anyone." He said that although he was not "read in" to the new secret surveillance program, "my people were brought in, and they told me, 'Can you believe they're doing this? They're getting billing records on U.S. citizens! They're putting pen registers'"—logs of dialed phone numbers—"'on everyone in the country!'"

Drake recalled that, after the October 4th directive, "strange things were happening. Equipment was being moved. People were coming to me and saying, 'We're now targeting our own country!'" Drake says that N.S.A. officials who helped the agency obtain FISA warrants were suddenly reassigned, a tipoff that the conventional process was being circumvented. He added, "I was concerned that it was illegal, and none of it was necessary." In his view, domestic data mining "could have been done legally" if the N.S.A. had maintained privacy protections. "But they didn't want an accountable system."

Aid, the author of the N.S.A. history, suggests that ThinThread's privacy protections interfered with top officials' secret objective—to pick American targets by name. "They wanted selection, not just collection," he says.

A former N.S.A. official expressed skepticism that Drake cared deeply about the constitutional privacy issues raised by the agency's surveillance policies. The official characterizes him as a bureaucrat driven by resentment of a rival project—Trailblazer—and calls his story "revisionist history." But Drake says that, in the fall of 2001, he told Baginski he feared that the agency was breaking the law. He says that to some extent she shared his views, and later told him she feared that the agency would be "haunted" by the surveillance program. In 2003, she left the agency for the F.B.I., in part because of her discomfort with the surveillance program. Drake says that, at one point, Baginski told him that if he had concerns he should talk to the N.S.A.'s general counsel. Drake claims that he did, and that the agency's top lawyer, Vito Potenza, told him, "Don't worry about it. We're the executive agent for the White House. It's all been scrubbed. It's legal." When he pressed further, Potenza told him, "It's none of your business." (Potenza, who is now retired, declined to comment.)

Drake says, "I feared for the future. If Pandora's box was opened, what would the government become?" He was not about to drop the matter. Matthew Aid, who describes Drake as "brilliant," says that "he has sort of a Jesus complex—only he can see the way things are. Everyone else is mentally deficient, or in someone's pocket." Drake's history of whistle-blowing stretches back to high school, in Manchester, Vermont, where his father, a retired Air Force officer, taught. When drugs infested the school, Drake became a police informant. And Watergate, which occurred while he was a student, taught him "that no one is above the law."

Drake says that in the Air Force, where he learned to capture electronic signals, the FISA law "was drilled into us." He recalls, "If you accidentally intercepted U.S. persons, there were special procedures to expunge it." The procedures had been devised to prevent the recurrence of past abuses, such as Nixon's use of the N.S.A. to spy on his political enemies.

Drake didn't know the precise details, but he sensed that domestic spying "was now being done on a vast level." He was dismayed to hear from N.S.A. colleagues that "arrangements" were being made with telecom and credit-card companies. He added, "The mantra was 'Get the data!'" The transformation of the N.S.A., he says, was so radical that "it wasn't just that the brakes came off after 9/11—we were in a whole different vehicle."

Few people have a precise knowledge of the size or scope of the N.S.A.'s domestic-surveillance powers. An agency spokesman declined to comment on how the agency "performs its mission," but said that its activities are constitutional and subject to "comprehensive and rigorous" oversight. But Susan Landau, a former engineer at Sun Microsystems, and the author of a new book, "Surveillance or Security?," notes that, in 2003, the government placed equipment capable of copying electronic communications at locations across America. These installations were made, she says, at "switching offices" that not only connect foreign and domestic communications but also handle purely domestic traffic. As a result, she surmises, the U.S. now has the capability to monitor domestic traffic on a huge scale. "Why was it done this way?" she asks. "One can come up with all sorts of nefarious reasons, but one doesn't want to think that way about our government."

Binney, for his part, believes that the agency now stores copies of all e-mails transmitted in America, in case the government wants to retrieve the details later. In the past few years, the N.S.A. has built enormous electronic-storage facilities in Texas and Utah. Binney says that an N.S.A. e-mail database can be searched with "dictionary selection," in the manner of Google. After 9/11, he says, "General Hayden reassured everyone that the N.S.A. didn't put out dragnets, and that was true. It had no need—it was getting every fish in the sea."

Binney considers himself a conservative, and, as an opponent of big govern-ment, he worries that the N.S.A.'s data-mining program is so extensive that it could help "create an Orwellian state." Whereas wiretap surveillance requires trained human operators, data mining is automated, meaning that the entire country can be watched. Conceivably, U.S. officials could "monitor the Tea Party, or reporters, whatever group or organization you want to target," he says. "It's exactly what the Founding Fathers never wanted."

On October 31, 2001, soon after Binney concluded that the N.S.A. was headed in an unethical direction, he retired. He had served for thirty-six years. His wife worked there, too. Wiebe, the analyst, and Ed Loomis, a computer sci-entist at SARC, also left. Binney said of his decision, "I couldn't be an accessory to subverting the Constitution."

Not long after Binney quit the N.S.A., he says, he confided his concerns about the secret surveillance program to Diane Roark, a staff member on the House Permanent Select Committee on Intelligence, which oversees the agen-cy. Roark, who has flowing gray hair and large, wide-set eyes, looks like a waifish poet. But in her intelligence-committee job, which she held for seventeen years, she modelled herself on Machiavelli's maxim that it is better to be feared than loved. Within the N.S.A.'s upper ranks she was widely resented. A former top N.S.A. official says of her, "In meetings, she would just say, 'You're lying.'"

Roark agrees that she distrusted the N.S.A.'s managers. "I asked very tough questions, because they were trying to hide stuff," she says. "For instance, I wasn't supposed to know about the warrantless surveillance. They were all de-termined that no one else was going to tell them what to do."

Like Drake and Binney, Roark was a registered Republican, skeptical about bureaucracy but strong on national defense. She had a knack for recruiting sources at the N.S.A. One of them was Drake, who introduced himself to her in 2000, after she visited N.S.A. headquarters and gave a stinging talk on the agency's failings; she also established relationships with Binney and Wiebe. Hayden was furious about this back channel. After learning that Binney had attended a meeting with Roark at which N.S.A. employees complained about Trailblazer, Hayden dressed down the critics. He then sent out an agency-wide memo, in which he warned that several "individuals, in a session with our congressional overseers, took a position in direct opposition to one that we had corporately decided to follow. . . . Actions contrary to our decisions will have a serious adverse effect on our efforts to transform N.S.A., and I cannot tolerate them." Roark says of the memo, "Hayden brooked no opposition to his favorite people and programs."

Roark, who had substantial influence over N.S.A. budget appropriations, was an early champion of Binney's ThinThread project. She was dismayed, she says, to hear that it had evolved into a means of domestic surveillance, and felt personally responsible. Her oversight committee had been created after Watergate specifically to curb such abuses. "It was my duty to oppose it," she told me. "That is why oversight existed, so that these things didn't happen again. I'm not an attorney, but I thought that there was no way it was constitutional." Roark recalls thinking that, if N.S.A. officials were breaking the law, she was "going to fry them."

She soon learned that she was practically alone in her outrage. Very few congressional leaders had been briefed on the program, and some were apparently going along with it, even if they had reservations. Starting in February, 2002, Roark says, she wrote a series of memos warning of potential illegalities and privacy breaches and handed them to the staffers for Porter Goss, the chairman of her committee, and Nancy Pelosi, its ranking Democrat. But nothing changed. (Pelosi's spokesman denied that she received such memos, and pointed out that a year earlier Pelosi had written to Hayden and expressed grave concerns about the N.S.A.'s electronic surveillance.)

Roark, feeling powerless, retired. Before leaving Washington, though, she learned that Hayden, who knew of her strong opposition to the surveillance program, wanted to talk to her. They met at N.S.A. headquarters on July 15, 2002. According to notes that she made after the meeting, Hayden pleaded with her to stop agitating against the program. He conceded that the policy would leak at some point, and told her that when it did she could "yell and scream" as much as she wished. Meanwhile, he wanted to give the program more time. She asked Hayden why the N.S.A. had chosen not to include privacy protections for Americans. She says that he "kept not answering. Finally, he mumbled, and looked down, and said, 'We didn't need them. We had the power.' He didn't even look me in the eye. I was flabbergasted." She asked him directly if the government was getting warrants for domestic surveillance, and he admitted that it was not.

In an e-mail, Hayden confirmed that the meeting took place, but said that he recalled only its "broad outlines." He noted that Roark was not "cleared to know about the expanded surveillance program, so I did not go into great detail." He added, "I assured her that I firmly believed that what N.S.A. was doing was effective, appropriate, and lawful. I also reminded her that the program's success depended on it remaining secret, that it was appropriately classified, and that any public discussion of it would have to await a later day."

During the meeting, Roark says, she warned Hayden that no court would uphold the program. Curiously, Hayden responded that he had already been assured by unspecified individuals that he could count on a majority of "the nine votes"—an apparent reference to the Supreme Court. According to Roark's notes, Hayden told her that such a vote might even be 7-2 in his favor.

Roark couldn't believe that the Supreme Court had been adequately informed of the N.S.A.'s transgressions, and she decided to alert Chief Justice William H. Rehnquist, sending a message through a family friend. Once again, there was no response. She also tried to contact a judge on the FISA court, in Washington, which adjudicates requests for warrants sanctioning domestic surveillance of suspected foreign agents. But the judge had her assistant refer the call to the Department of Justice, which had approved the secret program in the first place. Roark says that she even tried to reach David Addington, the legal counsel to Vice-President Dick Cheney, who had once been her congressional colleague. He never called back, and Addington was eventually revealed to be one of the prime advocates for the surveillance program.

"This was such a Catch-22," Roark says. "There was no one to go to." In October, 2003, feeling "profoundly depressed," she left Washington and moved to a small town in Oregon.

Drake was still working at the N.S.A., but he was secretly informing on the agency to Congress. In addition to briefing Roark, he had become an anonymous source for the congressional committees investigating intelligence failures related to 9/11. He provided Congress with top-secret documents chronicling the N.S.A.'s shortcomings. Drake believed that the agency had failed to feed other intelligence agencies critical information that it had collected before the attacks. Congressional investigators corroborated these criticisms, though they found greater lapses at the C.I.A. and the F.B.I.

Around this time, Drake recalls, Baginski warned him, "Be careful, Tom—they're looking for leakers." He found this extraordinary, and asked himself, "Telling the truth to congressional oversight committees is leaking?" But the N.S.A. has a rule requiring employees to clear any contact with Congress, and in the spring of 2002 Baginski told Drake, "It's time for you to find another job." He soon switched to a less sensitive post at the agency, the first of several.

As for Binney, he remained frustrated even in retirement about what he considered the misuse of ThinThread. In September, 2002, he, Wiebe, Loomis, and Roark filed what they thought was a confidential complaint with the Pentagon's Inspector General, extolling the virtues of the original ThinThread project and accusing the N.S.A. of wasting money on Trailblazer. Drake did not put his name on the complaint, because he was still an N.S.A. employee. But he soon became involved in helping the others, who had become friends. He obtained documents aimed at proving waste, fraud, and abuse in the Trailblazer program.

The Inspector General's report, which was completed in 2005, was classified as secret, so only a few insiders could read what Drake describes as a scathing document. Possibly the only impact of the probe was to hasten the end of Trailblazer, whose budget overruns had become indisputably staggering. Though Hayden acknowledged to a Senate committee that the costs of the Trailblazer project "were greater than anticipated, to the tune of, I would say, hundreds of millions," most of the scandal's details remained hidden from the public.

In December, 2005, the N.S.A.'s culture of secrecy was breached by a stunning leak. The *Times* reporters James Risen and Eric Lichtblau revealed that the N.S.A. was running a warrantless wiretapping program inside the United States. The paper's editors had held onto the scoop for more than a year, weighing the propriety of publishing it. According to Bill Keller, the executive editor of the *Times*, President Bush pleaded with the paper's editors to not publish the story; Keller told *New York* that "the basic message was: You'll have blood on your hands." After the paper defied the Administration, Bush called the leak "a shameful act." At his command, federal agents launched a criminal investigation to identify the paper's source.

The *Times* story shocked the country. Democrats, including then Senator Obama, denounced the program as illegal and demanded congressional hearings. A FISA court judge resigned in protest. In March, 2006, Mark Klein, a retired A.T. & T. employee, gave a sworn statement to the Electronic Frontier Foundation, which was filing a lawsuit against the company, describing a secret room in San Francisco where powerful Narus computers appeared to be sorting and copying all of the telecom's Internet traffic—both foreign and domestic.

A high-capacity fibre-optic cable seemed to be forwarding this data to a centralized location, which, Klein surmised, was N.S.A. headquarters. Soon, *USA Today* reported that A.T. & T., Verizon, and BellSouth had secretly opened their electronic records to the government, in violation of communications laws. Legal experts said that each instance of spying without a warrant was a serious crime, and that there appeared to be hundreds of thousands of infractions.

President Bush and Administration officials assured the American public that the surveillance program was legal, although new legislation was eventually required to bring it more in line with the law. They insisted that the traditional method of getting warrants was too slow for the urgent threats posed by international terrorism. And they implied that the only domestic surveillance taking place involved tapping phone calls in which one speaker was outside the U.S.

Drake says of Bush Administration officials, "They were lying through their teeth. They had chosen to go an illegal route, and it wasn't because they had no other choice." He also believed that the Administration was covering up the full extent of the program. "The phone calls were the tip of the iceberg. The really sensitive stuff was the data mining." He says, "I was faced with a crisis of conscience. What do I do—remain silent, and complicit, or go to the press?"

Drake has a wife and five sons, the youngest of whom has serious health problems, and so he agonized over the decision. He researched the relevant legal statutes and concluded that if he spoke to a reporter about unclassified matters the only risk he ran was losing his job. N.S.A. policy forbids initiating contact with the press. "I get that it's grounds for 'We have to let you go,'" he says. But he decided that he was willing to lose his job. "This was a violation of everything I knew and believed as an American. We were making the Nixon Administration look like pikers."

Drake got in touch with Gorman, who covered the N.S.A. for the *Baltimore Sun*. He had admired an article of hers and knew that Roark had spoken to her previously, though not about anything classified. He got Gorman's contact information from Roark, who warned him to be careful. She knew that in the past the N.S.A. had dealt harshly with people who embarrassed it.

Drake set up a secure Hushmail e-mail account and began sending Gorman anonymous tips. Half in jest, he chose the pseudonym The Shadow Knows. He says that he insisted on three ground rules with Gorman: neither he nor she would reveal his identity; he wouldn't be the sole source for any story; he would not supply her with classified information. But a year into the arrangement, in February, 2007, Drake decided to blow his cover, surprising Gorman by showing up at the newspaper and introducing himself as The Shadow Knows. He ended up meeting with Gorman half a dozen times. But, he says, "I never gave her anything classified." Gorman has not been charged with wrongdoing, and declined, through her lawyer, Laura Handman, to comment, citing the pending trial.

Starting on January 29, 2006, Gorman, who now works at the *Wall Street Journal*, published a series of articles about problems at the N.S.A., including a story describing Trailblazer as an expensive fiasco. On May 18, 2006, the day that Hayden faced Senate confirmation hearings for a new post—the head of the C.I.A.—the *Sun* published Gorman's exposé on ThinThread, which accused the N.S.A. of rejecting an approach that protected Americans' privacy. Hayden, evidently peeved, testified that intelligence officers deserved "not to have every action analyzed, second-guessed, and criticized on the front pages of the newspapers."

At the time, the government did not complain that the *Sun* had crossed a legal line. It did not contact the paper's editors or try to restrain the paper from publishing Gorman's work. A former N.S.A. colleague of Drake's says he believes that the *Sun* stories revealed government secrets. Others disagree. Steven Aftergood, the secrecy expert, says that the articles "did not damage national security."

Matthew Aid argues that the material Drake provided to the *Sun* should not have been highly classified—if it was—and in any case only highlighted that "the N.S.A. was a management nightmare, which wasn't a secret in Washington." In his view, Drake "was just saying, 'We're not doing our job, and it's having a deleterious effect on mission performance.' He was right, by the way." The *Sun* series, Aid says, was "embarrassing to N.S.A. management, but embarrassment to the U.S. government is not a criminal offense in this country." (Aid has a stake in this debate. In 1984, when he was in the Air Force, he spent several months in the stockade for having stored classified documents in a private locker. The experience, he says, sensitized him to issues of government secrecy.)

While the *Sun* was publishing its series, twenty-five federal agents and five prosecutors were struggling to identify the *Times*' source. The team had targeted some two hundred possible suspects, but had found no culprits. The *Sun* series attracted the attention of the investigators, who theorized that its source might also have talked to the *Times*. This turned out not to be true. Nevertheless, the investigators quickly homed in on the Trailblazer critics. "It's sad," an intelligence expert says. "I think they were aiming at the *Times* leak and found this instead."

Roark was an obvious suspect for the *Times* leak. Everyone from Hayden on down knew that she had opposed the surveillance program. After the article appeared, she says, "I was waiting for the shoe to drop." The F.B.I. eventually contacted her, and in February, 2007, she and her attorney met with the prosecutor then in charge, Steven Tyrrell, who was the head of the fraud section at the Justice Department. Roark signed an affidavit saying that she was not a source for the *Times* story or for "State of War," a related book that James Risen wrote. She also swore that she had no idea who the source was. She says of the experience, "It was an interrogation, not an interview. They treated me like a target."

Roark recalls that the F.B.I. agents tried to force her to divulge the identity of her old N.S.A. informants. They already seemed to know about Drake, Binney, and Wiebe—perhaps from the Inspector General's report. She refused to cooperate, arguing that it was improper for agents of the executive branch to threaten a congressional overseer about her sources. "I had the sense that N.S.A. was egging the F.B.I. on," she says. "I'd gotten the N.S.A. so many times—they were going to get me. The N.S.A. hated me." (The N.S.A. and the Justice Department declined to comment on the investigations.)

In the months that followed, Roark heard nothing. Finally, her lawyer placed the case in her "dead file."

On July 26, 2007, at 9 A.M. Eastern Standard Time, armed federal agents simultaneously raided the houses of Binney, Wiebe, and Roark. (At Roark's house, in Oregon, it was six o'clock.) Binney was in the shower when agents arrived, and recalls, "They went right upstairs to the bathroom and held guns on me and my wife, right between the eyes." The agents took computer equipment, a copy of the Inspector General complaint and a copy of a commercial pitch that Binney had written with Wiebe, Loomis, and Roark. In 2001, the N.S.A. indicated to Binney that he could pursue commercial projects based on ThinThread. He and the others thought that aspects of the software could be used to help detect Medicare fraud.

Binney professed his innocence, and he says that the agents told him, "We think you're lying. You need to implicate someone. " He believed that they were trying to get him to name Roark as the *Times*' source. He suggested that if they were looking for criminal conspirators they should focus on Bush and Hayden for allowing warrantless surveillance. Binney recalls an agent responding that such brazen spying didn't happen in America. Looking over the rims of his owlish glasses, Binney replied, "Oh, really?"

Roark was sleeping when the agents arrived, and didn't hear them until "it sounded as if they were going to pull the house down, they were rattling it so badly." They took computers and a copy of the same commercial pitch. Her son had been interested in collaborating on the venture, and he, too, became a potential target. "They believed everybody was conspiring," Roark says. "For years, I couldn't talk to my own son without worrying that they'd say I was trying to influence his testimony." Although she has been fighting cancer, she has spoken with him only sparingly since the raid.

The agents seemed to think that the commercial pitch contained classified information. Roark was shaken: she and the others thought they had edited it scrupulously to insure that it did not. Agents also informed her that a few scattered papers in her old office files were classified. After the raid, she called her lawyer and asked, "If there's a disagreement on classification, does intent mean anything?" The question goes to the heart of the Drake case.

Roark, who always considered herself "a law-and-order person," said of the raid, "This changed my faith." Eventually, the prosecution offered her a plea bargain, under which she would plead guilty to perjury, for ostensibly lying to the F.B.I. about press leaks. The prosecutors also wanted her to testify against Drake. Roark refused. "I'm not going to plead guilty to deliberately doing anything wrong," she told them. "And I can't testify against Tom because I don't know that he did anything wrong. Whatever Tom revealed, I am sure that he did not think it was classified." She says, "I didn't think the system was perfect, but I thought they'd play fair with me. They didn't. I felt it was retribution."

Wiebe, the retired analyst, was the most surprised by the raid—he had not yet been contacted in connection with the investigation. He recalls that agents locked his two Pembroke Welsh corgis in a bathroom and commanded his daughter and his mother-in-law, who was in her bathrobe, to stay on a couch while they searched his house. He says, "I feel I'm living in the very country I worked for years to defeat: the Soviet Union. We're turning into a police state." Like Roark, he says of the raid, "It was retribution for our filing the Inspector General complaint."

Under the law, such complaints are confidential, and employees who file them are supposed to be protected from retaliation. It's unclear if the Trailblazer complaint tipped off authorities, but all four people who signed it became targets. Jesselyn Radack, of the Government Accountability Project, a whistle-blower advocacy group that has provided legal support to Drake, says of his case, "It's the most severe form of whistle-blower retaliation I have ever seen."

A few days after the raid, Drake met Binney and Wiebe for lunch, at a tavern in Glenelg, Maryland. "I had a pretty good idea I was next," Drake says. But it wasn't until the morning of November 28, 2007, that he saw armed agents streaming across his lawn. Though Drake was informed of his right to remain silent, he viewed the raid as a fresh opportunity to blow the whistle. He spent the day at his kitchen table, without a lawyer, talking. He brought up Trailblazer, but found that the investigators weren't interested in the details of a defunct computer system, or in cost overruns, or in the constitutional conflicts posed by warrantless surveillance. Their focus was on the *Times* leak. He assured them that he wasn't the source, but he confirmed his contact with the *Sun*, insisting that he had not relayed any classified information. He also disclosed his computer password. The agents bagged documents, computers, and books, and removed eight or ten boxes of office files from his basement. "I felt incredibly violated," he says.

For four months, Drake continued cooperating. He admitted that he had given Gorman information that he had cut and pasted from secret documents, but stressed that he had not included anything classified. He acknowledged sending Gorman hundreds of e-mails. Then, in April, 2008, the F.B.I. told him that someone important wanted to meet with him, at a secure building in Calverton, Maryland. Drake agreed to the appointment. Soon after he showed up, he says, Steven Tyrrell, the prosecutor, walked in and told him, "You're screwed, Mr. Drake. We have enough evidence to put you away for most of the rest of your natural life."

Prosecutors informed Drake that they had found classified documents in the boxes in his basement—the indictment cites three—and discovered two more in his e-mail archive. They also accused him of shredding other documents, and of deleting e-mails in the months before he was raided, in an attempt to obstruct justice. Further, they said that he had lied when he told federal agents that he hadn't given Gorman classified information.

"They had made me into an enemy of the state just by saying I was," Drake says. The boxes in his basement contained copies of some of the less sensitive material that he had procured for the Inspector General's Trailblazer investigation. The Inspector General's Web site directs complainants to keep copies. Drake says that if the boxes did, in fact, contain classified documents he didn't realize it. (The indictment emphasizes that he "willfully" retained documents.) The two documents that the government says it extracted from his e-mail archive were even less sensitive, Drake says. Both pertained to a successor to Trailblazer, code-named Turbulence. One document listed a schedule of meetings about Turbulence. It was marked "unclassified/for official use only" and posted on the N.S.A.'s internal Web site. The government has since argued that the schedule should have been classified, and that Drake should have known this. The other document, which touted the success of Turbulence, was officially declassified in July, 2010, three months after Drake was indicted. "After charging him with having this ostensibly serious classified document, the government waved a wand and decided it wasn't so classified after all," Radack says.

Clearly, the intelligence community hopes that the Drake case will send a message about the gravity of exposing government secrets. But Drake's lawyer, a federal public defender named James Wyda, argued in court last spring that "there have never been two documents so benign that are the subject of this kind of prosecution against a client whose motives are as salutary as Tom's."

Drake insists, too, that the only computer files he destroyed were routine trash: "I held then, and I hold now, I had nothing to destroy." Drake, who left the N.S.A. in 2008, and now works at an Apple Store outside Washington, asks, "Why didn't I erase everything on my computer, then? I know how to do it. They found what they found."

Not everyone familiar with Drake's case is moved by his plight. A former federal official knowledgeable about the case says, "To his credit, he tried to raise these issues, and, to an extent, they were dealt with. But who died and left him in charge?"

In May, 2009, Tyrrell proposed a plea bargain: if Drake pleaded guilty to one count of conspiring to violate the Espionage Act and agreed to cooperate against the others, he would get a maximum of five years in prison. "They wanted me to reveal a conspiracy that didn't exist," Drake says. "It was all about the *Times*, but I had no knowledge of the leak." Drake says that he told prosecutors, "I refuse to plea-bargain with the truth."

That June, Drake learned that Tyrrell was leaving the government. Tyrrell was a Republican, and Drake was hopeful that a prosecutor appointed by the Obama Administration would have a different approach. But Drake was dismayed to learn that Tyrrell's replacement, William Welch, had just been transferred from the top spot in the Justice Department's public-integrity section, after an overzealous prosecution of Ted Stevens, the Alaska senator. A judge had thrown out Stevens's conviction, and, at one point, had held Welch in contempt of court. (Welch declined to comment.)

In April, 2010, Welch indicted Drake, shattering his hope for a reprieve from the Obama Administration. But the prosecution's case had shrunk dramatically from the grand conspiracy initially laid out by Tyrrell. (Welch accidentally sent the defense team an early draft of the indictment, revealing how the case had changed.) Drake was no longer charged with leaking classified documents, or with being part of a conspiracy. He is still charged with violating the Espionage

Act, but now merely because of unauthorized "willful retention" of the five documents. Drake says that when he learned that, even with the reduced charges, he still faced up to thirty-five years in prison, he "was completely aghast."

Morton Halperin, of the Open Society Institute, says that the reduced charges make the prosecution even more outlandish: "If Drake is convicted, it means the Espionage Law is an Official Secrets Act." Because reporters often retain unauthorized defense documents, Drake's conviction would establish a legal precedent making it possible to prosecute journalists as spies. "It poses a grave threat to the mechanism by which we learn most of what the government does," Halperin says.

The Espionage Act has rarely been used to prosecute leakers and whistle-blowers. Drake's case is only the fourth in which the act has been used to indict someone for mishandling classified material. "It was meant to deal with classic espionage, not publication," Stephen Vladeck, a law professor at American University who is an expert on the statute, says.

The first attempt to apply the law to leakers was the aborted prosecution, in 1973, of Daniel Ellsberg, a researcher at the RAND Corporation who was charged with disclosing the Pentagon Papers—a damning secret history of the Vietnam War. But the case was dropped, owing, in large part, to prosecutorial misconduct. The second such effort was the case of Samuel L. Morison, a naval intelligence officer who, in 1985, was convicted for providing U.S. photographs of a Soviet ship to *Jane's Defence Weekly*. Morison was later pardoned by Bill Clinton. The third case was the prosecution, in 2005, of a Defense Department official, Lawrence Franklin, and two lobbyists for the American-Israel Public Affairs Committee. Franklin pleaded guilty to a lesser charge, and the case against the lobbyists collapsed after the presiding judge insisted that prosecutors establish criminal intent. Unable to prove this, the Justice Department abandoned the case, amid criticism that the government had overreached.

Drake's case also raises questions about double standards. In recent years, several top officials accused of similar misdeeds have not faced such serious charges. John Deutch, the former C.I.A. director, and Alberto Gonzales, the former Attorney General, both faced much less stringent punishment after taking classified documents home without authorization. In 2003, Sandy Berger, Clinton's national-security adviser, smuggled classified documents out of a federal building, reportedly by hiding them in his pants. It was treated as a misdemeanor. His defense lawyer was Lanny Breuer—the official overseeing the prosecution of Drake.

Jack Goldsmith, a Harvard law professor who served in the Bush Justice Department, laments the lack of consistency in leak prosecutions. He notes that no investigations have been launched into the sourcing of Bob Woodward's four most recent books, even though "they are filled with classified information that he could only have received from the top of the government." Gabriel Schoenfeld, of the Hudson Institute, says, "The selectivity of the prosecutions here is nightmarish. It's a broken system."

Mark Feldstein, a professor of media and public affairs at George Washington University, warns that, if whistle-blowers and other dissenters are singled out for prosecution, "this has gigantic repercussions. You choke off the information that the public needs to judge policy."

Few people are more disturbed about Drake's prosecution than the others who spoke out against the N.S.A. surveillance program. In 2008, Thomas Tamm, a Justice Department lawyer, revealed that he was one of the people who leaked to the *Times*. He says of Obama, "It's so disappointing from someone who was a constitutional-law professor, and who made all those campaign promises." The Justice Department recently confirmed that it won't pursue charges against Tamm. Speaking before Congress, Attorney General Holder explained that "there is a balancing that has to be done . . . between what our national-security interests are and what might be gained by prosecuting a particular individual." The decision provoked strong criticism from Republicans, underscoring the political pressures that the Justice Department faces when it backs off such prosecutions. Still, Tamm questions why the Drake case is proceeding, given that Drake never revealed anything as sensitive as what appeared in the *Times*. "The program he talked to the *Baltimore Sun* about was a failure and wasted billions of dollars," Tamm says. "It's embarrassing to the N.S.A., but it's not giving aid and comfort to the enemy."

Mark Klein, the former A.T. & T. employee who exposed the telecom-company wiretaps, is also dismayed by the Drake case. "I think it's outrageous," he says. "The Bush people have been let off. The telecom companies got immunity. The only people Obama has prosecuted are the whistle-blowers."

*Jane Mayer has been a staff writer for the *New Yorker* since 1995. In recent years, she has written for that publication on money in politics, government prosecution of whistle-blowers, and the United States' Predator drone program. Mayer's latest book, *The Dark Side: The Inside Story of How the War on Terror Turned into a War on American Ideals* (2008), was a finalist for the National Book Awards.

Mayer, Jane. "The Secret Sharer: Is Thomas Drake an Enemy of the State?" *New Yorker*, May 23, 2011, 47–57.

Used by permission.